MINDWEAVE
Communication, Computers and Distance Education

Other Pergamon Titles of Related Interest

ERAUT (ed.)
The International Encyclopedia of Educational Technology

KIBBY & MAYES
Computer Assisted Learning: Selected Proceedings
from the CAL 87 Symposium

MOONEN & PLOMP
EURIT 86: Developments in Educational Software and Courseware

Related Journals of Interest

Computers & Education

Language & Communication

MINDWEAVE

Communication, Computers and Distance Education

Edited by

Robin Mason

and

Anthony Kaye

Open University, Milton Keynes, UK

PERGAMON PRESS

OXFORD · NEW YORK · BEIJING · FRANKFURT
SÃO PAULO · SYDNEY · TOKYO · TORONTO

U.K.	Pergamon Press plc, Headington Hill Hall, Oxford OX3 0BW, England
U.S.A.	Pergamon Press, Inc., Maxwell House, Fairview Park, Elmsford, New York 10523, U.S.A.
PEOPLE'S REPUBLIC OF CHINA	Pergamon Press, Room 4037, Qianmen Hotel, Beijing, People's Republic of China
FEDERAL REPUBLIC OF GERMANY	Pergamon Press GmbH, Hammerweg 6, D-6242 Kronberg, Federal Republic of Germany
BRAZIL	Pergamon Editora Ltda, Rua Eça de Queiros, 346, CEP 04011, Paraiso, São Paulo, Brazil
AUSTRALIA	Pergamon Press Australia Pty Ltd., P.O. Box 544, Potts Point, N.S.W. 2011, Australia
JAPAN	Pergamon Press, 5th Floor, Matsuoka Central Building, 1-7-1 Nishishinjuku, Shinjuku-ku, Tokyo 160, Japan
CANADA	Pergamon Press Canada Ltd., Suite No. 271, 253 College Street, Toronto, Ontario, Canada M5T 1R5

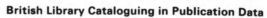

First edition 1989

Library of Congress Cataloging in Publication Data

Mindweave: communication, computers, and distance education/edited by Robin Mason and Anthony Kaye.
p. cm.
Based on a conference held at the British Open University, Milton Keynes, October 1988.
1. Distance education—Great Britain—Data processing—Congresses. I. Mason, Robin.
II. Kaye, Anthony, 1942– .
LC5808.67M56 1988 374'.41—dc19 89–31110

British Library Cataloguing in Publication Data

Mindweave: communications, computers and distance education.
1. Distance education
I. Mason, Robin II. Kaye, Anthony
371.3'07'8
ISBN 0–08–037755–6

Cover illustration based on the thought box logo, adapted from a design by David Alexander

Printed in Great Britain by BPCC Wheaton Ltd, Exeter

CONTENTS

Prologue
Students 'Conversing' about Computer-Mediated Communication...

PART 1: THEMES AND ISSUES

PART 2: COMPUTER CONFERENCING AND MASS DISTANCE EDUCATION

v

PART 3: RESOURCE FILE

Papers on Applications of CMC in Education

Papers Reflecting on CMC as a Medium for Education

ACKNOWLEDGEMENTS

This book is based to a large extent on an international conference on Computer-Mediated Communication (CMC) in Distance Education which we organised at the British Open University's central campus in Milton Keynes in October 1988. The chapters in Part 1 are based on invited plenary lectures given at this conference, and Part 3 of the book contains summaries of papers presented at a series of poster sessions.

The conference included sessions about a new Open University course with an annual enrolment of about 1300 home-based students, which represents the first attempt to integrate CMC into a multi-media distance education programme of this size. Part 2 of the book contains three chapters analysing the implications of this continuing experience. For those readers who are wondering why we believe that computer-mediated communication will have such an an important role to play in distance education, we recommend the Prologue. This is a transcript of a 'conversation' on the Open University's CoSy conferencing system between five of the most enthusiastic users of CMC on this course – students based respectively in London, Cambridge, Birmingham, Preston, and Troon (in Scotland). Without CoSy, they would never have met each other, 'electronically' or otherwise. We believe they are among the pioneers in the use of this technology for learning at a distance. *Mindweave* is dedicated to an exploration of the ways in which the benefits of computer-mediated communication, as experienced by these students, can be made more widely available to adult distance learners.

It is impossible for us to acknowledge individually the many colleagues who have contributed directly and indirectly to this book. However, in addition to those whose written contributions you will find in the following pages, we would particularly like to mention the cooperation and support we received during the conference from Tony Bates, Neil Costello, Geoff Einon, Ruth Finnegan, Paul Hare, Nick Heap and Christina Lay, with whom we have the pleasure of working on the Open University course *An Introduction to Information Technology: Social and Technological Issues*. We are also very grateful to the students (Mike O'Rourke, Pat Porter, Sharon Roberts, Maureen Walker, Howard Webber) and the tutors (Eric Deeson, Tony Edwards, David McConnell, Colin Shaw, and Mary Shepherd) from this course who contributed so actively to the panel sessions. And we want to acknowledge the valuable contributions from Angela Castro (of Deakin University, Australia), France Henri (of the Télé-Université in Quebec), Annette Lorentsen (of the Jutland Open University in Denmark) and James Baring (a 'mindweaver' *par excellence*), who played key roles as discussants during the conference. We would also like to thank Dacom Systems of Milton Keynes and Pace Micro Technology of Bradford (suppliers of modems to the Open University) as well as Apple Computer UK, for contributing part of the conference costs.

Finally, we would like to thank Paul Bacsich, team leader of the Open University's Electronic Publishing project, without whose help, patience, and goodwill we would never have got the camera-ready copy for this book to the publisher in time.

Mindweave was produced using Microsoft Word 3.01 on an Apple Mac II computer with output to an Apple LaserWriter II NT. Diagrams were drawn in CricketDraw, MacPaint and various other packages. Electronic text for many individual chapters and papers was sent to us on various conferencing systems – including EIES, Participate and CoSy (Guelph) – as well as through international academic email networks.

Tony Kaye, Robin Mason
Institute of Educational Technology,
The Open University

PROLOGUE

Students 'Conversing' about
Computer-Mediated Communication

==========================
514 ?/message #1, s-roberts, 1810 chars, 31-Oct-88 21:31
There is/are comment(s) on this message.

Having just completed my third Open University course, and my first experience of Computer Mediated Communication (CMC), I thought I'd like to share some of my feelings and enthusiasm with you, and some of the exciting differences between distance learning with and without CMC.

I have used the conferencing, conversation and mailing facilities almost every day from the beginning of the course until the end and have found the system an invaluable tool in helping with the course work, overcoming the initial technical difficulties and discussing the arguments surrounding the study of Information Technology (IT).

CMC has tremendous potential in creating impromptu tutorials and this course has been the first one to make me feel that the O.U. has a campus like the conventional Universities. DT200 [1] in a way has spoilt me, I am going to sorely miss active discussion whenever I like for the remainder of my courses - it will be like losing my right arm or a friend !

I've loved using the system, I really feel I've learned more and understood the aims and objectives better because of CMC and my marks have been consistently higher too, even though I've not put the time I should have put in because I've used the system so much, but I haven't lost anything, far from it, I've gained tremendously, not only in the education aspects, but socially too. One of the disadvantages of distance learning to me was the lack of contact with fellow students, you are lucky if you meet a handful studying the same course, and you rarely keep in touch throughout the course, CMC has altered all of that, I for one have made a few good friends and we hope to continue talking for a long time to come, particularly as some of us will be doing a course together next year.

Well, what do the rest of you think ?

Sharon.

===========================
51438/message #2, mb-walker, 3342 chars, 1-Nov-88 20:08
This is a comment to message 1
There is/are comment(s) on this message.

Yes Sharon, I would agree with you wholeheartedly. CMC has certainly made my year more enjoyable and the medium has come a long way to bridge the gap in distance education.

What amazed me, as a complete beginner, was how easy I found the system to learn. This was possibly due to the menu-based interface provided by OUCOM - I kept watching what was being automatically written for me by the program when I had made my choice from the menu. I then began entering the commands myself at the main prompts. I just kept saying to myself that the ONLY thing that can happen is that I lose information - I mean - the equipment wouldn't suddenly go up in smoke because I'd entered something incorrectly :-)

In fact what did happen was a message to the effect /no Maureen, 'fraid I don't understand what you're trying to tell me to do - what about trying one of this little lot / - followed by a list of acceptable commands. Easy.

By experimenting with these commands I quickly gained confidence and made the system work for me. .....[2]

I was thrilled when I received my first mail message and exhilarated when I first contributed to a conference. However it slowly dawned on me that not only was there the exciting possibility of making contact with others country-wide, but that this medium could provide the forum for discussion sadly lacking in the under-attended tutorials of the previous year. AND I could join in at a time which was convenient to me.

Like you Sharon, I used the system nearly every day sending mail and taking part in conferences and conversations. I quickly became aware of where the expertise lay within the student body in particular subject areas whether technical or social sciences. The discussions on each block were especially helpful in enabling me to view aspects of the course from differing perspectives. This was invaluable to me coming from a science /one answer/ background.

The social side seemed to evolve naturally with the use of the medium and I was surprised to find that personalities were very much in evidence. Friends /sensed/ when I was feeling below par and their light-hearted comments boosted me when the workload was heavy.This support, I would imagine, would be very much part of a conventional university.

As well as enabling support by fellow students, tutors and contact with the Course Team, CMC has engendered a sense of belonging which hitherto was missing in distance education. Isolation was rendered a thing of the past.

Indeed this feeling of unity will be difficult to do without in my future years with the Open University. We can only hope that there will be some restructuring of the system to allow this interaction to continue and give greater opportunity for more students to join the /virtual campus/.

How do you see the future of CMC within the Open University ?
Maureen.

===========================
51438/message #3, m-orourke, 3623 chars, 3-Nov-88 17:59
This is a comment to message 2

I came to the course with mixed feelings having taken two years off from studying for various (mostly emotional) reasons. I wasn't sure if I'd be able to get back into studying and I had no prior knowledge of CMC ... I remember logging on for the first time and the feelings of a) doubt that I was doing the right thing and b) hope that my first hesitant message would get through. The next day brought the exhilaration of a message (from K.T. Malone of course) and from then on I entered into the spirit of the conferencing facilities - I also experimented with Conv [3] as early as April though not many people responded. It was very frustrating, too, knowing that people were on line but not responding. The Conferences themselves were invaluable for providing solutions to the early teething problems - I never needed to phone the OU for Technical support - I either e-mailed Coco [4] or left comments in the conferences and action/further messages were always forthcoming from students tutors and/or Coco. As time went on so did the feelings of being part of a large open community. It was disappointing that my tutor group had only a regular following of tutor and three other students (the same, incidentally that regularly turned up at f2f tutorials) The difference between f2f and on-line was that the majority of the on-line messages were social ones between the "regular" students and our tutor.
The Conferences, however more than made up for this - there you were debating a point with a student from Scotland when someone else from Wales chipped in with a valid point - it was like being in a huge debate but with none of the usual feelings of shyness which often make you keep quiet in a large group situation. My initial fears that my lack of experience in Social Science subjects were wiped away by others in my situation or those with less of a technical background anxious for support. The power of "peer group teaching/tutoring" became very apparent and underlying this immense resource was the excitement of actually using the system. I have mentioned this before in another conference - the feelings I had whilst using the system are just like those you get when playing an adventure game - time passes you by - what matters most is getting through the next challenge - putting over your point - getting agreement or disagreement but most of all inter-acting with fellow students in the ways that you would in a normal campus-based University. Much has been said of the "CMC Campus" I can only endorse this view. The course has been extremely invigorating, very exciting, hard work but so rewarding. It has been the most enjoyable course of my degree. The only differences between it and the rest of the subjects I have studied are
a) The Social science content - without CMC this alone would have caused me to withdraw b) CMC
I think I have proved my point!
Mike

===========================
51438/message #4, vj-maine, 2675 chars, 6-Nov-88 18:40

Like you three I am also hooked on CMC, and see it as a vital component for distance education in the future. Unlike you all I have a totally non-technical background. My job involves nothing more technically revolutionary than a telephone, and in my three years with the OU I have not taken any courses with any science or technology content.

Like Maureen I was amazed how easy I found OUCOM to use, (once I had realised the non-functioning London node was not my fault) and how quickly I really began to feel part of something, as opposed to a lone student. Besides being able to communicate with students all over the country I also found I actually initiated more face to face contact with other students. I have never before telephoned my tutor or other students but this year was in frequent contact with several students, and not only those who used Cosy. I also went to Open Day, which was something I would not have done before!

The use of CMC for more serious purposes has also improved the quality of my studying. More frequent contact with a wider variety of students than I would meet at tutorials and access to members of the course team has widened my outlook on the various topics, and has brought the whole course to life. I have found that I have spent far more time studying, as well as spending time on-line, because I have wanted to follow up discussions.

For me the practical element of the course would have been impossible without CMC. I think that for people attempting to master skills in technical areas there is a great need to be able to communicate with others easily. Many times I would have given up if there had not been opportunity to scream for help in a conference where I knew I would not be interrupting someone's dinner! If people thought I was stupid they just ignored the message, which they couldn't do on the phone. I have found CMC a very non-judgemental medium to use in this way.

I was also interested in the way that I and all the others new to the system gradually expanded the way we used it. At first it seemed to be used mainly for practical, one answer type questions, and then as we got better at it we were able to develop our ability to use the medium for discussion of the social science side of the course. As my skills in using CMC grew there was plenty to discover in the way of conversations, new conferences and an increasingly full mailbox.

What upsets me is that I will be doing largely Social Science courses for the rest of my degree, and there will probably not be many fellow students around on Cosy to talk to, but I still intend to stay on line to reap all the other benefits.
Verity

============================
51438/message #5, ad-ford, 3774 chars, 9-Nov-88 22:36
There is/are comment(s) on this message.

TITLE: Sorry this is late... I was on holiday when all the fun started! CMC has changed my life. I have never met Maureen, Mike, Verity or Shaz face-to-face, but but we are all great friends ...well most of the time :-) Before studying with the Open University, I attended a college for 'A' levels. Then I had an accident which forced me to move to home-study. Studying at home is not the best method for many. There is even less motivation to work if you do not attend tutorials and meet with other students. Of course you can talk to tutors, and they will come to your home if you cannot get out and about very easily, but it does not replace contact with other students. This is where CMC is invaluable. It cuts down isolation, removes barriers and can help increase equality.

At college, tutorials were supposed to give students an opportunity to speak freely about problems, and receive guidance from the tutor or fellow students. The problem was, hardly anybody spoke, especially if the tutor had a sour face! Consequently, hardly anybody attended. CoSy is completely different. Everybody is given an equal opportunity to speak. Students can think carefully about what they want to say, and do not have to wait for somebody else to stop speaking before they can contribute. Thus each student can have a voice if they wish, and can paste their messages day or night. In a face-to-face tutorial, it is easy to feel shy and intimidated by the presence of other more educated students. On CoSy, students and staff are very supportive.

We could put a question or problem on a conference, and it was very common to receive several replies very quickly, sometimes within minutes of pasting it.

Everybody who contributes is concerned with everybody else's' problems. We have a community of students who care for each other and spur each other on to keep going, despite the problems that arise for the home-based student.

Like Mike, I have been concerned about the number of lurkers on the system. In a quest to find out why they look at the messages but do not contribute, I opened up a conversation with the aim of getting the students who regularly contribute to encourage those who lurk to try using CMC interactively.

The conversation was called The CoSy Chatline/Self-help Group, and had a very informal atmosphere. We added many students onto the conversation and addressed personal messages to a number of lurkers, in an attempt to give them a gentle push. Not all of them replied, but there were quite a few who started to feel their feet and eventually became as addicted to CMC as the CoSy personalities that Maureen mentioned. They were grateful for the encouragement (until they received their telephone bills!).

Conversations such as the Chatline are useful for socialising. It is possible to have on-line chats with other students. When a couple of people start talking, more and more join in, and before we know it, a large group of students and tutors are chipping in from all over the British Isles. It is not uncommon for students from England, Scotland, Ireland and Wales to all be conversing as though in the same room, but with the advantage of being able to edit each comment before it is transmitted.

This sort of contact has made me feel part of a real university for the first time, and has been a great source of encouragement. Many have said that if CoSy had not been what it is, they would have dropped out of the course. Before the exam, on-line conversations became more frequent, and after the exam, we celebrated (and commiserated) with a UK-wide on-line party.

I would dearly love to see CMC take an increasingly active role in distance-learning, to aid and support students in ALL courses.

Andrew.

```
===========================
```
51438/message #6, s-roberts, 260 chars, 10-Nov-88 00:14
This is a comment to message 5
There is/are comment(s) on this message.
There are additional comments to message 5.
```
--------------------------
```
I agree Andy, the chat/self-help-line was one of the big successes of the whole course for me, and the on-line post exam party was brilliant, there was contributions from quite a few students who had never said a word before, and your mum was tremendous !!
Shaz

```
==========================
```
51438/message #7, m-orourke, 714 chars, 10-Nov-88 21:29
This is a comment to message 6
```
--------------------------
```
.......I opened a conv back in July for a small group of COSY -philes who had all discovered each other in other convs. Our point of interest was IT in the workplace - from those small beginnings grew a large conv with over 90 messages which included details of people's own workplaces, working methods hardware and software used etc. CMC does have this tremendous advantage for getting like-minded people together to "talk" about a common subject - which in this case not only improved our knowledge on the course but was also invaluable for our use at work - indeed as the student population dwindles. I notice that the Conv is still thriving with the Walton staff.

```
==========================
```
51438/message #8, vj-maine, 354 chars, 10-Nov-88 21:52
This is a comment to message 5
There are additional comments to message 5.
```
--------------------------
```
Your message also brings out another advantage Andy - you can go on holiday and not miss a thing, it's all still there when you get back. I really like the 'time-warp' aspect. Not many people are overjoyed when you ring them to discuss a serious topic at 2 am, but with CoSy, no problem. You can even join in a party at 7 in the morning if you want, too!

```
==========================
```
51438/message #9, mb-walker, 1207 chars, 13-Nov-88 20:41
This is a comment to message 5
There is/are comment(s) on this message.
```
--------------------------
```
Yes Andy, I believe that the /conversation/ mode is the ideal environment in which to introduce the reluctant participants, i.e. the lurkers. The atmosphere is less formal than the /open/ conferences and people seem to feel more at ease in a confined group. You can experiment with the system and receive encouragement from your new- found friends thus gaining confidence before venturing into /the big wide world/ of conferencing.
I suppose too as in a face-to-face situation you need someone to gently prod others into action.
....
And I agree Andy, CMC should be a part of EVERY Open University Course. Having had the advantage of CoSy this year with DT200, I should feel sorely deprived if other courses did not follow suit.
Maureen.

```
==========================
```
51438/message #10, vj-maine, 622 chars, 13-Nov-88 22:24
There is/are comment(s) on this message.
```
--------------------------
```
Conversations are certainly a good way to get into the system. I did not feel nearly so vulnerable in them, as I KNEW who I was talking to. Also they can focus on different topics, as Mike points out. This year I have discussed everything from politics, religion, my cat's state of health and many other topics, both course related and otherwise!

Mail has also been useful to me...for some reason I feel able to e-mail people that I would normally hesitate to phone or write to. It does not seem so formal somehow. The different ways in which people use mail and conversations would be an interesting topic for study.

```
============================
```
51438/message #11, s-roberts, 661 chars, 23-Nov-88 00:27
This is a comment to message 9
There is/are comment(s) on this message.
```
--------------------------
```
I personally think that students who have to take distance learning courses (for whatever reason) should be encouraged as much as possible to use CMC if they are given the chance and the opportunity, I for one really feel I've missed out on a hell of a brilliant means of education for the first two years of study with the Open University, I had never heard of computer conferencing until this course, which brings me to ask - we know that CMC can and will revolutionise distant learning, but how do we make its possibilities known to all the students who would love it just as much as we do, but don't just happen to stumble across it via DT200?
Sharon.

```
============================
```
51438/message #12, m-orourke, 453 chars, 23-Nov-88 17:36
This is a comment to message 10
```
--------------------------
```
I agree re the phoning/writing - I guess sitting in front of a screen almost adds the visual medium that you cannot add in a letter or phone call. At the same time you keep your anonymity so that even if you say something daft - which gets picked up on - you can blush alone!
More importantly if you say something good, there is tremendous satisfaction in actually seeing the feedback as other people mention your contribution THERE in front of you!

NOTES

[1] DT200 is the course code for the Open University course *An Introduction to Information Technology: Social and Technological Issues*. It is the only OU undergraduate course which has a built-in CMC element: see Part 2 of this book. (ed)
[2] ....indicates where a section of text has been left out. (ed)
[3] This refers to the 'conversation' facility on CoSy which, in contrast to the 'conference' area, is an informal unlisted area for asynchronous discussion. (ed)
[4] COCO is a group ID used by the DT200 course team for responding to student queries; it stands for COsy COordinator. (ed)

PART 1

THEMES AND ISSUES

The eight chapters that make up Part 1 of this book explore the use and educational implications of computer-mediated communication (CMC) from a variety of different perspectives, but are to a large extent underpinned by the same major themes.

The first of these themes is the unique nature of CMC as a medium for communication – a medium which, whilst being essentially one of literary discourse, is also one of interactive, reflective, and asynchronous group communication. Andrew Feenberg, in Chapter 2, presents an analysis of the 'Written World' of CMC, and stresses the importance of the roles of the social network designer and conference moderator in initiating and maintaining group communication processes. Paul Levinson, in Chapter 3, places CMC within an evolutionary model of media, and makes interesting comparisons between CMC and other media used in education – namely face-to-face meetings, print, and audio-visual media.

The second main theme is that of distance education, and the various models of the educational process which underlie particular distance learning programmes. In this book, two different models are apparent:

- the large-scale multi-media distance teaching model espoused by the British Open University, into which CMC becomes an additional medium of communication (see Part 2)
- the 'virtual classroom' model, as exemplified by the on-line courses given at the Ontario Institute for Studies in Education (see Chapter 4, by Harasim, and Chapter 6, by Davie).

There is clearly no single 'right way' for using CMC in distance education, and many models intermediate between these two extremes will undoubtedly develop. Søren Nipper, in Chapter 5, points to one possible direction with the concept of 'third generation' distance learning, centred around the group processes which CMC permits.

A third major theme is the impact which CMC will have not only on the nature of the interactions between learners, tutors, and other resource people, but also on the organisational structures which support the educational process.

Elaine McCreary, in Chapter 8, describes some of the impacts that the widespread availability of the CoSy conferencing system has had on the University of Guelph's organisational culture.

Finally, in every discussion of current CMC systems, the question of the human-computer interface, and the ways in which it could be improved through specially tailored front-ends, hypertext-based local storage, and smoother integration of on-line and off-line functions, is a recurrent theme. Alexander and Lincoln, in Chapter 7, present a description of a workstation and communication system specially designed for distance learners, which represents one possible answer to the design problems of current systems.

CHAPTER 1

COMPUTER-MEDIATED COMMUNICATION AND DISTANCE EDUCATION

Anthony Kaye
Open University
Milton Keynes, UK

INTRODUCTION

This opening chapter has a number of functions. Firstly, it briefly defines the various on-line services available for education. Then it sets the scene for the rest of the book by reviewing the aspects of distance education which are important in examining the potential of computer-mediated communication (CMC), and outlines some of the principal arguments put forward for using this technology. The chapter concludes with an analysis of the implications of adopting CMC for education, with specific reference to learners, teachers, integration with other media, and overall organisational factors.

This chapter is also meant to provide a framework which can be used to navigate through the wide range of different ideas, concepts, and practices discussed in the book. Forward references are made to later chapters, or to papers in the Resource File (Part 3), whenever a more extended treatment of the issue in question can be found. The book has been edited, by the way, on the assumption that it will be read in a relatively eclectic manner, and this introductory chapter should be helpful in providing guidance for selective reading.

If there is one central theme to this book, it is the belief that CMC will ultimately emerge as a new educational paradigm, taking its place alongside both face-to-face and distance education; at the same time, it will change the nature of 'traditional' multi-media distance education. On-line education has unique attributes, even though it shares some of the features of place-based education (notably group interactivity) and of distance education (notably the freedom from time and place constraints). CMC has the potential to provide a means for the weaving together of ideas and information from many peoples' minds, regardless of when and from where they contribute. The educational potential of

3

such computer-mediated interactivity, and the open-ness to multiple discourse and perspectives which it can permit, is enormous. The chapters and papers collected together in this book represent some of the early, and often unsure, steps towards the realisation of this potential.

ON-LINE EDUCATION

Through on-line communication facilities, people can very easily contact each other, transfer text and data files, and obtain information from computer databases, regardless of space or time constraints, from their own homes or workplaces. All that is required is a telephone line, a micro-computer, a modem, and suitable word-processing and communications software. This technology, combined with access to suitable networks, has the potential to vastly enrich the range of resources available to the distance learner.

Three types of on-line service are currently being used in education. These are electronic mail, computer conferencing, and on-line databases. Each is briefly described below.

Electronic Mail

The basic unit of an electronic mail system is a 'message' – a discrete item of text produced by a sender and addressed to one or more named readers. Messages can vary in length from a few words to very many pages of text, and this means that electronic mail systems can be used both for on-line transmission of short messages as well as for the transfer of word-processed files that have been prepared off-line. Messages are routed by the system to the addressee's mailbox on the host computer, and wait there to be read the next time the addressee logs in to the system. At this point, the latter can then read the message, reply to it, leave it in the mailbox for later attention, delete it, forward it to someone else, or file it. Most electronic mail systems have a bulletin board facility which gives multiple read-only access to messages and documents. However, this represents a very limited form of group communication.

Computer Conferencing

Computer conferencing systems, although based on similar technology to electronic mail, use the filing and organising power of a host computer to support sophisticated group and many-to-many communication facilities. Individual users can join 'conferences' on specific subjects of interest; a given user may be a member of many such conferences, each conference containing the cumulative total of messages sent to it by the various conference members. As in electronic mail, conferencing on such a system is asynchronous – it does not require that all members be present and active at the same moment in time. Unlike face-to-face conferencing, or telephone or video-conferencing, participants are not obliged to respond immediately to questions and to other participants' interventions. These can be read and reflected on at ease, and one's own contribution sent in when it is ready and at a time which is convenient. The conference transcript becomes a valuable record which can be consulted at leisure, or edited and used as a basis for a collective group report, as all contributions to a conference are automatically stored on the system. Most conferencing systems offer a range of facilities for enhancing group communication and information retrieval; these include directories of users and conferences, conference management tools, search facilities, polling options, cooperative authoring, and the ability to customise the system with special commands for particular groups.

On-Line Databases and Information Banks

Information can be stored in databases on the same host computer which is used for an electronic mail or computer conferencing system, or alternatively, users can access a variety of existing public or private databases held on other computers. It is often more economic and efficient to search for specialist information on such electronic databases than it is to use more traditional information sources. Setting up a database can be relatively straightforward, although its maintenance and up-dating may represent a quite considerable commitment. However, even for small groups of widely dispersed members, it is often more economic to make information available in this way rather than through more conventional means such as photocopying and mailing. Users can locate required information with a variety of search methods and, if needed, download the material onto their own microcomputer for subsequent printing.

Computer-Mediated Communication

At the present time, the three types of on-line service mentioned above tend to be seen as separate, discrete, elements, partly because they have developed in different markets, serving different types of clientele. Electronic mail has been used mainly in computer and business environments, and is developing fast in this sector (with estimated annual growth rates in messaging traffic of from 68% to 100% in the USA). Educational databases have traditionally been seen as the province of libraries and other specialist information services.

The documented applications of computer conferencing suggest that its flat communication structure can cause problems in hierarchically structured organisations (Zuboff, 1988, ch 10), although it has been shown to be valued amongst communities of research workers in both commercial and academic environments (Hiltz, 1984). It is interesting to note that, although computer conferencing technology was first developed at about the same time as electronic mail, around 1970 (see Paper 20 in the Resource File, by Zorkoczy), its use is far less widespread than one-to-one electronic mail. Recently, however, an increasing number of companies have started to use conferencing as an aid to group decision-taking, and developments in business applications of software for computer-supported cooperative work (see, for example, Johansen, 1988) are likely to accelerate this process. In general, it is probable that on-line services will increasingly continue to replace many telephone calls, conventional mailings, and meetings. [1]

In this book, we are looking predominantly at the educational uses of electronic mail and computer conferencing, which we are subsuming under the general heading of computer-mediated communication (CMC).

Specific examples of educational uses of electronic mail, including the use of public mailboxes or bulletin boards, are given in the Resource File by Muzio (Paper 6), Riedl (Paper 10), Wingfield-Stratford (Paper 11), and Somekh (Paper 16). Various aspects of the use of computer conferencing systems, which always include electronic mail facilities, but have much greater functionality for group communication than public mailboxes, are analysed in each of the chapters in Parts 1 and 2. In the Resource File, the Papers by Gray (no 2), Grint (no 3), Lorentsen (no 5), Paulsen (no 7), Owen (no 8), and Van Duren (no 9) refer to specific examples of the use of computer conferencing for education.

Most of these examples concentrate on the use of CMC to enable participants in educational programmes to communicate with each other, although in some cases this use is combined with database access and transfer of data files (eg Paper 6 by Muzio in the Resource File). In the future, it is likely that there will be much more convergence of CMC for interpersonal communication with database access and with local, stand-alone, elements (eg CAL, hypertext, audio, video etc) to form components of a new generation of interactive multimedia and hypermedia systems which will have powerful educational applications (see, for example, Ambron and Hooper, 1988). In this book, Ehrmann, (Paper 19 in the Resource File) summarises some of the issues involved in integrating a variety of technological media into a distributed learning environment. And an example of a current research project into the design of a multi-purpose workstation specifically for distance learners (The Thought Box), combining both remote and local functions, is described by Alexander and Lincoln in Chapter 7.

However, although the next generation of hypermedia systems will have much improved interfaces, and enable the user to switch transparently between different functions (eg from local graphics, word-processing, or hypertext software, to remote communication and cooperative authoring), the basic principles of non-synchronous text-based group communication, which is a major feature of CMC, will remain the same. These basic principles are introduced and examined in depth by Feenberg, in Chapter 2, and form a major theme of much of the remainder of the book.

DISTANCE EDUCATION

Distance education, in contrast to traditional classroom or campus-based education, is characterised by a clear separation in space and time of the majority of teaching and learning activities (see, for example, Keegan, 1986). Teaching is to a large degree mediated through various technologies (print, audio, video, broadcasting, computers), and learning generally takes place on an individual basis through supported independent study in the student's home or workplace. The quality of the teaching materials and the level and variety of support for independent study depends on the nature and resources of the institution or organisation responsible for a given programme, and the available communications infrastructure. Well-financed organisations with large student populations can attract experienced faculty and tutorial staff, and are able to deploy a wide range of technological media and support services – including correspondence tuition, group meetings and residential seminars, radio and TV broadcasting, and various forms of teleconferencing.

Models of Distance Education Provision

Distance education courses at university level are offered in a variety of different ways. At one extreme, individual teachers in campus-based institutions may be encouraged to take on a small number of external students to whom they send copies of their reading lists and lecture notes, and maybe tapes of their lectures, and whom they tutor by correspondence, telephone, or electronic mail. At the other extreme are the dedicated distance teaching universities (see Harry and Rumble, 1982) which teach exclusively at a distance, often to large numbers of students. In between lie a wide range of 'mixed mode' institutions, which, whilst teaching on-campus students, also have specialised units or departments for organising the teaching and support of significant numbers of external students.

The British Open University is a leading example of an institution set up specifically to teach at a distance, and to provide cost-effective education for adults through the enormous economies of scale which it can achieve. In total, in its various programmes, it caters for around 170,000 students each year, employs 2,800 full-time staff (including 700 academic staff) and about 5000 regionally-based part-time tutorial and counselling staff. The University makes extensive use of media specialists (radio and television producers, graphic designers, editors, software developers etc) and runs its own national computer network. Because of the degree of technological support available in such an institution, and the large numbers of adult, home-based students it reaches, the Open University is a particularly significant instance of the potential of CMC in distance education. In Part 2 of this book, the chapters by Mason, Rumble, and Thomas look specifically at the pedagogical, economic and organisational factors involved in introducing CMC into a multi-media, distance education course with an annual enrolment of about 1300 students at the Open University.

Another dedicated large-scale distance teaching institution is represented in this volume by Athabasca University in Alberta, which caters for around 11,000 distance learners. Paper 9 in the Resource File, by Van Duren, analyses Athabasca's current and planned uses of CMC. The Jutland Open University (see Chapter 5, by Nipper, and Paper 5 in the Resource File, by Lorentsen) is a further example of a multi-media teaching institution set up specifically for distance learners.

Elsewhere in the book will be found examples of the other types of institution offering distance education opportunities. For example, Chapter 6, by Davie, analyses the use of CMC by the Ontario Institute for Studies in Education to support small groups of external students following graduate courses in education throughout the province. This and other cases (eg an electronic poetry workshop run by the Riverdale Collegiate Institute in Ontario, described by Owen in Paper 8 of the Resource File, and the use of electronic mail for class discussion at the University of Alaska, analysed by Riedl in Paper 10) are instances of initiatives taken, with institutional support, by individual instructors for their own particular groups of students.

Mixed-mode institutions, catering on a larger scale for both on-campus and external students, are illustrated here by the case of Guelph University in Ontario, which has around 11,000 full-time students, and 1,500 part-timers. Distance education provision, through correspondence, CMC, and occasional residential seminars, is used by many of these part-time students. In Chapter 8, McCreary touches on the ways in which CMC is used for external students, in her analysis of how use of the CoSy conferencing system (originally developed at Guelph) has modified the university's organisational culture. Further examples of mixed-mode institutions, described in the Resource File in Part 3 of the book, include the University of Victoria (British Columbia) Extension Studies Department, whose use of CMC is described by Muzio in Paper 6, and Rochester Institute of Technology (New York), where CMC support on telecourses for disabled students is analysed by Coombs, in Paper 1.

The Future Potential of CMC for Distance Education

The above examples, which are drawn from a small number of distance education programmes currently using CMC, represent only a tiny proportion of the total, and very diverse, number of institutions throughout the world providing distance education opportunities. The International Council for Distance Education has estimated that there are currently around 10 million students taking degree courses at a distance in the world. No organisation has attempted to estimate the numbers of people using distance education methods for other areas and levels of study, but they must be comparable, if not greater. In the USSR alone, some 1.5 million students take higher education courses at a distance. In China, in 1983, about 40% of the country's university population (around one million people) were studying at a distance – one third of these under the aegis of the Radio and Television University of China, the remainder with local TV universities and university correspondence programmes. In the last fifteen years, new institutions or organisations catering exclusively for distance learners have been established in Thailand, Indonesia, Japan, India, Italy, Holland, Spain, Venezuela, Costa Rica, Pakistan, Taiwan, Hong Kong, Sri Lanka, the UK, Canada, the USA, and several other countries (Kaye, 1988).

If the pioneering attempts at using CMC to improve distance learning provision are successful, there will be an enormous potential for further applications, which will grow in parallel with the development and increasing accessibility of national, and indeed global telecommunications and networking facilities. The 'globalisation' of education through CMC is one particularly interesting notion. Guelph University has already started using CMC extensively for academic links with educational institutions in Indonesia and other countries; and many examples now exist of international networking between secondary schools. Maybe because CMC is an interactive, personal, and self-enabling technology, it will be successful in providing more interesting educational opportunities at an international level than have earlier technologies (eg television, print), often criticised for being vehicles of cultural imperialism, providing imported models and information irrelevant to a country's true needs.

CMC and other new technologies have the potential for blurring the traditional distinctions between classroom-based and distance education provision. Smith and Kelly (1987, pp 1-11) suggest that, in general, methods of teaching in distance education and mainstream on-campus education are beginning to converge, and that traditional teaching methods are in some instances being abandoned or modified in favour of a resource-based approach which no longer emphasises the teacher as the main source of knowledge. It is also my experience that CMC is seen by some colleagues in distance teaching institutions as a way of returning to a more intimate and cooperative form of group-based learning ('real' university education), and by colleagues in traditional institutions as a way of extending the resources of the classroom to those unable to get to the campus.

It is my belief that CMC will act as a focus for educators from both types of institution to forge new teaching ideas, and a new educational paradigm (Mason and Kaye, 1989), based on a combination of the best features of independent study and group-based learning. The result will be the development of new educational models which will represent more than just a merging of classroom and distance education methods. This line of thought is reflected here by Linda Harasim (Chapter 4), who makes a case for on-line education as a new domain, and by Søren Nipper (Chapter 5), who presents his vision of 'third generation' distance learning.

Although this book, for obvious reasons, concentrates on the educational use of CMC and other on-line services, these technologies should not be considered as a substitute for existing media and methods which have already proved their worth for distance education. CMC will not in every case replace teachers, texts, telephone tuition, or residential seminars – for the majority of learners it will complement these earlier technologies, and in so doing vastly enrich the distance education experience. And for particular groups – the housebound, the handicapped (see Paper 1 in the Resource File by Coombs) – CMC may well become the major lifeline to interactive learning opportunities.

The remainder of this chapter attempts to define the nature of the enrichment that CMC can offer to the learning process, and to assess some of the implications of using on-line technologies in education.

EDUCATIONAL USES OF CMC: A RATIONALE

CMC is a relatively new medium in education, and like other new technologies (many of which have failed to live up to their supposed educational potential) it runs the risk of being over-promoted. Many educators, rightly cautious of the hacker culture, tend to equate computer conferencing with bulletin board chat-lines or CB radio, and do not see how CMC can be used seriously for educational communication. Furthermore, CMC requires access to the necessary equipment and telecommunications facilities (which has significant cost implications), and obliges students and teachers to master an unfamiliar medium of group communication. Why is it, then, that experienced teachers from a wide range of disciplines [2] are prepared to consider using this medium, despite the technological, economic, psychological, and institutional barriers which need to be overcome?

Many reasons for this high degree of interest will become apparent from reading the various contributions to this book; my purpose here is to try to organise them within some sort of framework, by looking in turn at the broad pedagogical, structural, and economic rationales that can be offered for the use of CMC in education.

The Pedagogical Arguments

It could be argued that the inherent pedagogical characteristics of CMC are independent of whether it is used in a distance or campus-based environment. They revolve around two very important features of this medium:
• it is essentially a medium of written discourse, which nevertheless shares some of the spontaneity and flexibility of spoken conversation
• it can be used as a powerful tool for group communication and for cooperative learning.
Evidently, these features take on increased importance when opportunities for verbal face-to-face communication are limited, as for example in distance learning courses, or, in a campus situation, because of class scheduling and time-tabling problems. However, the discipline of being obliged to formulate one's ideas, thoughts, reactions, and opinions in writing in such a way that their meaning is clear to other people who are not physically present, is of key importance in the majority of educational programmes. Most universities and colleges evaluate their students' progress and achievement to a large extent on the basis of the written materials (essays, term papers, reports) that they produce for their coursework or examinations. Any medium which gives students practice in developing their skills of written expression is beneficial – in fact many educators would claim that such skills have deteriorated over the last decade; maybe the use of word-processors and computer communications will lead to an improvement in literacy levels and writing skills.

The value of CMC for group-based and cooperative learning is a pedagogical argument whose strength depends both on the particular educational perspective adopted and, to some extent, on the nature of the specific discipline and the characteristics of the learners. Educational theorists and practitioners who emphasise the importance of debate, discussion, and group work in promoting meaningful learning (such as those mentioned by Harasim in Chapter 4, and by Davies in Paper 13 in the Resource File) will argue strongly for the use of CMC for distance learners, because it provides an opportunity for such experiences which may otherwise be completely lacking. And even in situations where there are no constraints on the use of in-person meetings, CMC can provide a valuable additional dimension to group work: for example, turn-taking tends to be more equally distributed in CMC discussions, inputs are often more thoughtfully composed because of the text-based nature of the medium, and a written record is maintained of discussions which can run continuously over a given period.

However, some academic disciplines lend themselves better to cooperative work, and to the use of discussion and debate as a teaching/learning strategy, than others. It can also be argued that the value of group interaction depends to a large extent on what the learners have to offer from their own store of knowledge and experience. Courses aimed at professionals (executives, teachers, etc) often place strong emphasis on the contributions which students and trainees can make from their own personal experience. Distance education programmes tend to attract relatively heterogeneous groups of adults, who often have specialist expertise in particular areas of the course which they can share with other students. CMC can be an ideal medium for this sharing (see, for example, the comments by Mason in Chapter 9 on the ways in which students helped each other via CMC on an Open University course).

The Structural Arguments

By 'structural' I mean, in this context, those arguments related to the technological characteristics of the CMC medium and the ways they match the nature of the distance education environment. The freedom from time and space constraints which characterises CMC as a technology is obviously well adapted to the needs and circumstances of adult learners studying independently at a distance. Such learners, whether their primary locus of study is their home or their workplace, organise their study activities in the light of their domestic and professional circumstances, their frame of mind, and their available time and the way it is distributed. In such circumstances, even fixed-time broadcasts (although accessible from home) represent a constraint which makes them unsuitable for many learners. [3] Face-to-face tutorials and meetings, or weekend or week-long residential sessions, are even more of a constraint, especially for adult students with professional and family responsibilities. CMC, however, provides access to human learning resources at any time of the day or night, and, theoretically, from anywhere in the world. By this token, it also provides a means for bringing inputs to a course of study from a range of experts (visiting 'electronic lecturers') and other resource people that would be impossible by any other means. [4]

Another structural advantage of CMC for educational interaction is the fact that all communications are stored on the system and are retrievable. Distance learners' and tutors' contributions to a conference discussion can be searched, downloaded, and perused at leisure: in fact they can form a valuable living database or information bank, which can complement and up-date the pre-prepared course materials (self-study texts, TV, tapes etc) which generally form the backbone of traditional distance education courses. The psychological significance of such retrievability should not be underestimated: gone is the pressure many students feel at face-to-face seminars to note down every word the tutor says; it is all there, with valuable comments from other students and peers, in the conference transcript.

The electronic mail feature of CMC systems can provide a convenient and rapid means of submitting homework to tutors, and obtaining their feedback. A major problem with much traditional correspondence tuition is the long turnround time when students' work and the tutors' comments are posted via surface mail. Three weeks turnround is considered good in most institutions, yet this is usually too late for the tutor's written comments to be of much educational value, as the student will by then have moved on to a later part of the course. Obviously, provided that the tutor's time is organised appropriately, electronic mail can reduce such turnrounds drastically (although this may bring other problems in its wake – such as unrealistic expectations from students as to the instant availability of their tutors!).

Finally, the structure of a CMC system permits serendipity – it provides a planned framework within which unplanned and unexpected events, meetings, and interactions can occur. On a CMC system, any student is able to find out about and contact any other student or user on the system, for example to follow up the comments and ideas made in group conferences. Any user can set up a conference on any subject, and see who 'out there' is attracted in. The potential educational and psycho-social value of this is enormous, especially for isolated learners: CMC can become for distance learners the electronic equivalent of the bar, the lounge, the cafeteria, the many other sites of social exchange which play such an important role in on-campus life.

The Economic Argument

The economic case for CMC is complex, and depends on the starting point for comparison, and on who pays which costs. Turoff (1982) has made out a convincing economic case for teaching entire courses electronically, assuming that:

- courses are at continuing education/post-graduate level
- student to faculty ratios are of the order of 20 to 1 (ie no economies of scale associated with mass distance education provision)
- there is no front-end investment in preparation of special self-study materials (print, video etc), and students use the same textbooks as they would on a comparable on-campus course, and pay for them themselves
- there is no face-to-face tutorial element in the course
- students pay all communications costs, and provide their own micro-computers, modems, and software; course fees might reflect these costs.

The savings, obviously, are associated with the abolition of any need for campus buildings and facilities (lecture theatres, libraries, seminar rooms, offices, car parks, cafeterias, residences, furniture, heating, lighting, associated salary and overhead costs etc). However, although totally on-line courses will certainly be attractive to some students (and, indeed, a very strong case is made for such a course model by Levinson in Chapter 3), other students may want additional media and channels of communication – and this, of course, has resource implications.

If one takes a successful, multi-media, distance teaching institution such as Athabasca University in Canada, or the British Open University, as a starting point for comparison, the purely economic argument for CMC is far less convincing. These institutions are already demonstrating significant cost advantages over traditional universities, because of a combination of economies of scale associated with extremely high enrolments on some courses, [5] and a reduction in the need for student-based campus facilities. Adding a CMC element to such courses, however convincing the pedagogical and structural arguments are, makes it more expensive for both the institution and the students (see Chapter 10 by Rumble for a cost analysis of the use of CMC on a British Open University course). If CMC is to be used without significant increments in costs, then the basic multi-media distance course model must be modified. Less resource will need to be allocated to development of high cost learning materials (specially prepared print, video, or CAL materials), and more resource made available for communications and tutoring. This point is argued more intensively by Thomas in Chapter 11.

IMPLICATIONS OF USING CMC IN DISTANCE EDUCATION

I want to end this chapter by briefly reviewing some of the implications for students and teachers of using CMC in distance education, and by looking at the ways in which the use of other distance education media, and associated organisational structures, might need to be modified if the educational potential of CMC is to be fully realised. [6]

The Students

The on-line student is a learner in many dimensions, often learning about the medium, the basic rules of language and discourse, and the subject-matter of the course at the same time. Only when a student has become familiar with the medium, and is able to participate in CMC discourse as transparently as in more familiar modes (such as face-to-face seminars and classes, independent study etc), will its potential as a learning tool be fully realised. At the present time, it is therefore necessary to consider the needs of two quite different groups of users: those who are complete novices to CMC, and those who have achieved technical and social mastery of the medium.

Those in the first group need to be able to overcome a series of barriers to CMC participation:
- economic barriers associated with the initial cost of the necessary equipment (micro-computer, modem, printer, telephone access) and the space for its use
- technological barriers, associated with learning to use the equipment and software in conjunction with existing telecommunications infrastructure
- social-psychological barriers, associated with the mastery of a new and unfamiliar mode of written communication.

In some cases, educational providers can offer some help in overcoming these barriers: OISE provides face-to-face induction sessions for new students (see Chapter 6 by Davie), WBSI and the Open University specially tailor their students' communications software with menu-driven front-ends (see Chapter 2, by Feenberg, and Chapter 9, by Mason), and the Open University subsidises some of its students' equipment costs (see Chapter 10 by Rumble). Most CMC course providers also try to help new students conceptualise the CMC environment by using familiar metaphors: Connected Education courses have an on-line 'café' and 'library' (see Chapter 3, by Levinson), the Open University has its 'electronic campus' with a 'mail building', a 'tutorial building', a 'student lounge', and a 'senior common room' (see Figure 9.1), and OISE on-line courses use the small graduate class or seminar as their educational metaphor (see Chapter 6, by Davie).

Once students have gained some initial mastery of the medium, there is still a major cost issue for many in terms of telecommunications charges, and who pays for them: the student or the providing institution. Current optimism about falling prices for on-line charges via, for example, packet-switched networks, or packet radio (see Paper 11 in the Resource File), or the use of high-speed modems, may or may not be justified. The fact remains that, at the moment, the high cost of on-line telephone and PSS charges is a major deterrent for many potential students. It is therefore essential to develop workstations and software for distance learners that will keep on-line costs to a minimum (see Chapter 7, by Alexander and Lincoln), and to lobby wherever feasible for lower cost access to telecommunications networks.

Assuming that cost, technology, and learning barriers can be overcome, the major issue of varying levels of motivation and 'comfort' with the medium remains. Educators and planners often seem to forget the fact that people are different, and differ just as much in their preferences for learning and teaching modes as they do in other areas of their life. [7] This is particularly the case with adult learners, where the scope for the development of individual differences and preferences in learning styles is much greater than amongst, say, school children or college students. It is thus absurd to assume that on-line education is going to suit all adult learners: some will benefit greatly from this medium; others – even though they have mastered its use – will prefer traditional teaching modes, and may in any case be resistant to the idea of cooperative learning and peer help (see, for example, Hiltz, 1987, p 95, p 77). In multi-media distance education programmes for adults, where learners can choose to use or ignore certain media, these differences become very clear. For example, there has always been a wide variation in use by students at the British Open University of broadcasts and face-to-face-tutorials. Not surprisingly, there have been similar differences amongst students in level of take-up of CMC, measured in terms of total on-line time, number of contributions, and opinions of the value of CMC (see Chapter 9, and Paper 3 in the Resource File). CMC is an open-ended medium, unlike broadcasting or face-to-face tutorials, which have finite time boundaries. This, combined with its 'time-intensive' nature, means it is even more likely that there will be a fairly wide spread of use, with some students spending considerable amounts of time on-line, and others the bare minimum needed to satisfy course requirements.

There is not yet sufficient research data available to draw conclusions about the extent of variations in preferences for on-line education amongst the adult population at large. It is clear that, amongst self-selected groups who have opted specifically for CMC-based courses, this is the preferred mode, and participation rates are high. Examples would be the management courses run by WBSI, OISE's on-line courses (see Chapter 4 for data on participation rates), and the Connected Education courses. In groups studied under research conditions (Hiltz, 1987), or amongst large student populations enrolled in multi-media courses, there is a wider range in preference and in participation rates.

CMC and the Teacher

It is reasonable to assume that, just as with students, there will be individual differences amongst any given group of teachers or tutors in preference for, and ability in, on-line teaching. The skills required for successful conference moderating (see Chapter 2 by Feenberg, and Figure 2.2) have to be learnt, and then applied to a specific educational environment (as described, for example, in Chapter 6, by Davie). Some people have a natural flair and talent for this type of work, others have to make major efforts to learn to use the medium effectively; yet others will fail regardless of how much training and support they receive. Selection of on-line tutors and facilitators is therefore of key importance. Factors such as the following are possible predictors of success:
- some prior familiarity with the technology – at least at the level of word-processing on micro-computers, and use of electronic mail
- an interest in the educational potential of networking and CMC
- a commitment to the values of group work and cooperative learning
- sufficient time, not only actual on-line time, but, more importantly, the time to consider students' contributions and react to them appropriately.

At a practical, structural, level, the potential of CMC for enhancing and broadening the range of tutorial provision for on-line students is enormous. Resource people (potentially from anywhere in the world) can be brought in as electronic 'guest lecturers'; other students and members of a conferencing system may volunteer advice and help as well as the formally appointed tutor; busy faculty members can use spare time to contribute as part-time tutors from home, as can retired teachers who would otherwise be unable to maintain links with their institutions.

However, as Søren Nipper points out in Chapter 5 of this book, the use of CMC as a major element of a course almost inevitably implies that the locus of control shifts from the teacher to the group and the group processes. The teacher who sees her/his role principally as a facilitator of learning and as a 'networker', putting learners in touch with the resources (human and otherwise) that they need, is liable to be more successful as an on-line tutor than the one who tries to be the sole arbiter of learning and dispenser of knowledge.

The success of the on-line classes run by OISE (see Chapters 4 and 6) may well be due in large measure to the cultural and educational traditions of the graduate seminar class on which the on-line pedagogy is modelled, which puts the emphasis on group discussion, and the tutor as facilitator. Conversely, the relative lack of success of the tutor group conferences at the Open University (see Chapter 9) may partly be due to the dominant pedagogy of the institution. This is essentially based on individual study of highly structured print and broadcast course materials, with very little emphasis on group work and discussion-centred learning; the tutor is commonly perceived as the individual student's trouble-shooter and evaluator, rather than as a facilitator of group learning processes.

Integration of CMC with Other Distance Education Media

CMC as a medium is in principle sufficiently robust to adapt to a wide range of different 'media mixes', ranging from the course that is completely on-line, to integration into a traditional multi-media distance education environment. However, care must be taken at each end of the spectrum: the totally on-line course may well put too much reliance on CMC, whereas poor integration into a multi-media course may result in a loss or dilution of its specific advantages.

The ways in which CMC might be used in conjunction with other educational media should focus on the two specific aspects stressed earlier: the text-based nature of the medium, and its potential for group interaction. Although there is nothing unique about text as a medium of communication, to a certain extent it is the absence of the other media that enhances the value of CMC as a pure exchange and record, as well as permitting the advantages of deferred-time or interrupted access to be gained without any loss of data or context. Text can be read at whatever speed the reader chooses: sound and pictures demand a more continuous observation at a determined pace to achieve their planned impact. However, there seems to be agreement that it is not desirable to replace print and audio-visual materials with CMC media, although, in the future a case could be made for integration of some audio-visual and CAL materials with CMC on the same workstation (see Levinson, Chapter 3).

Conferencing is primarily about interaction, so in considering the role of CMC, one needs to look at the interactive media normally available to distance learners. Most distance education systems use three principal channels of interactive communication: correspondence tuition, telephone contact, and face-to-face meetings. To these one can add, in some countries, phone-in links to broadcast radio and TV programmes, as well as two-way radio and facsimile transmission of written documents. The ways these media of communication are used – singly and in combination – vary from one distance teaching situation to another, but group tutorial meetings, correspondence tuition, and telephone contact remain the three principal forms. Should CMC be used to supplant some of these channels of contact, or conversely, is it a complementary medium?

There is some evidence to suggest that the introduction of computer conferencing into dispersed groups may lead to an increase in other forms of communication amongst some of those involved (see for example, Kerr and Hiltz, 1982). The increased level of communication which conferencing permits might lead to an increased demand for face-to-face and telephone contact, so it could well be inappropriate to imagine that conferencing will be a substitute either for face-to-face meetings, or even for postal contact and telephone calls.

Electronic mail could replace written communication between tutors and students – after all, it can be more convenient, is much more rapid, and is not necessarily any more expensive. However, as the main function of written correspondence tuition is for tutors to evaluate, annotate, and grade written work submitted by students, there are certain advantages to using paper – students receive their work back with the tutor's comments and annotations against the relevant parts of the text. When assignments are submitted electronically, current CMC software requires the student's text (eg an essay) to be sliced into a series of discrete messages, so that the tutor can make message-based comments. Furthermore, assignment work in many disciplines requires sketches, graphs, and other diagrams, and, once again, current CMC systems cannot cater for these functions adequately, just as they cannot cater elegantly for written comments in the margins of electronically submitted text.

Conferencing can certainly replace a certain proportion of the telephone communications that take place between tutors and students. Telephone contact is generally used by students to report difficulties with specific parts of the course material, or with particular assignment questions. If, instead, students send their queries into a group conference space, it will mean that the tutor will not have to deal with the same problem with each student separately, and that other students will be able to contribute their own explanations and views. The mere psychological factor of realising that others in the group are having similar problems, and that one is not alone in experiencing difficulties, is very motivating. And the asynchronous nature of computer communication has certain clear advantages over voice telephone calls, when there is always the possibility that the person called will be unavailable, or preoccupied with other matters.

However, CMC is not a substitute for certain properties of voice telephone communication – especially the intimacy and the spontaneity of response. Telephone conversations provide the opportunity for an informal chat, as well a chance to clear up difficulties rapidly. The introduction of CMC into a distance education course can lead to an increase in telephone contacts between and amongst students and tutors, particularly at the beginning of the course, when people are learning how to use the system (see Chapter 9, and the reference to the value of telephone help lines for students in difficulties with the new

MW—C

technology). New CMC users often want to use a more traditional medium such as the telephone to check whether a message has been received, to talk about the message, to apologise for mistakes in its formatting, or simply to receive reassurance.

Organisational Implications

The introduction of any new technology – even into traditionally conservative educational organisations – is bound to have implications for the ways in which the organisation functions (unless, of course, the technology is rejected, in which case it is often taken up and exploited by new organisations, who compete for the same clientele, or use the technology to open educational opportunities to new clienteles). The earliest distance education courses (in shorthand) were started by Isaac Pitman in England in 1840, when a national postal system with a standard tariff throughout Britain was introduced: this was the beginning of correspondence tuition, the first distance tutoring technique (Dieuzeide, 1985, p 31). As other media and technologies became available, so they have been incorporated into distance education: newspapers, radio, television, telephones, satellite transmission, electronic publishing (see Paper 17 in the Resource File, by Bacsich), have all had major impacts on the ways in which distance education provision is organised.

CMC is no exception to this generalisation. However, the extent of its organisational impact will, of course, vary depending on the scale and nature of its use, and on the type of institution. In primary and secondary schools for example, it is clear that attempts to use CMC to allow children in different schools to communicate directly with each other is liable to cut across many of the basic assumptions and authority structures which underpin the school organisation (see Paper 4, by Guihot, and Paper 16, by Somekh, in the Resource File). In the case of on-campus universities or colleges, where use of CMC on local area and wide area networks is developing, it is still not clear what the organisational and social repercussions will be: what is certain is that the innovation process needs to be handled with care (see Paper 14 in the Resource File, by Florini and Vertrees; and Paper 19, by Ehrmann).

McCreary, in Chapter 8, analyses the influence that the CoSy system has had on the University of Guelph's organisational culture over the five years since its introduction, and concludes that it has had "a positive, but not unequivocal" impact on organisational vitality. It has certainly led to significant increases in both internal and external networking – with the development of new communities of interest, and a new means of implementing and enriching the University's many overseas links. It has led to changes in role requirements and expectations within the University, in particular to higher expectations of cooperation in working groups.

CMC has also led to the development of entirely new types of organisation. One of these is Connected Education (see Chapter 3), which teaches group-based courses entirely on-line on the EIES computer conferencing system, drawing on part-time electronic faculty from a wide range of sources. Another is the

Electronic University Network in the USA, which provides home-based learning opportunities through a combination of print materials, electronic mail, and database access, in collaboration with a number of existing universities, colleges, and suppliers of on-line information services (Electronic University Network, 1987).

It is perhaps too early to tell what sort of impact CMC might have on the large-scale dedicated distance education institutions such as the British Open University, or Athabasca University in Canada. In the traditional – and often very individualistic – distance education context, the use of CMC by students and tutors could have many far-reaching implications. Firstly, it provides a democratic, relatively status-free, environment for group interaction and learning. This not only gives students and tutors ready communication channels to course development staff, but also provides an environment for peer teaching, and a chance for students who may know more about certain aspects of the course than the tutors or faculty members, to demonstrate this knowledge publicly. On the other hand, it also provides opportunities for students who have misconceptions to propagate them at the flick of a switch, thus misleading others and creating difficult situations for the tutor and the group as a whole to disentangle.

Secondly, conferencing opens the door to unplanned events and interactions within systems where a great deal of time, money, and human resource is invested by course development teams in planning, structuring, and packaging mediated course materials, and 'optimal' learning sequences. Informal communication networks which may run counter to this pre-structuring can develop amongst students and other users; successful conferences thrive on suspense and surprise (Feenberg, 1987), and the unexpected can become the order of the day. What are the implications of these factors for course design?

Thirdly, any significant use of computer conferencing (as opposed to other on-linc applications such as database access) could radically change the cost structure of distance education as it is practised by institutions such as the Open University. Up to now, such systems have relied on amortising investment in high front-end course development costs by enrolling very large numbers of students, and keeping student-related costs to a much lower level than in conventional institutions (Rumble, 1986). Conferencing is likely to require more inputs, and more time, from tutors than the traditional distance education situation. It also requires more administrative support – if one puts a user-friendly and effective communication medium at students' disposal, there is an obligation to invest staff resources in answering and dealing with the messages that are transmitted by the medium.

These factors become very significant in considering the role of distance education institutions in providing mass higher education. Will it be possible to adapt an establishment geared to the mass production of distance-learning materials, to the management of distance learning on computers – to turn 'second generation' distance education institutions into 'third generation' ones (see Chapter 5)? Will it even be possible to integrate the use of conferencing with the *existing* features of mass distance education courses (see Part 2 of this book)? Maybe the increasing use of electronic publishing technologies for the preparation and up-dating of printed distance teaching materials by many 'second generation' distance teaching institutions will be associated with related developments in using computer communication for interactive teaching and learning on large population courses (see Paper 17 in the Resource File by Bacsich). On the other hand, it may be more likely that the effective applications of CMC will develop in the context of low population post-graduate and specialist courses for professionals (of the sort described by Harasim in Chapter 4, and Davie in Chapter 6).

CONCLUSION

In introducing a technology such as CMC, the creation of new forms of learning is likely to be in conflict with the desire for tradition and continuity. This can – quite reasonably – give rise to the fear that technology itself might dictate the nature of future syllabi and educational structures. Whilst this real danger must be recognised, it is important to ensure that the desire for continuity does not prevent the emergence of new, innovative learning and teaching techniques that the medium makes possible. Few would claim that current educational systems and techniques are producing satisfactory results for the required number of people, either in initial or continuing education and training. I hope that the examples, practices, and concepts discussed in the remainder of this book will provide some pointers to the ways in which CMC might improve existing educational provision in ways that could help meet society's needs.

NOTES

[1] IBM research indicates that 70% of business phone calls fail to achieve their goal. 'Which?' reports that 2 out of 5 first class letters posted in Britain do not arrive the next day.
[2] This book includes contributions from university and college teachers of philosophy, history, electronics, education, linguistics, rural extension studies, poetry, management studies, computer science, media studies, information technology, economics, and sociology.
[3] Many Open University TV and radio broadcasts are transmitted at times which do not always coincide with students' states of 'learning readiness': eg late on weekday evenings, or early on weekday mornings.
[4] For example, the annual management course run by WBSI from La Jolla, California, includes a session tutored electronically by a faculty member from the London School of Economics in England. The Connected Education course 'Computer Conferencing for Business and Education', run on the EIES system in New Jersey, in its Winter 1988-89 presentation, included guest inputs from two British Open University students.
[5] Annual enrolments on each of the five multi-disciplinary first year Foundation Courses at the British Open University average between 4,000–7,000 students.
[6] This final section is based to some extent on the many valuable contributions made by panel members, discussants, and rapporteurs at the CMCDE conference held in Milton Keynes in October 1988. I would particularly like to acknowledge the extensive report prepared by James Baring, and uploaded into the 'cmcde/book' conference on the OU CoSy system.

[7] The fact that, in most so-called civilised societies, we oblige children between the ages of 6 and 16 to spend six to eight hours a day in school classrooms, and prosecute the parents of those children who try to escape, does not mean that the majority of people would choose a classroom as their preferred mode of learning!

CHAPTER 2

THE WRITTEN WORLD:
ON THE THEORY AND PRACTICE OF COMPUTER
CONFERENCING

Andrew Feenberg [1]
Western Behavioral Sciences Institute
La Jolla, California, USA

TEXTUAL MEDIATIONS

Writing and Personal Presence

In our culture the face-to-face encounter is the ideal paradigm of the meeting of minds. Communication seems most complete and successful where the person is physically present 'in' the message. This physical presence is supposed to be the guarantor of authenticity: you can look your interlocutor in the eye and search for tacit signs of truthfulness or falsehood, where context and tone permit a subtler interpretation of the spoken word.

Plato initiated our traditional negative view of the written word. He argued that writing was no more than an imitation of speech, while speech itself was an imitation of thought. Thus writing would be an imitation of an imitation and low indeed in the Platonic hierarchy of being, based on the superiority of the original over the copy. For Plato, writing detaches the message from its author and transforms it into a dead thing, a text. Such a text, however, can cross time (written records) and space (mail), acquire objectivity and permanence, even while losing authenticity (Derrida, 1972a). That we still share Plato's thinking about writing can be shown in how differently we respond to face-to-face, written, typed and printed forms of communication. These form a continuum, ranging from the most personal to the most public.

The new phenomenon of computer mediated communication (CMC) appears to represent a dramatic step toward total impersonality. For example, authorship seems drastically reduced when messages entered into the computer's memory are accessed in accordance with the recipient's interest rather than the writer's agenda.

But is it true that CMC is a sterile imitation of thought, devoid of the personal touch? Computer bulletin boards, electronic mail, computer conferencing, videotex and synchronous dialogue programs are now employed by millions of people all over the world. Yet experienced users of the new medium usually deny that it obstructs human contact. It turns out that many ordinary individuals possess a compensatory 'literary' capability to project their personality into writing destined for the computer screen.

The strangest thing about CMC is not its purported inhumanity, but rather its lively, rapid iterations, almost rapid enough to recall spoken conversation. The speed with which messages are exchanged makes it possible to use computer communications to manage a project, say, or teach a class, or meet new people. With practice, the computerised mediation of such pursuits comes to seem a normal part of daily life.

Yet no matter how thoroughly we banalise the on-line environment it remains unpredictable and surprising because it violates many deeply ingrained cultural assumptions we make about communication. For example, we may no longer assume that writing is more formal and less personal than speech. This and other strange consequences must be taken into account in any on-line setting.

The core of the new CMC medium is computer conferencing, which makes it possible to create discussion groups with access to a topic of mutual interest. Typed messages are transmitted over phone lines to a central computer where they are classified and stored. Participants 'sign on' at times of their own choosing, using the central computer as a 'meeting place' for an 'asynchronous' conversation that may last weeks or months. Life in such a 'written world' gives rise to many unfamiliar problems and possibilities.

Communication Anxiety

Engaging in face-to-face conversation involves complex forms of behaviour called 'phatic' functions by semiologists. When we say "Hey, how's it going?" we signify our availability for communication. We usually close the conversation with another set of rituals, such as, "I've gotta go. See you later." Throughout our talk, we are continually sending phatic signs back and forth to keep the line open and to make sure messages are getting through. For example, we say such things as, "How about that!" or reply, "Yes, go on." Looks and facial expressions tacitly reassure interlocutors that they are still in touch, or on the contrary carry a warning if the communication link is threatened by technical difficulties or improprieties. All such phatic signs are bypassed in computer conferencing. Even standard codes for opening and closing conversations are discarded.

Communicating on-line involves a minor but real personal risk, and a response – any response – is generally interpreted as a success while silence means failure. Additionally, the sender of a message needs to know not only that it was received, but how it was received. It is disturbing to do without nods of the head, smiles, glances, tacit signs which in everyday conversation often take the place of words. An on-line acquaintance once wrote me that he found himself "almost begging this machine to recognise me." The paucity of phatic expression in CMC amplifies certain social insecurities that no doubt were always there, but which now come to the fore.

The problem is aggravated by the asynchronous character of the medium. Here, computer conferencing resembles letter writing, another medium in which phatic functions are quite weak. It is less rude to leave a letter unanswered than to refuse to reply to a direct question in face-to-face conversation. Similarly, if we fail to answer an on-line message, it is without the embarrassment we would certainly feel were we to ignore an acquaintance on the street. But a poor correspondent may be excused because of the delay and uncertainty of ordinary mail, while CMC messages are never 'lost in the mail'. They are lodged instantly in the central computer. As a result when we leave a message in computer memory we feel an intense need for response.

This technical improvement, which makes rapid exchanges possible, also makes unusual delay a sign of rejection or indifference since there is no mechanical excuse for silence. Paradoxically, then, speeding up and improving asynchronous exchanges causes unexpected distress. This explains why on-line communities place such an emphasis on active participation and are often critical of passive readers who are pejoratively called 'lurkers'. This concern with participation may even become obsessive, revealing the surprising depths of anxiety of unrequited authors.

The Management of Identity

Computer conferencing is one of several new technologies which create novel forms of identity. Electronic bulletin boards, dialogue systems and computer conferences present their users to each other only through explicit written language. When writing, it is easier to choose a tone and attitude than it is in speech, dress and gesture. The social subject is profoundly modified by the generalisation of such highly controlled forms of self-presentation. The written 'I' is not the same 'I' who appears in face-to-face encounters. This new 'I' has increased its distance from the world and itself.

An extreme form of self-definition occurs in 'chatting' systems, where people make dates through an exchange of pseudonymous messages. These systems represent an interactive form of classified personal advertisement. In France, where such systems have developed on a large scale, this is a popular way to meet people (Marchand, 1987; Bruhat, 1984). [2] As with newspaper 'personals', lonely individuals have the impression they fully command all the signals they emit, unlike risky face-to-face encounters where such control is difficult and uncertain. Thus the use of writing makes possible elaborate identity games. As Claude Baltz (1984, p 185) writes, "instead of identity having the status of an initial given (with which the communication usually begins), it becomes a stake, a product of the communication."

The experience of pseudonymous communication calls to mind Erving Goffman's (1982, p 31) double definition of the self as an 'image' or identity, and as a 'sacred object' to which consideration is due: "the self as an image pieced together from the expressive implications of the full flow of events in an undertaking; and the self as a kind of player in a ritual game who copes honorably or dishonorably, diplomatically or undiplomatically, with the judgemental contingencies of the situation." By increasing the individuals' control of image, while diminishing the risk of embarrassment, computer talk alters the sociological ratio of the two dimensions of selfhood and opens up a new social space.

The relative desacralisation of the subject weakens social control in computer-mediated communication. It is difficult to bring group pressure to bear on someone who cannot see frowns of disapproval. Communication by computer thus enhances the sense of personal freedom and individualism by reducing the 'existential' engagement of the self in its communications. 'Flaming' (the expression of uncensored emotions on-line) is viewed as a negative consequence of this feeling of liberation. And so is the diminished sense of the reality of other people.

Chatting systems, like 'hacking', (Turkle, 1984) are bizarre social innovations that accompany and subvert the mainstream of technological innovation on which they depend. Marc Guillaume (1982, p 23) has introduced the concept of 'spectrality' to describe these new forms of interaction between individuals who are reduced to anonymity in modern social life, and yet succeed in using that anonymity to shelter and assert their identities.

The Relationship to Discourse

These changes in the management of identity take on their full significance against the background of changes in the role of language in CMC. A group which exists through an exchange of written texts has the peculiar ability to recall and inspect its entire past. Nothing quite like this is available to a community based on the spoken word. The modification of language by CMC can best be understood as a new variety of 'social memory' comparable to such other mediated memories as storytelling, books, and mass communications. Each medium supports recall of the past through different types of 'iteration', with different social implications (Derrida, 1972b; Goody and Watt, 1968). [3]

We can distinguish generally between retrievable and repeatable discourse. Retrieval involves access to a permanent text, such as a book or diskette. In principal there is no reason why such access should not be entirely under individual control since the technologies of retrieval do not require the presence of other human beings. Texts 'stored' in human memory, however, are 'accessed' through 'repetition' or performance. In cultures which rely heavily on repetition of basic texts, the function of performance is frequently assigned to special individuals, and access to the text is not under individual control but regulated socially through participation in public functions and audiences.

There is a long theoretical tradition of study of the relation between 'oral' and 'literate' cultures in which retrieval is identified with writing, and repetition with speech. But today the difference between retrieval and repetition no longer correlates neatly with the distinction between writing and speech: answering machines routinely present us with speech as a retrievable text, computer dialogue systems allow synchronous written conversation, and sophisticated phonemail systems and computerised voice management technology, and will soon shift the balance toward retrievability in all domains. This shift has remarkable social implications.

It has only been a short while since Marshall McLuhan announced the end of literate culture and the rise of a new 'oral' culture based on electronic broadcasting. Certainly McLuhan was right in identifying a steady devaluation of the written word in modern societies. Recent years have seen the proliferation of remedial writing courses in colleges and the gradual decline of the childhood pastime of reading for pleasure. In this context, computer-mediated communication seems to promise that writing will once again become a universal form of expression.

One powerful hypothesis about modern individualism holds that it grew with the emergence of printing and literacy – what I have called retrievable forms of discourse (McLuhan, 1964; Ong, 1977). The spread of written discourse fosters the corresponding spread of a new subjectivity: the eye (I) of the reader is an individual. The organic community of speech, based on repetition and performance, gives way to the privacy of the modern individual, suddenly distanced from the language of the community. In this new position the individual gains control of a personal language, which is 'doubled' because the speaker/writer is no longer identified with his own words but uses them for 'effect'. This distance is the essence of modern individuality. According to this hypothesis, the loss of distance in the pseudo-synchronous broadcasting of performance accounts for the decline of individuality in mass society (Ong, 1971, pp 284-303; Katz, 1980, pp 84-89).

McLuhan (1964, pp 50-51) was not afraid of the political consequence of this thesis, essentially the demise of Western individualism. He predicted the rise of a new form of collectivism based on the replacement of "literate, fragmented Western man" by "a complex and depth-structured person emotionally aware of his total interdependence with the rest of human society." But what if the dominant medium of the next century is not structured like broadcast television but like CMC? Such an environment, based on generalised retrievability, suggests a different future in which a new form of 'post-modern' individualism emerges, not as a retrograde reminder of the dying past, but in response to the most advanced methods of mediating experience (Lyotard, 1979, pp 103-104).

Absorption

Computer conferencing is frequently said to build community, but the idea of community implies bonds of sentiment that are not always necessary to effective on-line communication. A group of interested individuals may produce a successful conference whether they form a community or just a temporary gathering. Rather than focusing on the concept of community, it would make sense to study the dynamics of conferencing on its own terms. This may open a way to understanding the sociology of the conference group, its specific 'sociability'.

Conferencing dynamics involve the management of time, both the personal time of the participants and the overall time of the conference. Sometimes these dynamics are determined by extrinsic factors, such as job deadlines or the urgent need to accomplish a mission. Conferences are surprisingly fragile, however, and no amount of external time pressure saves hopelessly mismanaged on-line groups. To a lesser extent, we see something similar in face-to-face meetings, which require not only an extrinsic *raison d'etre* but also skillful leadership to insure a hearing for all those with something to say.

The social cohesion of conferences therefore depends not only upon the extrinsic motives participants bring from their off-line lives, but also the intrinsic motives that emerge in the course of the on-line interaction. To understand these intrinsic motives, we must discover how the conference empowers its members to speak up and provokes others to reply.

The sociability of conferencing resembles that of sports or games where we are drawn along by interest in the next step in the action. Every comment has a double goal: to communicate something and to evoke the (passive or active) participation of interlocutors. We can say that playing at computer conferencing consists in making moves that keep others playing. The goal is to prolong the game and to avoid making the last move. This is why computer conferencing favours open-ended comments which invite a response, as opposed to closed and complete pronouncements.

Erving Goffman introduced the term 'absorption' or 'engrossment' to describe the force that draws us into an encounter such as a game (Goffman, 1961). The concept of absorption refers to the sharing of purpose among people who do not form a community but have accepted a common work or play as the context for an intense, temporary relationship. The term nicely describes participants' feelings about an exciting conference. They are 'absorbed' in the activity as one might be in a game of poker or bridge.

To the extent that social organisation is increasingly projected onto the electronic world of CMC, this peculiar agonistic structure of on-line human relations will tend to be generalised as well. Those observers of contemporary society who see movement away from institutional and sentimental stability toward more fluid, temporary 'contracts' will find here a confirmation of their thesis. CMC is a privileged technological scene where we may observe the "atomisation of society into flexible networks of language games" (Lyotard, 1979, p 34).

GROUPWARE

Social Network Design

If computer conferences resemble games, then how are they organised, by whom, and on what sort of 'field' of play? These are practical questions, to be sure, but more is needed than a simple list of 'do's and 'dont's'; a theory of mediation must inform our approach.

It would be a mistake to treat this as essentially a technical issue. Although technology is important for any mediated activity, it cannot 'automate' what is in reality a social encounter based on specific social practices. These social practices are unusually complex because of the difficulty of mediating organised group activity in a written environment. Failures and breakdowns occur at the social level far more often than at the strictly technical level.

Until recently, it was possible to ignore rejection of the on-line experience because the disappointed users of CMC entered and left the system on a one-by-one basis as subscribers to information utilities or synchronous dialogue programs. Today, however, individuals often enter the CMC environment collectively, along with co-workers or fellow students in highly structured groups. Dissatisfaction in this context visibly affects group performance and must be addressed. A new profession – the social network designer – has emerged to solve the problems of organising and leading on-line groups. The success or failure of on-line groups depends initially on decisions such as:

- the selection of systems, training techniques and materials adjusted to the proficiency of the group.
- the selection of software and systems with the features best adapted to the needs of the group.
- the construction of conference architecture by breaking down the various concerns of the group into separate discussion forums.
- the provision of leadership, and development of moderating skills amongst members.
- the starting of conferencing activities with all the members of the group clear on the agenda and procedures.

Organising groups in the 'written world' demands an unusual insight into group processes as well as an awareness of the technical features of communications systems. The social network designer needs both these skills in order to build specific software structures out of available programs and features. Such structures are called 'groupware' by Peter and Trudy Johnson-Lenz:

"Groupware = intentional GROUP processes and procedures to achieve specific purposes + softWARE tools designed to support and facilitate the group's work." (Johnson-Lenz, 1982). The term 'groupware' refers to the combination of group process and software that characterises a network as a communications system.

Understanding Social Factors

Computer conferences create electronic social environments every bit as complex as the buildings serving the social activities that go on in face-to-face encounters. There is no generic answer to the question of where to put the walls, doors and corridors of a building. Architects and interior designers must devise solutions corresponding to the anticipated needs of the users. So too, designers of CMC systems must anticipate the requirements of the users of their products. The software's social architecture determines the success of group communication just as the location of chairs, tables, blackboards, podiums, affects more traditional forms of human interaction.

'Human factors' research tries to identify inherent constraints on product design with regard to human nature. By analogy, research into 'social factors' seeks to identify constraints on the design of products for this or that social group or category. These social considerations are generally known to well-informed product designers, marketing executives, and on-line group leaders but there is no one field where social factors are studied systematically. As a result, they are more likely to be misunderstood or overlooked than human factors.

This is a matter of great consequence for computer-mediated communications. Despite their complexity and variety, conferencing systems are not yet designed as social environments. Designers and users still tend to view CMC as merely one more communications technology, competing with the telephone and mail or available as a convenient travel substitute. From this standpoint, the social network designer resembles the designer of a device such as a telephone, who must adapt the equipment to human hearing, dexterity, etc. The search for generic solutions to the problems of the typical 'human' user obscures the fact that groups are realities in their own right, with socially specific needs that must be served by CMC technology. Often rationalistic assumptions blind designers to the specificity of group needs. They believe that they can understand and organise communication 'logically', on *a priori* grounds, rather than sociologically, in terms of the realities of actual social experience (Winograd and Flores, 1986).

Typically, products designed as generic solutions are offered to users in much the same way a new phone system or FAX machine would be. System administrators try to get people on-line with the hope that once they connect something will happen. This approach to CMC leads to disappointing results. It ignores the most profound potential of the medium, which is to provide electronically for groups to achieve a common purpose.

Tailored Conferencing Systems

The value of software features is relative to group needs and so varies widely. For certain groups, the addition of a specific feature may have little importance, while for other groups that feature can turn out to be vital (Vallee, 1984).

Educational conferencing systems, for example, are fairly limited in their ability to handle mathematical symbols. Not surprisingly, then, educational conferences are almost entirely to be found on the non-mathematical side of the campus. Here one might conclude that conferencing is best suited to qualitative discussion, but this conclusion would be premature if the systems simply cannot transmit graphics and mathematical symbols (Hiltz, 1986).

Does this mean that the best system is the one that offers the most features? The most complex and powerful conferencing systems do in fact offer ways of meeting multiple needs, but their sophisticated commands are too difficult for many users. Powerful systems, frequently trade off ease of learning for additional flexibility (Goodwin, 1987). Unfortunately there is no correlation between the level of proficiency of on-line groups and the specificity of their on-line needs. In fact, most users need both an extremely simple interface and one that tackles specific tasks. For such users, the far-ranging power of an adaptable system is likely to be experienced as a weakness, a fatal design defect.

To be effective for many purposes, CMC products must employ simple, group-specific interfaces for unskilled users. I believe that the best way of accomplishing this would be the creation of tailored systems based on a powerful, mutable program. This program must incorporate software tools that respond to both standard and specialised needs. Each tailored version of the basic program must share a common list of constant features and differ from others only in the variables it offers.

For most purposes a simple interface should be designed that will direct users toward the features they are likely to need. These features are 'foregrounded' by being placed in routinely visible menus while the others remain accessible in the background. The size of the foreground in each case will be determined by the competence and experience of the group.

The task of creating these tailored interfaces appears daunting. The variety of groups and tasks is so immense that it is difficult to imagine suiting them all. And yet the fact is that in many design fields this vast diversity is simplified with great success. For example, interior designers manage to accommodate all sorts of groups with just a few arrangements of walls, windows, corridors and doors. Something similar is possible in the field of CMC. The task is to map the variety of social situations into a limited number of communication environments. Many different groups and activities will turn out to require identical designs. The difficulty, while real, is manageable.

The concept of communication requirements stands as a link between the sociology of group behaviour and the technical capability of CMC. Communication requirements are group needs which can be addressed by the appropriate configuration of communication systems. Thus an instant 'message waiting' signal might be needed by certain groups, or secure communications, graphs and charts, or form filling capabilities by other types of groups. Figure 2.1 sketches a preliminary classification of such communication requirements.

PRODUCTION

Access Private and group messages/private and public conferences/bulletin boards

Group Process Action support/contextualisations/moderating/ interaction rate (synchronous/asynchronous)

Relevance Conference architecture/overload protection/length of contributions

RETRIEVAL

Time Alarms/reminders

Reference Indices/keywords/title displays/ conference architecture/ search programs/hypertext

Sharing Data/programs/lists/documents

PRAGMATICS

Friendliness Syntax/learning/help/error control

Identity Public (real names)/private (anonymous, pen names)/subscriber information (directories)

Safety Security/secrecy/reliability

Inputs Mathematics/texts/graphics

MANAGEMENT

Accounts Opening/grouping/billing/enrolling in conferences/updating

Tailoring Help files/command prompts/opening screens/system architecture

Figure 2.1 Communication Requirements

Selecting Conference Architectures

Ideally, conference architecture should be constructed according to the social characteristics of different groups. Today this is possible only to a limited extent. Each CMC program strives for an unattainable social neutrality and, in falling short, favours one group more than others. The network designer needs to be aware of these differences between programs, and must be able to take advantage of their strengths.

Conference architecture classifies incoming and archived messages and distributes tasks among groups or individual conferences. Here the metaphoric identification of conference architecture with interior design is most clearly relevant since each conference on the network is a bit like a room in a building. Network design and interior design both pose the same question; "Who needs to communicate with whom about what?" Then, equipped with the answer, it asks, "How many conference 'rooms' of what 'size' are required for the tasks of the group?" We must make our choices carefully: while it is less difficult to change conference architecture than the interior of a building, it can be confusing for a group to find the structure of its message system altered in mid-stream.

The implied sociology of conferencing software differs widely. Most designs today are either group-centred or topic-centred. A group-centred system promotes the cohesion of stable groups around a common discussion, the topic of which may evolve and change with time. Topic-centred systems, on the other hand, organise shifting groups of participants around the topics under discussion, occasionally forcing members to branch off to new conferences to discuss new issues. These different software structures reflect contrasting views about how best to file or classify on-line texts: in terms of a group process from which the text emanates and to which it contributes, or by subject which, presumably, will determine interest in the text whatever its source.

The Electronic Information Exchange System (EIES) and Participate represent two extreme cases, with other systems such as CONFER and VaxNotes offering a compromise based on item/reply branching. These latter systems are interesting for what they reveal about the problem of social network design. Each text designated by the author as an 'item' can become the starting point for a sequence of 'replies' addressed to the topic it raises. In practice, this means that after reading each new item, the user is prompted to choose to respond to it or to introduce a new topic.

This software feature can be used for two very different communicative functions, which I call 'contextualising' and 'classifying'. In the first case, each new item serves as a context for the replies it engenders. The most appropriate replies are brief texts quickly offering recognition or asking questions. As soon as users pass on to new items they cease to reply to old ones, even if the subject discussed in the old item is broached again. This application of the item/reply structure resembles a group-centred system. In the second case, where the item/reply structure is used to classify subjects of discussion, each participant uses the structure to maintain a logical organisation by topic, as in a branching, topic-centred system.

Technically, the two applications are identical, but socially they are very different. The correct choice in terms of group competences and needs may make the difference between success and failure. The social network designer should therefore select a configuration that fits the conversational style of the group. A large group of specialists collaborating on many complex projects might find branching essential to managing large masses of information. On the other hand, a group which values the process of discussion in itself might prefer a group-centred format for its activities.

The Moderator

Like other small groups, computer conferences are most successful when skillfully led. The technical conditions for this are usually defined in the conference program as a 'moderating function', ie setting up groups of participants as 'conference members', establishing and naming a file in the central computer in which to store discussions, and occasional deletion of irrelevant messages from the file.

These technical powers represent, however, only a small part of the moderating groupware, which Hiltz and Turoff (1981, pp 23-24) describe as follows:

> In order for a computerized conference to be successful...the moderator has to work very hard at both the 'social host' and the 'meeting chairperson' roles. As social host she/he has to issue warm invitations to people; send encouraging private messages to people complimenting them or at least commenting on their entries, or suggesting what they may be uniquely qualified to contribute. As meeting chairperson, she/he must prepare an enticing-sounding initial agenda; frequently summarize or clarify what has been going on; try to express the emerging consensus or call for a formal vote; sense and announce when it is time to move on to a new topic. Without this kind of active moderator role, a conference is not apt to get off the ground...

The moderator's role can also be considered as a literary equivalent of the 'intermediary' described by Luce Giard and Michel de Certeau (1983, p 11) in their discussion of neighbourhood life. But this is an intermediary active in new electronic 'localities'. In these new spaces there is a need for someone to serve as a "translator who decodes and recodes fragments of knowledge, links them together, transforms them by generalisation, handles each conjuncture of events by comparison with a previous experience and puts together in their own way, by an everyday practice, a...logic of the general and the practical, of action and of time."

It is strange to contemplate communication without a tacit dimension. Strong leadership must compensate for the missing cues. What I call 'contextualising' and 'monitoring' functions are explicit substitutes for the tacit signals that guide talk in everyday settings. These two functions complement each other. In contextualising, the moderator establishes a general arena of topicality, speaking in the name of the group. Monitoring offers verification of the accuracy of each participant's judgements about the nature of the communication context so defined.

The moderator's most basic task is to choose at the outset a 'communication model' for the group. Human relationships (the 'pragmatics' of communication) differ for example, in meetings, courses, informal conversations, parties, doctor's visits, and so on. As soon as we enter a room, we orient ourselves according to the tacit cues of the conversation we are about to join. These contextual cues establish a mood from which flow norms, roles and expectations. In the absence of visible cues, on-line moderators must make an explicit choice for the group they lead, reducing the strangeness of the medium by selecting a familiar system of roles and rules derived from everyday life.

Contextualising has the unusual semiological property of proceeding largely through the use of 'performative utterances'. These are statements which bring about the very reality they describe. An example would be the Principal's statement to the assembled scholars to the effect that "School is now open for the new term." Such an utterance effectively 'opens' the school and so is called 'performative'. Performatives appear frequently in the contextualisation processes of ordinary speech (Austin, 1962; Turner, 1970).

In most face-to-face interaction, performatives play a secondary role because so much tacit information is available to define the communication model. In computer conferences, on the other hand, performatives are usually the principle or only means of defining the communication model. Unless someone opens the conference by saying "This is a meeting", "This is a class" or "This is a support group" the participants have no way of being sure what kinds of contributions are relevant.

The moderator's contextualising functions relieve some of the anxiety participants experience in an electronic setting. Once a communication model has been chosen, the moderator must play the leadership role implied in that model, such as chairperson, host, teacher, facilitator, entertainer, and so on. This role will involve monitoring conformity with the communication model by reassuring participants that their contributions to the discussion really fit that model.

Meta-Communication and the Art of Weaving

Moderators also play an important role in initiating and sustaining meta-communication, ie communication about communication. Meta-communication is particularly valuable for strengthening a weak communication link by calling attention to problems in the process of discussion. Although, we occasionally engage in explicit meta-communication, as for example, when we ask our interlocutor to speak up or to come to the point, cues we give with our bodies and tone of voice are so effective that we can usually carry on complex conversations without employing much meta-talk. Not only can we get along without uttering our meta-messages, it is often embarrassing or disruptive to do so.

But in computer conferencing the only tacit sign we can transmit is our silence, a message that is both brutal and ambiguous. The solution to this dilemma is explicit meta-communication. Whenever communication problems arise, participants must overcome their inhibitions and demand further explanation of unclear remarks, call attention to information overload, request clarification of emotional tone and intent, suggest changes in the rules of the conference, and so on.

Meta-comments concerning the content of the discussion are called 'weaving' comments. These summarise the state of the discussion, identifying its unifying themes and points of disagreement. These comments reveal an important benefit of textual mediation for social interaction. Writing a weaving comment involves a relation to discourse which is characteristically literary and encourages a command of the written world 'from above'.

Many conferences lack weaving because no one has the time or the talent to perform the function for the group. This is unfortunate since, as a written medium, conferencing offers a unique opportunity to reflect upon the agenda of the group. The conference moderator or another participant can review printouts, harkening back to earlier discussions, clarifying confused expressions, identifying the themes, making connections, 'indexing' the material mentally.

Such weaving comments supply a unifying overview, interpreting the discussion by drawing its various strands together in a momentary synthesis that can serve as a starting point for the next round of debate. Weaving comments allow on-line groups to achieve a sense of accomplishment and direction. They supply the group with a code for framing its history and establish a common boundary between past, present and future.

Figure 2.2 provides a summary list of the moderating functions discussed above (Feenberg, 1986; Kerr, 1986).

CONTEXTUALISING FUNCTIONS

Opening Discussion: Carefully designed opening comments should announce the theme of discussion, and identify any shared experiences or symbols which can clarify content and purpose

Setting Norms: A familiar communication model should be selected to establish tacit expectations about conference behaviour, and to suggest rules of behaviour

Setting Agenda: The moderator controls the order and flow of discussion topics, and generally shares part or all of the agenda with participants at the outset

---

MONITORING FUNCTIONS

Recognition: The moderator refers explicitly to the participants to assure them that their contribution is valued and welcome, or to correct any misapprehensions about the context of discussion

Prompting: To solicit comments from participants, either publicly or through private mail messages; might be formalised as 'assignments' in some conferences

---

META FUNCTIONS

Meta-commenting: To remedy problems in context, norms or agenda, clarity, irrelevance, and information overload

Weaving: To summarise the state of the discussion and to find unifying threads in participants' comments; it encourages these participants and implicitly prompts them to pursue their ideas

---

Figure 2.2 Moderating Functions

Recognising, prompting, weaving and meta-commenting are listed as moderating functions, but that is not because there is only room for one person to perform them. Rather it is to ensure that there be at least one person who accepts responsibility for keeping the group alive. Discussions are most absorbing and successful when the members of the group share these functions with the moderator.

THE FUTURE OF COMPUTER CONFERENCING

Integrated CMC

Computer conferencing is an example of what Gilbert Simondon (1958) calls progress through 'concretisation'. Technological advance often proceeds by the integration of apparently separate, externally related functions in a new and more 'concrete' whole. Conferencing can be considered as a concretisation of mail and filing technologies.

The mail system relies on orderly filing of received messages. Only a message that has been filed can be re-accessed later, not only by the recipient but also by his associates locally. While the means of transmission have advanced rapidly over the last century from the pony express to packet switching, filing technology has remained stable, requiring the recipient to open the letter and insert it into an appropriate folder. Even electronic mail systems force individual senders and recipients to be responsible for the local disposition of messages.

With computer conferencing the central computer serves as a remote filing cabinet where all participants can see and respond to the latest additions to the discussion. No longer is it necessary for a local recipient to dispose of the message; instead, the sender can place it directly in a virtual locus which is shared by all participants. Computer conferencing 'concretises' the previously separate functions of transmission and archiving. The social structure of mail as a basically one-to-one means of transmission is scrapped and replaced by remote group interaction.

But this technological advance exacts a price: creating a purely electronic or 'virtual' meeting space results in a loss of context. Contextualisation is the weak link in computer conferences, far more so than in familiar communications systems. The absence of tacit cues and coded objects strands participants in a contextual void that may leave them literally speechless. The uncertainty of a poorly contextualised communication leads to defensive withdrawal.

Decontextualisation is an essential effect of writing as a medium. Familiar uses of writing, such as record keeping and literature, are based on the advantages of the abstract written word. Never before, however, has writing been used as the primary support of small group activity. When writing is adapted to this purpose, it becomes clear that it is not self-sufficient but needs to be supplemented by other means of expression.

CMC writing may be compared to vocalised communication in a face-to-face encounter: both media carry the semantic content of the exchange. But the sound of voices alone is insufficient for effective communication, and, as we have seen, gestures and facial expressions are needed to provide additional cues. The bandwidth of writing is even narrower than that of voice. CMC thus suffers comparable limitations when it is confined strictly to the exchange of written text.

Given these limitations of CMC, the contextualisation of computer conferences must be carefully planned. Only a few elements are available as substitutes for all that is lost in the narrow band of electronic communication. The most effective contextualising brings the group together for a face-to-face discussion. At such a meeting, participants learn about network design, initiating friendly exchanges and practicing their technical skills. Meanwhile, the trainer develops personal contacts which will be helpful later, when offering reassurance and advice on line. The face-to-face meeting can also synchronise the commencement of the on-line exercise through a ritualised initiation to the conference. Where it is impossible to hold such a meeting, the mail and telephone calls may substitute for it.

The fact that contextualisation in CMC often requires a face-to-face meeting is an admission of defeat. Computer conferencing still depends on face-to-face contact. Clearly, with the present technology, conferencing is not fully autonomous, but is only a fragment of a more developed CMC medium to come. In the future, programs will generate a rich and varied environment where electronic group activity will be significantly enhanced. The new CMC medium will take advantage of the computer's capabilities by integrating media such as hypertext, videotex, film, and audio recording.

This perspective on CMC's future finds support in the history of other technologies. The cinema as we know it is the product of the seamless merging of photographic and recording technologies. The automobile fuses a half dozen distinct technologies. Something similar is happening today with CMC. But it requires imagination as well as technical experience to see into CMC's future.

The Client/Server Model

Conferencing systems still rely on a traditional timesharing model of networking in which users access an intelligent host with a dumb terminal. These designs persist even today, when more and more users have abandoned dumb terminals for microcomputers capable of taking the first step in the direction of integrated CMC.

This step introduces the 'client/server' model of networking in which small computers, are linked to large ones. In such a distributed system, many problems of social network design will be palliated by creating a richer, more complex, yet manageable, environment.

In future conferencing systems, a transparent client/server model will replace the current, clumsy process of connecting and disconnecting two separate computers. These systems will offer a common interface so that users will hardly be aware of whether they are working on the terminal or the host. They will be offered sophisticated communications and word processing software which will make it easy to sign on and download, by automating all or part of the relevant commands. These facilities can be complemented with an efficient script language in which to write 'macro' commands combining sequences in the host system command language. Network designers can even download programs and directories periodically to groups of users at remote locations, re-tailoring their communications software as the conferencing schedule advances.

In the client/server model, the user's own terminal can become a source of contextualising information that would otherwise be lacking or which would have to be supplied at a costly face-to-face meeting. If all conference participants are supplied with program disks or videodisks containing such things as a database, an image bank or an educational program, then they share not only common access to an on-line conference, but also information delivered in a sophisticated form which can provide a richer background for their discussions. Similarly, if the conference archive is indexed and reconstructed using hypertext programs, then the group's own past becomes readily available to it as a context for its future. The early experiments with these systems are most likely to occur in the field of distance learning, which has been at the leading edge in CMC ever since the introduction of this technology. [4] [5]

Conferencing already offers the possibility of accelerated exchange between teacher and student. In the electronic classroom, students can interact and watch each other interact with the teacher. The next step may see computer-assisted instructional diskettes or videodisks designed to be accessed from within a computer conferencing program. The teacher could assign work on portions of the disks and carry on discussions with the students on-line, responding to their questions and providing motivation. Here many of the advantages of CAI could be combined with the traditional benefits of classroom teaching.

CONCLUSION

The elements described in this chapter constitute an ensemble of practices for successful computer conferencing. Let us recall some of the principles on which these practices are based:

- Computer conferencing is a technology which, for the first time, allows small groups to form and communicate through inexpensive and technically simple electronic mediation.
- Many types of conferencing environments exist, depending on the sociology of the interacting group. For example, conferences may be based on a subject (of teaching or research), on a project (management, negotiation), or on the communication needs of the group itself (information exchange, mutual support), and so on.
- In the written world of textual mediation, many of the ordinary conventions and rituals of small group communications are lost. Their reconstruction involves passing from 'natural' communication to an 'artificial', consciously designed pragmatic.

• This new type of communication must be organised and sustained by designers and moderators.

Finally, we must remember that CMC is a technology in process. Designers and users should involve themselves in the invention of the systems they require rather than passively accepting what they are offered as a final product.

NOTES

[1] I would like to thank Matthew Robbins for his help in preparing this chapter.

[2] The erotic charge of new communications technology in France today curiously parallels early experience with the telephone in that country. See Catherine Bertho (1981, pp 243-245).

[3] Derrida's (1972b, p 392) discussion of the concept of iterability, reminds us of the relativity of the distinction between speech and writing, and shows that speech is no more original than writing. Thus we can agree with his remark on McLuhan, to the effect that "we are not witnessing an end to writing which would restore transparency or immediacy to social relations according to McLuhan's ideological representation." Yet, a non-ideological reconstruction of the distinction generally covered by the difference between speech and writing is needed. This is what I attempt in the remainder of this section.

[4] The first course taught using computer conferencing seems to have been a writing course offered by David Hughes for Colorado Technical College in 1981. In 1982 The Western Behavioral Sciences Institute (WBSI) became the first institution to employ computer conferencing as the primary vehicle for the delivery of an educational program. The WBSI program is described in Rowan (1986, pp 71-74).

[5] See chapter 7 for a description of a prototype for a distance learner workstation combining CMC with CAL, hypertext, and other media.(ed)

CHAPTER 3

MEDIA RELATIONS: INTEGRATING COMPUTER TELECOMMUNICATIONS WITH EDUCATIONAL MEDIA

Paul Levinson
Connected Education, Inc.
and The New School for Social Research
New York City, New York, USA

INTRODUCTION

The question of media integration in education – what kinds of communication technologies should be used for what kinds of learning, in what proportions and mixtures – is much more than a question of hardware or technical knowledge. The question gets directly to issues in human cognition: what sorts of communication encourage or inhibit what kinds of learning, what kinds of ideas, what scales and rates of knowledge growth? The question of media integration is thus really a question of applied epistemology: what can we do to improve the ways we know?

This chapter examines, and speculates about, the impact of computer-mediated communication (CMC) in an educational environment dominated up to now by in-person communication and books (what I call 'place-based book-paced' education), and occasionally augmented by one-way audiovisual media. The salient features of CMC or computer conferencing include:

- instantaneous access to information from any place in the world and at any time (or the obsolescence of space and time as limiting factors)
- capacity for interactivity with the contributors of on-line information (the on-line text thus remedies part of Socrates' critique of the written word: one can ask the on-line text a question) [1]
- asynchronous dialogue, or the ability of people to take part in conversations at different times (eg John makes a comment on Monday, Mary responds on Tuesday, James responds to John and Mary on Wednesday, Mary responds to

James later that day, still later that day John responds to the comments of Mary and James, etc) [2]

Such features can then be assessed from two standpoints:

- the extent to which they encourage, inhibit, or have no effect upon aspects of human cognition (for example, what effect does asynchronous dialogue have on creative processes, logical processes, group dynamics, etc)
- how they compare with, and what impact they are likely to have upon, traditional media already in educational use (for example, asynchronous dialogue permits continuous discussion throughout the duration of a course, whereas the in-person classroom allows discussion only during the specific times the class is in session).

Adequate consideration of such a wide range of consequences and comparisons would require several book-length manuscripts at the very least; here we will but point to and lightly sketch what I see as a few of the main possibilities. These sketches derive both from my practical experience with CMC in education [3] and years of contemplation and study of the historical development and dynamics of media systems (what I call 'media theory'). [4]

Before considering the interaction of CMC with traditional educational media, we thus need to examine some of the properties of mixed media environments and systems in general, and their impact on human life.

DYNAMICS OF MIXED MEDIA SYSTEMS

The Profound and Often Invisible Impact of Media

The low profile of communication structures, as opposed to the content they convey, has been explored by many media theorists, most prominently McLuhan (1962). The example I often use is that of the Roman numeral system [5]. I offer an 'A' to any student in my class who can do a simple multiplication via Roman numerals, without conversion into Arabic numerals. I do this with no fear of contributing to grade inflation, because I know the task is impossible to perform in a system lacking the placeholder zero. And this lack of multiplicative ability makes all higher mathematical operations impossible. Division, algebra, the calculus that was the basis of Newton's equations, and the Lobachevskian math that is the circulatory system of Einstein's work, were all unattainable to the Romans. Was this the reason that they failed to develop an industrial society despite their superb engineering skills? Perhaps. [6] The point is that this feature, or lack of feature, of a communication system was utterly invisible to the Romans, and yet perhaps had profound impact on its (and our) subsequent civilisation.

When attempting to construct a media integrated environment for education, we need to be as aware as possible of the hidden deficits, and advantages, of the specific media we employ.

The Transformational Effect of Adding one Medium to Another

The addition of a drop of blue dye to a glass of water results not in blue dye plus water, but in blue water: a new reality. As McLuhan and others have often pointed out, the inculcation of the habit of literacy results not in a preliterate world plus readers, but in a literate world: a new world in which everything is seen through the eyes of literacy. Seeing (rather than hearing) becomes believing, written documents take precedence over oral agreements, and published constitutions become the bedrock of democratic and other political power. [7]

The moral for the introduction of new media into educational settings is that the new medium will almost always transform the educational setting, with the consequence that prior structures may perform quite differently – for better or worse – or perhaps not at all. In view of the need for improvement in our processes of education, this consequence is more likely a source of hope than a cause for alarm.

A Mixed Media Environment is Only as Strong as its Weakest Link

This principle countervails the above principle of media transformation: in the real, multi-dimensional, slow and imperfectly moving world, we rarely get complete blue water immediately after the introduction of blue dye. Instead we get some blue water – perhaps mostly blue water- but with some residual clear water and blue dye tenaciously swirling around on the peripheries. And the overall performance of the new, transformed system can be inhibited or strengthened by the continued presence of elements of the original system.

Electronics, for example, endow text with instant and global transmissibility, infinite revisability, interactivity, and a whole host of qualities not possible in text written or printed upon paper. But the moment electronic text is fixed on paper – in computer-printed transcript or typeset book – the text becomes just another printed document. This document has a highly interesting provenance, having been brought into being electronically, but it is in the end no more or less than any other printed document as far as its capacity for transmission, revision, interactivity, and the like. (An analogous situation arises when final assignments for on-line courses are required on paper, rather than via electronic submission.) If printed texts have worthwhile qualities unavailable in electronic media, then their continuance in an educational media environment would be beneficial; if, on the other hand, the older medium is in all significant ways improved upon by the new one, then the continuance of the older medium is so much excess baggage on the plane of progress.

Media Survive only to the Degree that they Uniquely Meet a Human Need

New media of course can accentuate human patterns of communication, and to a degree even bring new needs into being (for example, the need of a literate person to read). But, by and large, media seem to survive depending on how well they satisfy cognitive (and other) needs that are already in place in the human psyche, whether by biological (most likely) or extended social encouragement. [8]

Consider the case of silent movies and radio, one dimensional media (sight-only and sound-only) that held sway earlier in this century. Each was soon confronted by audio-visual competition that performed the same functions, but with a fuller sensory array. Silent movies soon withered and disappeared in the environment of talking motion pictures (sight-and-sound). Much the same was feared for radio in the age of television (sight-and-sound). But the result was different: radio not only survived TV competition, but is now the most lucrative medium (in terms of return on investment) in operation.

Why? In my 'Human Replay: A Theory of the Evolution of Media' (Levinson, 1979), I suggest an answer. The world grows dark every night, but never silent; we can easily close our eyes, and our ears remain open, but we cannot do the same for our ears (we have no 'earlids'); in short, hearing without seeing is a fundamental human process, whereas seeing without hearing is not. Thus, radio survived because it accommodated a human pattern of communication already in place: eavesdropping or just listening. This accommodation was quite unintended – when first developed, radio was the only mass broadcast game in town (the only simultaneous mass medium experience then possible was via sound-only radio). The reasons for radio's ultimate success thus do not become clear (at least to me) until the introduction of television.

This life and death dynamic of media will doubtlessly obtain in the introduction of new media in education. Earlier structures whose tasks are performed better by new media, and which have no residual unique function, will probably fade. Should we be concerned about this? Only if nostalgia rather than human betterment is our central concern. For example, if the book as a medium of communication were to disappear in favour of electronic text, this would happen only because the book served purposes that could all be better served by electronic text (ie the book was a 'silent movie' not a 'radio'). Of course, an institution could, by social fiat, insist that a medium be retained despite its functional disadvantages. Similarly, the enormous social and economic and even political structures in place that consciously and unconsciously support current media would work against the supplantation of old by new media on purely functional grounds. Nonetheless, the real progress in education would be most marked in environments that facilitated functional evolutionary change – the accommodation of media to human functional niches – rather than imposed social structures that militated otherwise. This brings us to the introduction of CMC into traditional educational media environments.

INTEGRATION OF CMC INTO EXTANT EDUCATIONAL ENVIRONMENTS

The dominant media in education, now and prior to the arrival of computer conferencing, are (in descending order of importance): in-person classes, books and related printed documents, and audio-visual media (recorded and broadcast). Note that I am considering an in-person class a 'medium', in that it entails technological structures including chairs, desk, and blackboard. Indeed, I consider speech itself a medium. [9] Note also that recently established distance teaching organisations such as the National Technological University in the USA, and EuroPACE, reverse the descending trajectory, making audio-visual media primary.

We will consider the impact and relations of CMC in each of these three media environments (in-person, print, audio-visual). Since virtually all educational environments are animated by at least two of these media, my comments about the impact of CMC on any one of them must be tempered by the recognition that other media present may amplify, diminish, or otherwise alter the consequences.

Integration with the In-Person Classroom

In-person education has so long been the basis of all education (well before educational institutions arose, the in-person tutor and teacher were staples of the ancient world), that education without some in-person exchanges seems impossible.

This is not the case.

When we apply a genuinely open and critical eye to the essence of education, we find that this essence – entailing the exchange of information, the stimulation of original and associative thinking, the development of intellect and feeling – is not in the slightest dependent upon physical presence. To be sure, many aspects of human life are. Making love, dining in a fine restaurant, walking hand in hand on a windswept beach, hugging a loved one, are examples of the many human activities severely impoverished by a lack of physical presence. Certainly specific aspects or disciplines of education are subject to the same needs. I often say that were I in need of brain surgery (some people no doubt think that I am), I would not want to be operated upon by a Connect Ed graduate in surgery, or anyone trained in brain surgery exclusively in an on-line CMC environment.

But medical and sophisticated 'hands-on' skills are but a part of the world's educational curriculum, and vast traditional areas of education – philosophy, literature, history, psychology, the liberal arts and the social sciences in general – are eminently learnable via a text-only electronic computer conferencing environment. When we add to this environment the imminent arrival of vivid, electronically conveyed, graphics and sound, the fine arts become similarly accessible.

But does this non-essentiality of in-person presence for many areas of education mean that CMC must replace the in-person classroom or meeting entirely? No, it does not, and indeed it should not, unless (as discussed above) the in-person class has no qualities that are not better performed on-line.

At this early juncture in the development of CMC and education, most CMC programs require some in-person meetings. Nova University's on-line doctorate (DA) requires several in-person meetings per year. The Western Behavioral

Sciences Institute's non-degree seminars similarly require several in-person meetings. Connected Education is alone in not requiring any in-person meetings at all [10] – but we do this not out of contempt for such meetings, but out of a desire to have all of our students, including those as far away as Tokyo and Singapore, participate in our programs on an equal footing. Requirement of in-person meetings would effectively disenfranchise students who live far away and could not afford the cost of travel.

Further, the reasons often cited by casual observers for the need to meet face-to-face are not generally valid. A frequent reason given is that such meetings are needed to verify the identity of the students in an on-line class. But no instructors that I know of ever trouble to confirm the identity of students who sit in their classrooms, and for all they know, the gentleman who appears week after week before them as John Smith may in fact be James Brown (or Brown may in fact be writing Smith's papers).

Still, in-person meetings can make important contributions to on-line exchanges. Knowing what someone is like in person can help avoid misunderstandings in on-line environments where social cues are more limited. (For example: anyone who has seen me in person knows I smile a lot – in an on-line environment, I'm obliged to qualify many of my facetious comments with a [smile], so readers do not misunderstand). Although mixtures of media can draw energy away from the media when used individually, on-line and in-person exchanges seem to be synergistic, or mutually increasing of energy. On-line exchanges frequently result in in-person friendships and travel, and in-person meetings often result in an increase in on-line activity among participants who now know each other personally.

The rules of thumb would seem to be:
• try not to make education hostage to in-person meetings, and explore the extent to which CMC can suffice and even be superior to in-person education (for example because of the increased access it can provide)
• be open to the unique contributions which in-person education can make, in tandem with on-line activities.

Integration with the Book

If the face-to-face meeting has been the staple of all education since ancient times, the book has been the stimulant and bedrock of the institution of public education since the Renaissance. The very availability of books made possible by the printing press created an urgent public need to learn how to read, and the institution of public education arose to fulfil this need. [11] (Learning how to read and write are still the most essential tasks of early education, and school systems which fail in this regard are quite rightly condemned, regardless of what other positive contributions they may make.)

The book itself has undergone considerable evolution since the printing press, and has proved quite adaptable to changing media times. In 1800, the average book cost about one week's wages for the average working person in America (Whetmore, 1988, p 22) with the result that only the Bible and one or two cherished volumes found their way into most literate homes. Improvements in printing technology made the book a mass market item by the middle of the 19th century, with the result that the novel and the popular science tract alike had their heyday. In the 20th century, the inexpensive paperback has allowed books to keep pace with flashier audio-visual media, and in the educational market, paperbacks and hardcovers continue as unquestioned staples.

The current state of the electronic revolution is incomplete – many classic volumes are not yet available on-line, or in electronic disk or CD-ROM media – and thus the traditional book still serves an essential need. In my on-line course *Ethics in the Technological World*, I assign Kant's Critique of Practical Reason, at a cost of $2.00. The universally accessible paperback edition of this work is by far the most efficient medium for its presentation to students.

However, we can expect the availability of classic texts on-line (or on disk) to steadily increase in the near future. Given the choice of Kant on disk (or on-line) or in paperback, and at equivalent prices, what advantages would the paperback version have? None that I can see, save the nostalgic one of 'cuddling up with a good book'.

Can one cuddle up with a good disk, on a cosy laptop? I don't see why not. Costs of on-line storage and access may for a long while be such that off-line access to an electronic text will be far more cost-efficient than on-line access. But as to the advantages of non-electronic versus electronic off-line storage, these again seem to be nil.

The plain fact is that books are in many ways very inefficient. Their pages can contain but one set of text, whereas an electronic medium can in principle contain anything and everything written into it and over it; books take up considerable space in libraries and bookstores, whereas electronic media can be much more easily stored, and thus accessible to greater numbers of people. Defined as an off-line text, my guess is that the book, in electronic disk or CD-ROM form, will be an integral partner of on-line education for some time to come. Defined as a print-wedded-to-paper text, my guess is that the book's days are numbered both in on-line and in-person educational environments. If in-person environments are 'radio' to CMC's TV, then the paper book seems, alas, the silent movie to CMC's talkies. [12]

Integration with Audio-Visual Media

The educational hopes for audio-visual media go back quite some time – at least as far as the 1920s in the USA. [13] The logic of these optimistic expectations seems quite sound: a picture is worth a thousand words, a moving picture with sound and colour should be worth far more, the audio-visual extension can transform any classroom or living room into a panorama of the world.

So went the logic. But with the exception of the Open University and a few isolated places, the realisation of this logic never came. The reasons are many. Film, radio, and television are one-way media – receivers of information through these media cannot use the media to ask questions and refine their knowledge. This pitches the educational process back into the in-person class, and dependent upon the talents of the in-person teacher. Furthermore, as Neil Postman and others have emphasised (to a fault) the literal, emotional quality of sounds and images in mass media can be distracting rather than enhancing of some aspects of cognition (Postman, 1979). Postman sees television in particular as disruptive of rationality (I disagree, but admit that, in general, literal images are not the most conducive to the deepest kinds of contemplation and rational analysis [14]). Postman also argues that the process of watching one-way television engenders habits which are incompatible with genuine two-way dialogue: you can turn your back on the screen, or fall asleep in front of it, etc. Again, I disagree as to the ruination of dialogue, but certainly agree that any one-way medium leaves a lot to be desired as an educational tool.

The British Open University and similar institutions have sought with some success to surmount these problems by integrating audio-visual (and print) media with a wide range of tutoring and in-person interactive relationships. Ironically, this may make such institutions more resistant than traditional universities to the introduction of CMC. For while the traditional universities are naturally protective of the great stake they have in place-based education (the sanctity of the campus, in situ faculty) [15] some also recognise that progressive efforts are needed to make their universities viable in the 21st century. The Open University, on the other hand, has already made a major commitment to a new type of education – multi-media distance teaching – and to make yet another commitment, to CMC, may be asking too much.

Yet the integration of CMC and audio-visual media is likely to be much less difficult than the integration of CMC with the in-person environment. Computer conferencing is an ideal vehicle for discussion of materials experienced in one-way media broadcasts, and the inherent distance advantages of CMC seem more complementary to the distance qualities of audio-visual media than are the rigours of in-person meetings, which are often uncomfortably integrated into distance education at the Open University.

Furthermore, the very technologies of television and computer conferencing share a common screen. The convergence of audio-visual presentations, electronic text, and computer conferencing on a single computer screen and keyboard apparatus will provide hardware endorsement for an integration that already makes much pedagogic and social sense. [16]

HUMAN COGNITION IN MEDIA-INTEGRATED ENVIRONMENTS

Human cognition – reason, imagination, emotion, and the whole host of our mental processes – is the most supple and powerful force that we know of in the universe. Through our imagination, we can travel to Mars and back in an instant, faster than the speed of light; when our imagination is tempered by reason and applied to the construction of technological devices, we begin to understand other powerful forces in the universe, and can even begin to change these forces in our favour.

The notion that a force so multidimensional as human cognition can be adequately served by any constellation of media at hand is conceit at its worst. The current servants of our intellect were chosen not because they are the best possible vehicles for education and the expression of ideas, but because they happened to be available. The best testimony of the value of current and past media is that they foster climates which bring forth new, and in many ways better, media for education.

Computer-mediated communication, and the advent of personal electronic interactivity in general, rank with the alphabet and the printing press as signal developments in cognitive media. Unlike literal audio-visual media that replicate the content of human communications – the colours, shapes, images, and sounds of the world, all crucial components of human communication – the media of text give expression to the process of human communication, and its aspiration for contact with any idea ever thought, any person, anywhere, and at any time. Alphabetic manuscripts and books were the first realisations of this aspiration, for the reader of the book is in communion with its author, regardless of where and when the author lived. But the connectivity of the book pales in comparison to the possibilities of CMC.

The capacity of any human being on the planet to tap into and contribute to intellectual dialogue is still far from fully realised, but its first expressions are already at hand. So compelling and promising is this creation of a real (not just metaphoric) global mind, so energising of the intellect is the ability to express oneself from any place and at any time, that I believe educational institutions will either learn how to effectively integrate this new tool, or fail in the next century.

NOTES

[1] See Phaedrus, 275-276, for Socrates' critique of writing, and Levinson, 1988 (pp 109-110), for a discussion of this critique.
[2] See See Levinson, P. 'Social Impacts of Computer Conferencing', Plenary Address, Second International Conference on Computer Conferencing, University of Guelph, Canada, June 1987 (published acoustically on audio-tape by The Powersharing Series, Riverside, CT, no 161, editor: Charles K.Mann)
[3] My practical experience in the use of computer conferencing for education comes from my Presidency and Direction of Connected Education, Inc., a not-for-profit corporation that has been offering on-line courses for academic credit in conjunction with The New School for Social Research in New York City since 1985. For more on Connected Education, see: Levinson (1988), pp 216-217; Brian Smith, 'The Electronic University', New Jersey Monthly, January 1987, pp 38 ff.; Paul Levinson, 'Connected Education and the International Community', International Informatics Access, November-December 1986, pp 1-2; Brock Meeks, 'The Quiet Revolution, BYTE, February 1987, pp 183 ff.; Paul Levinson, 'Connected Education: The First Two Years', Learning Tomorrow, Winter 1988, pp 205-220; Gail Thomas, 'Electronic Campus a Reality with Computer Conferencing', Bulletin of the American Society for Information Science, April-May 1988, p 23; and Thomas B. Allen','Bulletin Boards of the 21st Century Are Coming of Age, 'The Smithsonian, September 1988, pp 83-93.

Note that Connected Education (r) and Connect Ed (r) are registered US trademarks of
Connected Education, Inc.

[4] Representative writings of mine in the field of media theory include: 'Mind at Large:
Knowing in the Technological Age' (Greenwich, CT: JAI Press, 1988), 'Information
Technologies as Vehicles of Evolution', in Philosophy and Technology, II, ed. C. Mitcham
and A. Huning (Boston: Reidel, 1986), pp 29-47; 'Technology as the Cutting Edge of Cosmic
Evolution', in Research in Philosophy and Technology, vol. 8, ed. P. Durbin (Greenwich,
CT:JAI Press, 1985), pp 161-176; 'Human Replay: A Theory of the Evolution of Media',
Ph.D. diss., New York University, 1979; and 'Toy, Mirror, and Art: The Metamorphosis of
Technological Culture', in Technology, Philosophy, and Human Affairs, ed.L. Hickman
(College Station, TX: Ibis Press, 1985), pp 162-175 (essay first published in 1977).

[5] See Levinson, 1988 (p.102) for more on the significance of Roman numerals

[6] ibid

[7] The UK would be an exception to this. The declaration by the government of Margaret
Thatcher in October 1988 that restricted BBC broadcasting of terrorist speech, and allowed
silence to be used as evidence of guilt in some court cases, is an example of what can happen
to basic human rights when they are not articulated and codified in a body of externally
written principles such as the United States' Bill of Rights.

[8] See Levinson, 1979, ch. 6: 'Principles of Media Evolution: Survival of the Closest Fit' for
more on my explanation of media survival in terms of how well they accommodate already
existing human needs and patterns of communication.

[9] See Levinson, 1979, ch. 6: 'The Persistence of Abstraction'; and Levinson, 1988, ch. 6:
'The Agony and The Ecstasy of Abstraction'.

[10] For more on Nova University, see Lynie Arden, 'Earning a Degree OnLine', Home
Office Computing, Nov 1988, pp 102 ff; for more on the Western Behavioral Sciences
Institute, see Levinson (1988) ch 8, and Margie Ploch, 'Earning a Degree at Your PC', High
Technology, Sept 1986. These articles also contain descriptions of Connected Education (see
also note [3] above).

[11] See Levinson (1988) p.134

[12] See Paper 18, by Dunn, in the Resource File, for a summary of some recent research with
school children which demonstrated a clear preference for reading text in a CRT as opposed to
a print environment, as well as higher comprehension test scores with CRT. (ed)

[13] See, for example, Don Carlos Ellis and Laura Thornborough, 'Motion Pictures in
Education', New York, Crowell, 1923.

[14] See Levinson, 1988, p 160, for my critique of Postman, and of the more vituperative
critic of TV, Jerry Mander. (Personal note: Postman was my doctoral mentor at New York
University.)

[15] See Paul Levinson, 'The Economic and Political implications of CMC in Education',
Keynote Address at the International Conference on Computer-Mediated Communication and
Distance Education, held at the Open University, Milton Keynes, October 7-11, 1987
(available in the on-line Connected Education Library, The Electronic Information Exchange
System (EIES) of the New Jersey Institute of Technology).

[16] One possible embodiment of such a single-screen system is described in Chapter 7 below.
(ed)

CHAPTER 4

ON-LINE EDUCATION: A NEW DOMAIN

Linda Harasim
Ontario Institute for Studies in Education,
Toronto, Ontario, Canada

A NEW DOMAIN

This chapter is based upon the premise that on-line education (by which I mean, predominantly, computer conferencing) represents a unique domain of educational interaction. It shares attributes with both face-to-face and distance learning, but the nature of the medium is distinct in its implications for education.

Until now, educational computer conferencing has been approached from one of two traditional perspectives: as a variant of distance education or as an extension of classroom activities. However, neither perspective is entirely adequate or appropriate; in fact, holding on to traditional perspectives may limit our understanding and realisation of the full potential of this new medium. The key attributes characterising this new domain are that it is an asynchronous (time independent), place independent, many-to-many interactive communication medium. This combination contributes to making on-line education a new and unique domain, distinct from that of face-to-face and/or distance education (Harasim, 1989).

Face-to-face education, as shown in Figure 4.1, facilitates many-to-many interaction, but it is time and place dependent. Even though classroom activities support group interaction, such activities require that the participants are together in the same location at the same time. On the other hand, while distance education is not dependent on place, and time is quite flexible, it is predicated on a broadcast (one-to-many) or tutor (one-to-one) model, rather than a many-to-many mode of interaction.

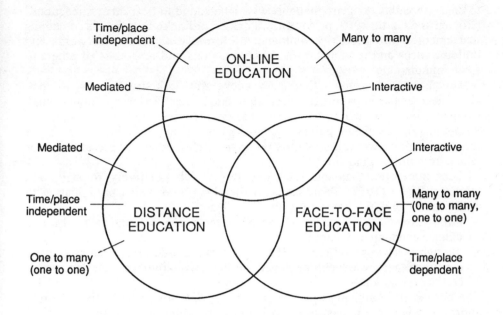

Figure 4.1 On-line Education as a New Domain

Theoretical or practical models drawn from either domain are not in themselves adequate to inform or explain activities in on-line education. It is necessary to approach on-line education as a distinct and unique domain. The group nature of computer conferencing may be the most fundamental or critical component underpinning theory-building and the design and implementation of on-line educational activities.

This chapter examines on-line collaborative learning, drawing upon data generated from courses at the Ontario Institute for Studies in Education (OISE), as well as research results from other OISE activities such as non-credit professional development activities for teachers and international collaboration. [1]

A DOMAIN FOR COLLABORATIVE LEARNING

Collaborative or group learning in the traditional face-to-face classroom refers to a set of instructional methods in which students are encouraged or required to work together on academic tasks (Johnson and Johnson, 1975; Slavin, 1986). It is the interaction among learners that distinguishes collaborative settings from other learning environments. Collaborative learning theories view the learner as an active participant in the learning process, involved in constructing knowledge through a process of discussion and interaction with learning peers and experts. "An optimum context for learning provides learners with frequent opportunities to create thoughts, to share thoughts with others, and to hear others' reactions" (Bouton and Garth, 1983, p 76). Knowledge according to this view is something that emerges through active dialogue, by formulating ideas into words and building ideas and concepts through the reactions and responses of others to these formulations.

Collaborative learning activities use cooperative task structures based upon active learner participation and peer interaction in achieving a common goal. Cooperative task structures may be seminar-type group interaction with focussed discussion and exchange guided by the teacher; or they may involve a shared reward, such as a workgroup jointly preparing a class report or presentation for which they will be graded.

Peer interaction has multiple functions which positively impact upon learning. Webb (1982) identifies two general ways in which participating in collaborative activities helps group members learn:
• through mediating variables which may create an emotional or intellectual climate conducive to learning
• through mechanisms directly affecting cognitive processes, such as actively constructing knowledge through verbalisation, cognitive restructuring, and/or conflict resolution.

The on-line environment is particularly appropriate for collaborative learning approaches which emphasise group interaction. Much more than a technical device for exchanging information, computer conferencing facilitates the sharing of knowledge and understanding among members of a group who are not working together at the same time or place. Computer conferencing was developed expressly to facilitate the interactivity of group communication, maintaining an ongoing common transcript of the interactions among the many people discussing a topic. Each conference is a file that is built and shared by the members of that conference. The system automatically files notes into topical discussions and updates members on new comments in a topic. Access can be configured to reflect the way in which the conference participants need to communicate: users can meet, break into small groups, complete assigned tasks, and discuss issues or readings – all through the computer.

The common file of a conference provides participants with a 'shared object' which focuses and organises the group discussions and interactions. The text-based, archived transcript of the interaction facilitates not only the transmission and sharing of ideas, but opportunities for reflective interaction. Moreover, by providing opportunities for time- and location-independent participation and interaction, computer conferencing offers opportunities for learning collaborations that have hitherto been impossible.

Nevertheless, if the computer conferencing system offers potential for active group participation and interaction, it does not guarantee it. While some reported cases of on-line education achieved high rates of learner participation and group interaction (Hiltz, 1986; Harasim, 1987a), other researchers have found that achieving an active membership (in which members are actively writing as well as reading notes) has been a problem in on-line educational activities (Umpleby, 1986). Haile (1986), analysing computer conferencing in a set of distance education courses, found that the activities were teacher-centred with little evidence of student interaction.

Research undertaken by and at OISE has identified the importance of conference (course) design and instructional techniques for facilitating active collaborative learning within the on-line domain (Harasim, 1988; Harasim and Wolfe, 1988). Factors such as the nature of the task, the subject matter, the nature of the group, and individual characteristics such as background and attitude of the learner and the instructor are important. However, careful design of the on-line educational environment is critical to ensure that learners will engage in active and purposeful learning interactions.

Designing the on-line environment is a key component which affects the quality, nature and volume of interaction. Educational designs based on collaborative learning provide motivational and cognitive benefits. Collegial collaboration reduces uncertainty as learners find their way around complex tasks and also encourages a connectivity to the learning process. Discussion, debate and multiple perspectives which arise within an on-line conference activity may contribute to higher developmental levels in the learners than if they were working alone.

On-line collaborative learning approaches which we have found particularly appropriate and successful are the 'on-line seminar' (both plenary and small group); 'on-line working groups', 'learning partnerships', and 'team debates'. Figure 4.2 presents the collaborative learning horizon, illustrating some of the key group learning activities supported by the on-line medium: learning dyads, small groups, and seminars.

Experience suggests that learning approaches taken from face-to-face designs, however, need to be reformulated or reconceptualised to take into account the unique characteristics of the on-line medium (Feenberg, 1989; Harasim, 1988). Attributes such as asynchronicity, text-mediation, and place-independence have important implications for designing on-line collaborations.

Careful design of the on-line domain has contributed to creating a collaborative learning environment in which the opportunities for active, interactive, and equitably distributed communication are augmented. Results illustrating aspects of collaborative learning on-line are presented below.

Active Learning

Active participation in learning activities has been one of the major outcomes of on-line collaborations at OISE. Students log on regularly (several times each week); not only do they remain current with the discussions by reading comments, but they actively participate by writing messages to the various conferences.

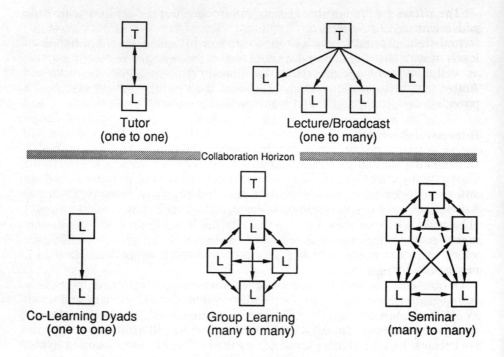

Figure 4.2 The Collaborative Learning Horizon

Active learning in the on-line environment can be measured by the level or amount of participation, such as the number of conference messages written, and the quality and significance of these messages. On-line activity offers the educational researcher a unique opportunity to analyse learning activities, since the interactions are text-based and archived on the system. Moreover, most systems generate usage statistics which can be used to measure the amount of interaction.

Usage analysis indicates active learner participation (the following data do not include personal notes which were not tracked). One course of 38 participants generated 3,132 conference messages during the 12 week session, averaging approximately 7 messages/person/week (Harasim, 1986). Other on-line courses based on collaborative learning showed similar results. For example, a graduate level course with 29 participants generated 3,177 conference notes over the 12 week session, approximately 9 notes per person per week; another course with 7 participants generated 542 conference notes during the session, approximately 6.5 notes per person per week. The average number of messages per student per week during a 12 week session ranges from 6 to 10 messages/person/week in the courses analysed. On-line courses generate transcripts with thousands of contributions from the learners. [2]

The nature of the on-line domain contributes to enabling and supporting active learning. Students actively present ideas and respond to one another's formulations, a process which contributes to facilitating higher developmental levels of understanding. The acts of formulating and verbalising one's own ideas as well as responding to ideas by one's peers are important cognitive skills. Active participation also creates a particularly information-rich environment, providing each student with multiple perspectives on an idea or theme.

Interactive Learning

Our research shows that on-line learning is not only active, but it is interactive. Conferencing exchanges in the courses are student-centred, involving dynamic and extensive sharing of information, ideas, and opinions among learners. Knowledge building occurs as students explore issues, examine one another's arguments, agree, disagree, and question positions. Collaboration contributes to higher order learning through cognitive restructuring or conflict resolution, in which new ways of understanding the material emerge as a result of contact with new or different perspectives.

Whereas in the face-to-face classroom environment up to 60-80% of the verbal exchange during class time comes from the teacher (Dunkin and Biddle, 1974; McDonald and Elias, 1976), this pattern is reversed in on-line courses. Analyses of various on-line course conferences indicates that the instructor contributes 10-15% of the message volume and of the number of conference messages (Harasim, 1987b; Winkelmans, 1988). Analysis of interaction patterns shows active learner-learner exchange. Transcript analysis of an on-line seminar, for example, indicates that the interaction is highly student-centred with over 80% of the messages referencing one another. Within an on-line seminar, initial activity has as its referent specific course reading(s) assigned for that period. The first 2-3 days of a 7 day session (representing approximately 20% of the total message volume) are primarily devoted to responding to the assigned material and identifying key issues from that material. This initial activity however serves to provide a framework for subsequent on-line interaction: having presented their position or argument in relation to the readings and to the topic, student comments become interactive, making specific reference to previous notes, agreeing, disagreeing, extrapolating, questioning, illustrating, expanding, and synthesising upon ideas presented by their class colleagues.

Inter-message reference analysis of electronic seminars at OISE further substantiates that messaging within an educational conference is interactive: notes refer back to and build upon previous messages. The IRA methodology, developed by Levin, Kim and Riel (1989), looks at references to previous notes in each message within a conference and draws a 'message map' of inter-referenced messages. This allows the identification of organised groups of messages and the representation of the influence that a given message has on the interaction. Message networking and interaction can be visually mapped.

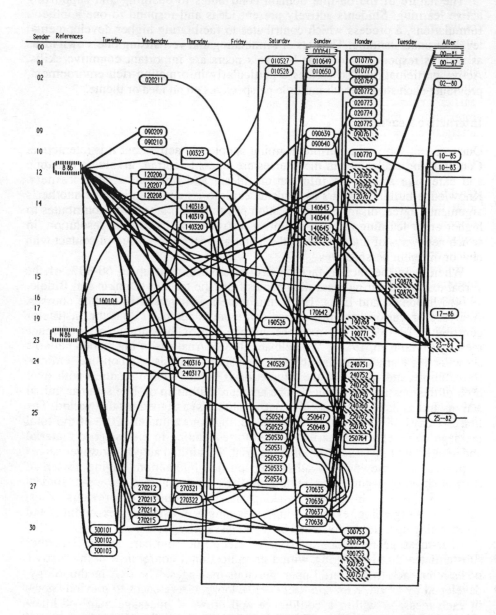

Figure 4.3 An Example of a Message Map (Winkelmans, 1988)

The message map presented in Figure 4.3, generated by Winkelmans (1988), provides a visual snapshot of the interaction between student participants, source readings, and the course instructor during a small group discussion which was part of a one week on-line seminar. Message map analysis shows a complex web of interaction composed of many interconnected linkages. This visual mapping of the comment linkages supports reported observations that on-line discussions are not linear and that complex referencing occurs. Moving from left to right (following the calendar sequence), initial comments can be seen as referencing the course readings. However, within a few days, the interaction pattern changes: students are referencing one another's messages, expanding and building upon earlier comments and analyses. Collaborative learning is predicated upon interaction; analyses of on-line courses indicate highly synergistic and interactive learning patterns. There is dynamic interaction and weaving of ideas.

Equitable Distribution of Communication

On-line courses designed around collaborative learning approaches generate more than active and interactive learning: it appears that a more equitable pattern of communication among class members also occurs. Analysis of usage data suggests that communication among class members in on-line courses is relatively equitably distributed (Harasim, 1987b).

In typical face-to-face classroom communication, participation rates are unequal. Firstly, the instructor takes up most of the available class time. Class discussion, if and when this occurs, is often characterised by one or two students dominating the discussion with the majority remaining silent. In the on-line courses at OISE, however, generally most students are participating and within each group the volume of contribution is relatively equally spread. We have found it especially revealing to prepare boxplots of usage over participants by segments of a course. Boxplots can show distribution in the amount (volume) of messaging, that is, the actual range of contribution per person over time. Analyses of three on-line courses indicated that all users were participating regularly and that the distribution of communication amongst members of a course was relatively equal: the amount of input per user is not highly divergent within a course (Harasim, 1987b).

Learning is Independent of Time and Place

Learning activities within the on-line environment are neither time nor place-dependent. Time-independence refers to the fact that communication within most computer conferencing systems is based upon asynchronous (that is, not real-time) communication. Unlike face-to-face or telephone interaction which is real-time, conferencing messages are stored in the central computer data base where they await access by the addressee(s). Although the design of the on-line course may have some guidelines as to organisational time frames, it is not necessary that the activities be simultaneous: there is far greater flexibility as to when the user may participate and for how long. This asynchronicity augments access, since users can participate at a time and at a pace convenient to them; our research indicates that users do access this learning environment 24 hours a day and seven days a week.

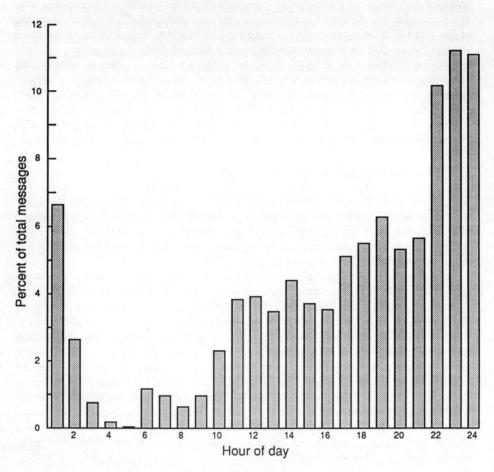

Figure 4.4 Class in Session: Percentage of Messaging by Hour of Day

Analysis of the transcripts of an on-line course (the system records the time and date of each) shows that the only time that the system was not being used was at 5 am (see Figure 4.4). Usage tends to be heaviest in the late evening; after a brief respite, the system is again actively engaged by the early risers. On-line learning interactions take place day and night.

As Figure 4.5 shows, learners access the system seven days per week, including week-ends. This diagram, displaying the percent of messaging by day of the week for an on-line graduate course, shows that usage peaks on a Monday. Participation ebbs somewhat on Fridays and Saturdays; during the remainder of the week, activity is quite high. This usage pattern is probably indicative of the course design, in which the electronic week began on a Tuesday and concluded the following Monday. Many participants in this course were part-time students and this design allowed for students with full-time jobs to have the week-end to finalise their input and weave their concluding statements for that week's topic. Hence, there is higher level of activity on the Sunday and Monday. Activity remains high with the opening of a new topic/focus for discussion. The pattern of on-line access may well differ according to such factors as the class design, the type of students, and the nature of the task. Nevertheless the overall outline of seven-day per week access is probably a typical characteristic of on-line learning.

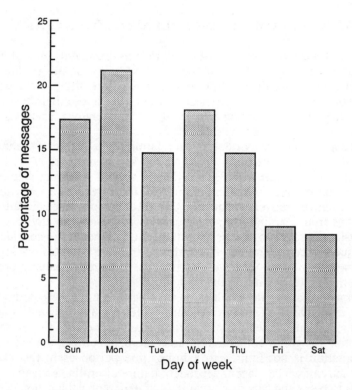

Figure 4.5 Class in Session: Percentage of Messaging by Day of Week

These access patterns are consistent with data from other educational interactions, such as the international on-line Educational Research Workshop, in which 20 participants from three countries took part in on-line collaborations over a period of two and one half months. Analysis of the time (local time for each participant) and day of system access reveals a similar pattern of 24 hours per day, seven days a week interaction (Harasim and Winkelmans, 1988).

On-line learning is independent of place, as well as time. Participants in OISE's on-line courses are geographically-distributed, located in urban and rural areas across several provinces in Canada. Learning collaborations are facilitated through the conferencing system, regardless of where each user is located. At

OISE, the conferencing system is used for communication among those located in the building; it is also employed to link peers located on different continents: such as a project linking educational researchers in Latin America with one another and with their colleagues at OISE, or the On-line Educators' Association, linking educators in Canada, the USA, Europe, and Japan. Time and place of access is no longer an inhibiting factor for collaborative learning or work.

AN AUGMENTED DOMAIN FOR COLLABORATIVE LEARNING

On-line education represents an augmented environment for collaborative learning and teaching. The asynchronous, text-based nature of the medium allows user control over the time, place, pace and nature of the interaction. Since the classroom is open '24 hours per day' users can choose their best readiness time for engaging in the learning activity; they can, moreover, spend as long and return as often as they need or wish.

Users have more control or options in relation to the nature of the interaction than in either face-to-face or distance mode learning: they can respond immediately or take time to reflect, perhaps access a reference book or some other information resource, and compose their response. Asynchronous communication, moreover, enhances opportunities for increased attention to contributions from learning peers. Discussions in the on-line environment may be read on-line or saved to disk or to printer for more thoughtful consideration or for subsequent reconsideration. The archived transcript invites organising and reorganising of the corpus of ideas contained in it, thereby enabling purposeful, active cognitive interaction with the content.

The amount of class time available to each participant is increased: unlike the finite time available in a face-to-face class, which must be 'shared' amongst all participants, the on-line learner can participate to the extent she or he wishes. Opportunities for group collaboration and interpersonal contact are enhanced, since interaction is not limited to a finite time period as in face-to-face or telephone activities. The place-independent nature of on-line education supports user access to peers and expertise regardless of geographical location. Computer-mediated communication overcomes boundaries of place, suggesting a kind of 'panoptic power', an ability to be or to see everywhere, transcending geographical limitations.

The text-based nature of on-line education enhances our interaction with one another (reducing discriminatory communication patterns based on physical and social cues such as gender, race, socio-economic status, physical features, etc). Text-based communication also augments our interaction with ideas generated through the discussions. Not only do we focus on the message, more than the messenger, but the availability of an archived transcript of the proceedings facilitates review of previous comments and discussion, for focussing on important ideas and concepts.

These are some of the ways that on-line education augments learning opportunities, particularly collaborative learning. Generally, we have come to recognise that computer conferencing enables and augments the generating and collecting of group input. As a medium it is particularly conducive to information-sharing, brainstorming, networking and group synergy: that is, to generating an information-rich environment.

While there are many ways in which computer conferencing augments learning opportunities, there are also important limitations to how learners and teachers can use the on-line medium most effectively. One of the major issues that needs to be addressed is the productive organisation of on-line collaborative activities. Although computer conferencing augments our ability to interact with one another, the medium is limited in providing tools to organise and manage group activities. For example, computer conferencing does not easily facilitate group problem-solving or decision-making (Harasim, 1987a). Asynchronous communication, in fact, can negatively affect decision-making, particularly in situations which are time-dependent. Such situations may require a synchronous group communication facility. More than that, however, as Stefik *et al* (1988, p 361) point out, while computer conferencing provides shared files, archiving, electronic mail, voting, and editors, these systems do not provide structures for the conferences based upon any models of group problem-solving processes. Computer conferencing facilitates information-exchange but there is no model to support decision-making. Developments in group decision support tools may be insightful and could perhaps be incorporated or interfaced with computer communications systems. [3]

A second critical area requiring research and development lies in the need for tools to facilitate productive organisation of the rich corpus of information generated in the on-line environment. On-line learning contributes to creating and augmenting group synergy and information-sharing, but it lacks tools to manage and focus this resource. Tools for tracking ideas and themes and navigating within the information-rich on-line space are limited.

Computer conferencing may be viewed as a primitive form of hypertext (Wolfe, 1989), but tools to organise, reorganise, and search the conferencing database are weak and rudimentary. New hypertextual environments might be interfaced with conferencing systems to produce a more advanced communication and education medium. John Seeley Brown, for example, calls for an advanced medium that breaks away from a fundamentally linear structuring of ideas "to start to experiment with ways to transcend the straightjacket of linear documents through an electronic medium that captures the more weblike structure of complex ideas" (Brown, 1985, p 198).

Parallel but increasingly converging sociotechnologies such as hypertext and hypermedia introduce new tools to enhance on-line education. Hypertextual interfaces to computer conferencing (both for the individual user and the group) suggest an important direction for developing on-line education to augment our capacity for knowledge building and knowledge networking.

CONCLUSION

On-line education is more than a new delivery mode. It is a new learning domain which enables us as educators and as learners to engage in learning interactions more easily, more often and perhaps more effectively, but also to develop qualitatively new and different forms of educational interactions. If we approach this new domain from old mindsets (such as theoretical frameworks underpinning traditional face-to-face or distance mode education), we may be applying metaphors that are not only limiting as a perspective but perhaps even misleading. We need to recognise the distinct nature of on-line education in our work as educational designers, implementors, researchers, and as learners if we are to realise the potential of this new domain for augmenting educational options and opportunities.

NOTES

[1] For more information on OISE and its activities (especially in graduate education) see the Introduction to Chapter 6, by Davie. (ed)
[2] For another example of actual interaction data from CMC class discussion, see Paper 10 in the Resource File, by Riedl. (ed)
[3] See Paper 13 in the Resource File, by Davies, for more on the research issues associated with the development of computer-supported cooperative learning tools. (ed)

CHAPTER 5

THIRD GENERATION DISTANCE LEARNING AND COMPUTER CONFERENCING

Søren Nipper [1]
Aarhus Technical College and DEUS Consortium
Aarhus, Denmark

COMMUNICATION STRUCTURES IN DISTANCE LEARNING

In this chapter, the terms first, second, and third generation distance learning refer to three models of distance education, which are linked historically to the development of production, distribution, and communication technologies.

Another name for 'first generation' distance learning is correspondence teaching. The medium in this case is written or printed material. First generation distance learning has in fact been practised throughout the history of Western civilisation, but it expanded in terms of quantitative efficiency when, by the end of the nineteenth century, new printing techniques and the railway system made possible the production and distribution of teaching materials in large quantities to geographically dispersed learner groups. Student-teacher and teacher-student feedback processes are slow, sparse, and mostly restricted to the periods when the learners submit scheduled assignments.

'Second generation' distance education is also called multi-media distance teaching, and has been developed since the late 1960s, integrating the use of print with broadcast media, cassettes, and – to some degree – computers. Feedback processes are very similar to those of 'first generation' systems, but include telephone counselling and some face-to-face tutorials.

The main objectives of the first and second generation systems have been the production and distribution of teaching/learning material to the learners. Communication with the learners has been marginal, and communication amongst the learners has been more or less non-existent.

From a certain point of view this could be explained by the technologies available up to now: they are one-way or two-way communication technologies. More interactive technologies have not been available outside the laboratories.

So in one sense the technologies of first and second generation distance education systems have had one extremely important advantage: they have been widely available, and it could have been expected that this accessibility would eliminate any bias in the social recruitment of learners. But by giving very low priority to the process of communication, by making it one-way or very restricted two-way, the result has *in fact* been a strong social bias in first and second generation distance education. It has mostly appealed to groups of educationally already privileged learners, and it has to a certain extent 'expelled' the educationally or socially weak learner. [2]

The question of production, distribution, and communication in distance teaching and learning is not merely a historical issue concerning the available technologies – whether they be one-way distribution channels or limited two-way communication technologies. It is first of all related to the basic pedagogical, social, and institutional concepts of adult learning. To use a phrase taken from Ger van Enckevort, [3] it is a matter of the degree of 'noise' accepted by the institution. The more communication there is with and amongst the learners, the more 'noise' there is in the system.

The media available and the communication processes accepted in first and second generation systems imply a specific approach to distance teaching and learning processes. To put it provocatively:

* Teaching is the process of structuring and distributing information about certain subjects in the form of printed and/or broadcast learning material. Communication takes the form of approving or disapproving comments on the answers given by students to the questions on the pre-printed assignments. This type of communication is in some cases taken care of by computers which mark the students' assignments.
* Learning is the acquisition of the information given by the study material. What the learner communicates is what he/she supposes to be the right answers to the questions in the pre-printed homework assignments.

Thus there is very little communication in the real sense of the word between the process of producing and distributing learning material, and the process of acquiring the information which it contains.

The teaching/learning process is thus defined by the very problem of geographical distance, and this problem is simply solved by implementing effective presentation and distribution methods. Learning is not seen to be a social process as well, and therefore does not imply dynamic interaction with or between the learners and teachers – on the contrary. In terms of the traditional classroom-based situation, the first and second generation concepts can be said to open the classroom. But because there is no interactivity, the classroom is not extended in the social and cognitive sense of the word, but dis-integrated. Learning is turned into an individual instead of a social process.

However, *communication*, and learning as a social process, will be the key elements in the conceptual development of third generation models of distance learning. It is not possible to promote the notion of learning as a social process without access to interactive communication facilities. In this respect we are now technologically ready (or almost so) to make the move from first and second generation to third generation systems.

However, once again, the issue is a pedagogical and institutional one, rather than a purely technological matter. At least, that is how we saw the question in Denmark, some six years ago, when we designed our initial 'third generation' distance education model. And that was how we arrived at the concept of distance learning using computer conferencing.

FROM 19TH CENTURY RURAL SUMMER SCHOOLS TO COMPUTER CONFERENCING

Modern distance education in Denmark started with the Jutland Open University (JOU) in 1982. Up till then, distance education had been a very marginal phenomenon, completely dominated by first generation correspondence schools. JOU, which is a joint venture between three of the five Danish universities, was the first and is the biggest open university activity in Denmark. Outreach teaching is done by all universities in the form of extra-mural classes and extension courses, but only at JOU have distance teaching and learning methods been implemented systematically. In fact, as described later in this chapter, JOU has promoted distance education as a viable model for many types of adult learning in Denmark, even though, traditionally and conceptually, adult learning in Denmark has so far been dedicated to everything but distance learning.

The tradition of group-based adult learning in Denmark goes back to the beginning of the nineteenth century, when the farmers' and peasants' liberation movement built up a very strong cultural and educational network. The ideology of this movement was learning by 'the living word', as opposed to the written word, where the latter was also the language of the authorities. Accordingly, the Danish tradition of adult education has always stressed the importance of personal, face-to-face contact and dialogue in the learning process, just as it has stressed the importance of learning in groups. Learning by communicating in groups also put the learners and their teacher(s) in an open, more fluid, and more equal relation to each other than is experienced in more traditional classroom-based teaching for children. Adults should be treated, not just as learners, but as *adult* learners, with experience, knowledge, and self-esteem.

Although more than 150 years old, this concept of adult learning is an active, living, pedagogical reference and idiom in Denmark: learning processes are seen by definition as social processes. Historically, however, distance education has been the opposite of all this:

- It is authoritarian, as it imposes text or broadcast material upon the learners as if the learning material comprises the eternal truth about the given subject. (Traditionally, distance education does not provide communication channels for those learners who disagree, or who just want to elaborate upon a certain statement.)
- It is non-interactive.
- It isolates learners from each other.

Accordingly, it has been said that distance education turns the learning process into something very individual. It could be argued that learning is always and of its very nature an individual matter. From my cultural perspective, I would say the contrary. Learning – although a very *personal* matter – must never be an *individual* matter – one learns best by and with others.

In order to integrate distance education with our cultural tradition of adult learning, new organisational and pedagogical concepts had to be developed by the Jutland Open University. In brief, the JOU model of distance education had three basic elements:
* regular face-to-face seminars
* a high degree of learner influence in the design and continuing adjustment of the learning material (JOU does not operate with an academic division of labour – the teachers are researchers and lecturers at one and the same time)
* project-oriented and group-based processes, where learners jointly define the subject of the assignments, and prepare them together.

The major problem was how to secure communication and socialising in learner networks between the seminars. It was obvious that traditional measures such as telephone conferencing were insufficient and hard to manage. But it was also evident that information and telecommunications technology had to be able to offer solutions to this problem, which would be more spectacular, efficient, and creative than that which could be accomplished by traditional means. What was required was a system which would allow for asynchronous group communication for learners without previous knowledge of how to use computers.

That was how computer conferencing was introduced as an integral part of JOU's model for third generation distance learning – even before such a thing as computer conferencing was known to the designers and planners involved. It was the pedagogical and social requirements derived from our conception of the learning process that led to the idea of implementing CMC services for distance education...not the other way round. In fact the social and educational requirements which were first formulated in the rural summer schools of the early nineteenth century are being fulfilled by a technology from the last part of the twentieth century. [4]

COMPUTER CONFERENCING FOR CONTINUING EDUCATION, VOCATIONAL TRAINING AND PROFESSIONAL PEER GROUPS

As well as attempting to integrate computer conferencing into some of its courses for home-based learners, JOU has also promoted this technology for post-graduate and vocational continuing education, using PortaCOM at Aarhus. [5] These distance education courses are inspired by the same pedagogical principles as those adopted and developed by the Jutland Open University for its non-vocational courses.

The first postgraduate courses utilising computer conferencing emerged in 1983. They were part of a formal upgrade of approximately 400 teachers from polytechnics all over the country, and they ran for almost four years. Following the not entirely successful experiences from the first courses, computer conferencing has been extended to a large variety of educational and para-educational environments and settings.

The Danish experiences up to 1988 thus include formal and non-formal education, postgraduate and in-company courses, higher education as well as professional training, short as well as longer courses. Parallel to this, computer conferencing has been adopted in quite varied organisational and social contexts: research environments, trade unions, senior students courses, unemployed, municipal and state offices, enterprises (blue and white collar environments), evening schools, in-service teacher training, open university degree courses, industrial peer groups, project development groups etc.

Experience from these activities evidently is very mixed and ambiguous, but has clearly identified some of the problems faced when establishing CMC as a communication tool for learners who are both unfamiliar with the use of computers, and who are unaccustomed to expressing themselves in writing. Computer conferencing clearly represents a threat to some learners, and may cause experiences of personal defeat, frustration, and educational inadequacy. In this respect, CMC may have very destructive and negative effects on the individual learner. The measures to be taken in such a situation seem to be of an exogenous nature – ie outside the system and its use. Not even the handiest and most user-friendly interfaces can neutralise the learner's fear of being a learner. Local, regional, or company-based self-support groups may be helpful, for example, by letting people connect to the system jointly, and prepare messages and conference entries collectively.

On the other hand, it has also been observed – both in this course and in others run on PortaCOM at Aarhus – that computer conferencing in happy moments may help learners to overcome their fear of computers. For many learners, there is an initial period of 1-2 months spent in chatting (via CMC), not related to the subject-matter of the course, but to the use of the medium. This period of testing and getting acquainted with the system is irritating and frustrating to the dedicated teacher and conference moderator. However, the process is a very important one for the learners, as it permits them to get in touch individually with the system, and to define collectively a specific social and working environment. [6] This process of building a productive and structured environment with a social and subject-related consensus takes time, even for experienced CMC users, and must be allowed for in the design of the course.

Surprisingly enough the learners' appreciation and/or rejection of computer conferencing apparently does not fully apply to the patterns of social constraints and bias experienced in first and second generation distance learning described above. To put it very generally, to many computer illiterate or inexperienced learners, computer conferencing represents a social extension and enhancement of the learner situation; whereas more experienced and well-equipped learners have expressed difficulties with coming to terms with the medium and its educational and social potentials.

This is a paradox. To understand this paradox it is, in our experience, extremely important to look closely at the exogenous factors in the learner situation and learner environment. It will be equally important, by way of in-depth linguistic, semantic and structural analyses, to describe the very tricky and hidden links between the nature and structure of the exogenous factors and the design of the CMC software in use. Such links, although not evident, may have a major impact on communication among learners and tutors – even to the extent of structuring and tailoring that communication.

An example of this is the problem generated by very poor navigation tools in current computer conferencing software. Poor navigation tools, or lack of structural transparency, is a common constraint in computer conferencing systems as we know them today. To the experienced user of the system it will be fairly easy to cope with such constraints by defining individual procedures and routines. The highly motivated, disciplined and experienced learner may also be able to find his/her ways of overcoming the design constraints and enhance the educational and didactic efficiency of the system. But poor navigation tools and design constraints in general may increase the problems of the ordinary distance learners, who have no prior experience of CMC, and therefore possess no tools or measures whereby they can organise the learning situation. The use of the system may subsequently be very unstructured and educationally inefficient.

It is too early for us to present the results of such analyses, but they are urgently required, basically because we have not yet really understood the nature of the cognitive and social processes generated by the medium. Another reason is that at the same time as we are trying to come to terms with the educational application of current CMC technologies, new, more advanced and powerful systems, are being developed and implemented. We have, for instance, already conducted trials with interconnection of distributed computer conferencing systems, and from these tests we know that the classical information overload and navigation problems are being multiplied. We have, in other words, the potential for distributed conferencing, but we do not yet know how to manage and organise distributed environments.

HOME-BASED LEARNERS AND COMPANY-BASED LEARNERS

Looking back over almost six years of using computer conferencing in distance learning, we have reached a point where we have to seriously question the models we have developed. Parallel to enhancing the learner tools by enhancing systems design, we need to examine much more carefully the exogenous structures within which the learner is studying – namely his or her cultural and social environment.

It is our firm conviction that the social factors may turn out to have a much greater impact on the learner than anticipated. [7] However, although we do not yet have the appropriate analytical tools to enable us to fully understand their impact, we have seen a pattern in the ways in which different types of learner groups act in a computer conferencing environment. Generally speaking and simplifying quite a lot, this pattern relates to two different environments – the home environment and the corporate environment – which we can define as follows:

- The home environment is socially speaking a private environment, where the learners are seen as individuals acting in accordance with their personal and private educational objectives.
- The corporate environment is a public or semi-public environment, where the learners are seen in their professional and vocational roles, and where individual or social profiles are a function of their professional identities (the company based learner is pursuing professional objectives which may or may not correspond to private objectives, but which are defined by the subject of the course and the corporate function of the learner).

In my experience, the home-based learner and the company-based learner communicate in very different ways (see Figure 5.1).

COMPANY-BASED LEARNER Memo Style	HOME-BASED LEARNER Letter Style
subject-triggered	process-triggered
short and to the point	long, diffuse, and associative
neutral	personal
passive	dynamic
formatted	messy, unformatted

Figure 5.1 Communication Styles

Emphasising that this is a very general description of different learner profiles in the computer conferencing environment, it is tempting to extend these characteristics to the differences between written and oral communication. It would also be very tempting to go one step further and apply the concepts of social publicity and social privacy to the two different learner styles.

The memo style of the company-based or corporate learner reflects an understanding of the conferencing environment as being public, where users and their communications are highly visible, and thus have to meet specific requirements for public communication. The corporate learner is reflecting a set of standards for public communication which may very well mirror policies applied to professional and in-company communication – representing not only professional position and ambitions, but a much more basic philosophy of publicity. The strength of the corporate learner, educationally speaking, is the disciplined and focussed way in which he/she uses the medium, by making relevant contributions to the subject-related discussions in the electronic classrooms. The weakness of the corporate learner is that, while applying the quality requirements for public communication, he/she at the same time is following a hierarchical and passive approach, consistent with perceptions of public or in-company communication.

There are, however, other and much more tangible factors that determine the way in which the corporate learner uses the medium. The time and cost factor is the most obvious – corporate learners in many cases log on from the workplace and during working hours. Interactivity with fellow learners and teachers has to be squeezed in between work tasks and does not allow for elaborate socialising. Work pressures often only allow the learner to read and browse and occasionally enter short comments, not to prepare elaborate comments or messages. One of the major constraints when implementing distance courses as on the job learning is simply that corporate culture is still not prepared for supporting learning by employees.

In this respect the home-based learner is in another position, being able to log on whenever convenient and assign more time to on-line activities. Communication costs, naturally, will constrain on-line activity for most private learners, but the private learner has the obvious advantage of being on-line late at night or during weekends. The private environment and the timing of on-line activity away from work hours may also be one of the reasons why the interactivity of the home-based learner is, to a large degree, of a more personal and subjective nature.

But more important from a pedagogical viewpoint is that the predominant 'letter style' of the home-based learner, is reflecting a need for – and a personal commitment to – a socially coherent and integrated learner environment. Socially speaking this is a tremendous strength, and stresses the potential for developing models for group-oriented distance learning by means of CMC. Didactically speaking, however, the small talk and socialising overshadows the educational objectives, disintegrates subject discussions and imposes low on-line discipline in the electronic classrooms. The educational environment becomes sloppy, and the learner loses perspective.

Many of the problems we have experienced with installing and maintaining the educational focus in on-line courses can be traced back to the lack of experienced on-line teachers, who are committed to make the courses a success, and who are good on-line pedagogues. In one sense, this is 'just' a matter of time, as the necessary experience is slowly being accumulated, and we can benefit from the results achieved by excellent and experienced on-line teachers in North America.

But we are still puzzled by coping with a learner environment which is so oral, and where the process of social interactivity overshadows the educational focus. The kind of oral discourse found in CMC learner environments is mimicking the sense of being together within a group, and is emulating the synchronous presence in ordinary classrooms. What is ambiguous is that the medium starts to generate a feeling of simultaneous presence, where the learner is reflecting a need for social presence and transparency that cannot in fact be met.

So, looking at our two learners we have on the one hand the very dynamic, but also very personal, unfocussed and undisciplined environment of the home-based learner and, on the other hand, the organised, elaborated, structured, but also very passive environment of the company-based learners. On the one hand the Tower of Babel, on the other hand the Darkness of Silence. The question is: how do we discipline the home-based learner to integrate social dynamics with the educational efficiency of the electronic classroom, and how do we encourage the corporate learner to play a more dynamic and interactive role in the on-line classroom?

That is a challenge – if it is met successfully, CMC may very well change the traditional concepts of distance learning.

CONCLUSION: POTENTIALS AND OBSTACLES

The primary aim of implementing computer conferencing in adult learning is to overcome the problem of the social distance between learners and teachers, not just geographical distance. In this respect, the Danish experiences, although quantitatively limited, clearly indicate the potential of CMC in distance education. Although specific implementations will always reflect institutional infrastructures as well as educational and cultural traditions, a certain number of generalisations can be made concerning the impact of CMC on distance education.

Computer conferencing is likely to allow for much more openly structured curricula, thus not only reducing the production and storage costs that are traditionally associated with distance learning material, but also making possible much quicker updating and revision, and even individually tailored courses. In this respect, third generation distance education will be adjusted to the specific needs of the individual learner or learner group, something which is becoming increasingly important – especially within the field of continuing vocational education and training.

As a result, the concept of fixed curricula in adult learning may very well change. This does, however, imply rather dramatic changes in the type of large-scale, distribution-based, distance education institutions that were developed during the 1970s. [8] These types of institution are in fact rather vulnerable to changes in the attitudes and needs of adult learners. They are, as van Enckevort puts it, not good at coping with noisy learners.

And noisy learners will be (at least from a Danish point of view) one of the positive outcomes of third generation distance education. Noisy learners are active and creative learners. It might be expected that the implementation of an open and democratic medium such as computer conferencing will move the locus of control in distance education from the teacher and the teaching material to the group and the processes generated by the group. The implementation of computer conferencing may contribute to less authoritarian concepts of learning and teaching.

This will also imply changes in the role of the teacher. The teacher will not be redundant in third generation distance education. On the contrary, the teacher will, for different reasons, be an extremely important figure in the process of the course. One of the consequences for the teacher's role as course and process moderator is likely to be a merging of the roles of the academic course developer and the intermediary – the tutor. Traditional distance education practice has been based on a very hierarchical division of labour between the subject-matter experts and the pedagogical intermediaries.

However, the most important function of the teacher in computer-mediated distance teaching will be to keep track of the processes taking place and developing throughout a course. One very negative effect of the change in locus of control is that the sense of overview and perspective, both within the individual learner and within the group, may vanish, disappearing behind the dark of the terminal screen. The teacher will have a very important function in securing continuity in the learning process, according to the overall aims and objectives of the course. Open communication structures and open learning processes may otherwise result in confusion and disintegration. [9]

Implementation of computer conferencing may thus be the means by which the traditional problem of social distance in distance education is solved. But, although by its nature a very open, democratic, easily accessible, and easy to use medium, computer conferencing may, for many learners, turn out to be very 'closed'. As has already been said, CMC may well contribute to the breaking down of authoritarian models in distance learning, but it will not necessarily be able to counter the elitist characteristics of many distance learning systems. Computer conferencing may turn out to be a two-edged sword in this respect.

Distance education has always advantaged the highly motivated, and often educationally privileged, adult learner. In important respects, this feature is exaggerated even further by CMC. It is a (hidden) prerequisite in computer conferencing that users are able to cope with communication processes that are textual – are able to express themselves clearly and analytically in writing, and keep track of cognitive and social processes effected as written messages. This is difficult enough for most people, but to the educationally disadvantaged user it may represent a barrier that cannot be overcome without help. If such problems are perceived by the tutor, the institution, or fellow learners as a private, individual, issue, and not as a collective and organisational matter affecting the whole course, then the inevitable result will be drop-outs and painful failures.

It is important not to overestimate the initiating and structuring power of the medium itself. To a large degree, the motivation, initiation, and structuring of distance learning processes will have to take place outside or before the implementation of computer conferencing into a given course. The value of supplementary social networks, based regionally or at the workplace, or established via audio-conferencing or face-to-face meetings between learners and teachers, must not be overlooked. It would, in our experience, be unproductive to conduct a distance education course entirely on-line.

Furthermore, it will not be possible to implement computer conferencing in future distance education programmes without radical changes in the way we organise both our working life and our family life. We cannot as yet grasp the full potential of computer conferencing. It will in many respects change the very process of learning in distance education, and it will most definitely change institutional models and infrastructures. That process may well turn out to be very cumbersome, but it is unavoidable.

These general statements about the potential of, and the obstacles to, the use of computer conferencing in distance education are perhaps only a reflection of a specific Danish small-scale approach to distance education, and may be limited to Danish pedagogical traditions in adult learning. However, this may turn out to be to our advantage: computer conferencing is not being implemented within a prior established distance education provision. Distance education is as new to us as computer conferencing, and computer conferencing has been from the very start an integral part of our concept of distance education. Although rooted in the rural summer schools of the nineteenth century, this gives us a freedom to build our own models for the integration of computer conferencing into adult learning.

NOTES

[1] This chapter is an updated version of a paper presented at the Second Symposium on Computer Conferencing, held at the University of Guelph, Ontario, in June 1987.
[2] See also Paper 12 in the Resource File, by Boyd for a supporting view on the 'excluding' effects of 'second generation' distance teaching media. (ed)
[3] Ger van Enckevort is leader of the Department for Research and Development at the Dutch Open University.
[4] However, for financial and/or political reasons JOU was not able to apply computer conferencing to its courses until 1987, when JOU and IBM Denmark launched a joint project to design and test a prototype multi-media computer conferencing system, integrating conventional tools with graphics and pictures. The project involves experiments with commercially available computer conferencing software (PortaCOM) and IBM products, as well as tests and design of two new computer conferencing systems, TEIES and EIES/2, in cooperation with New Jersey Institute of Technology. The cooperation with NJIT has been made possible through the Computer Conferencing Cooperation of Aarhus (CCCA), a joint venture between Aarhus Technical College and Jutland Technological Institute, established as a commercial operation in 1984. CCCA is one of several operations and projects within the Danish DEUS Consortium. In 1987 CCCA was invited by New Jersey Institute of Technology to become its partner in the TEIES and EIES/2 projects.
[5] PortaCOM is the portable version of the Swedish COM computer conferencing system, and was the subject of a field trial arranged by the Danish PTT in 1982-83. PortaCOM Aarhus is now run as an open service for approximately 1000 users by the Computer Conferencing Association of Aarhus (CCCA).
[6] Graddol, in Paper 15 in the Resource File, argues that the informal chat so often seen on CMC systems is in fact highly structured, and represents a valuable context for learning. (ed)
[7] See also Chapter 2, by Feenberg, and the section on 'Groupware', for further discussion of social factors and CMC environments. (ed)
[8] See Thomas, Chapter 11, for an analysis of the implications of using CMC in the British OU's large-scale system. (ed)
[9] See the next chapter, by Davie, particularly the section on 'Facilitation Techniques', for a detailed analysis of the role of the on-line tutor. (ed)

CHAPTER 6

FACILITATION TECHNIQUES FOR THE ON-LINE TUTOR

Lynn Davie [1]
Ontario Institute for Studies in Education
Toronto, Ontario, Canada

INTRODUCTION

This chapter has three objectives: in the first section, I want to talk about roles of facilitation for the tutor, teacher, or facilitator of learning. In addition, I want to examine closely the goals for graduate education that I am trying to achieve in our computer mediated courses. In this section I will not talk about management or administrative concerns, but rather focus on the concerns of facilitating learning.

In the second section I want to look at some of the considerations that need to be taken into account when designing educational applications of CMC. This section will look at some of the limits of the medium as it exists and how these limitations influence the design of on-line courses.

The final section will discuss a number of techniques which might be used by the tutor or facilitator to support desired learning. This paper extends some earlier thinking on facilitation techniques summarised by Peggy Palmer and myself (Davie and Palmer, 1985).

However, it might first of all be helpful to describe the learning setting in which I have designed and facilitated on-line courses. The Ontario Institute for Studies in Education (OISE), has three major functions: graduate instruction leading to master's and doctoral degrees; research into education; and field development, by which we mean both the dissemination of research findings and professional consultation pertaining to the improvement of education in Ontario. We are affiliated with the University of Toronto and our graduate degrees are granted by that university.

Our major building is located in downtown Toronto, but we maintain eight small field centres throughout Ontario. Ontario is an immense Province with about 3000 kilometres between its eastern and western borders. The greatest proportion of its population is located in the southern third of the province.

To serve the graduate study needs of students outside Toronto, we offer off-campus courses, by which we mean that we fly an instructor into the community once a week to meet classes. In recent years, we have developed a small, but important set of distance education courses to supplement the off-campus courses. Within this context, we have been experimenting with courses offered solely or mostly through CMC. The effort has been small (about 3 courses a year) and experimental.

The courses are master's level courses and the students receive regular credit for completing them. Typically, the courses have had enrolments of ten to twenty students, who meet once or twice in a face-to-face meeting with the remainder of the course conducted on-line. Linda Harasim [2] is the facilitator of two of the courses each year, and I facilitate the third. A number of other faculty are beginning to experiment with CMC as a module or part of their off-campus courses. Some of these courses might eventually develop into full CMC offerings.

For our educational metaphor, we have chosen the small graduate class or seminar. Almost every graduate program, ours included, occasionally has large lecture courses, and these courses are also worthy of study, but we have begun with the smaller seminar for a number of reasons. First, at OISE, the small seminar is the typical experience. Second, our faculty believe that the primary goals of graduate education include the development of research and analytical skills. These skills are probably best developed in one-to-one supervision, as in the writing of a master's thesis. However, our institution, like most graduate schools, needs to organise its interactions with students in courses or seminars for reasons of economy. We believe that the small seminar or course is the next best thing to individual supervision.

Our educational objectives for both CMC and face-to-face courses must support our goals for the Master's degree. I design and conduct CMC courses that are capable of being judged by the same criteria used to judge any other course, either on or off campus. I intend that the CMC courses be acceptable as a regular part of a student's curriculum and that each course contribute to developing the skills, attitudes, and knowledge that we desire in our Master of Education or Master of Arts graduates. The CMC courses simply cannot be a second best experience.

Graduate Education Objectives

My perceptions of graduate education objectives are:
- to develop an awareness and understanding of the major theories and research findings in the student's field of study
- to develop research skills for searching for and identifying research appropriate to the student's topic
- to be able to analyse a scholarly publication in terms of identifying important concepts; linking these concepts to the concepts of other scholars; developing

or learning standards for the appraisal of other's work; and applying these standards to the work that they are analysing
- to be able to select and develop a problem or topic worthy of investigation
- to be able to create a synthesis containing both the results of their analysis and new ideas independently created
- to be able to develop and present an academically sound argument in support of their synthesis.

How do we go about trying to develop these objectives in a face-to-face course or seminar? Approaches, methods, and structures vary widely depending on the level of the student, the predisposition of the instructor, and the availability of resources. Typically, a small graduate course or seminar will include some mix of lectures by the instructor, discussion or debate, the writing of academic papers, and occasionally the presenting of student work to the seminar for comment, critique, and defense. In addition, many small courses or seminars may include a wide variety of other educational techniques, such as role plays, small group presentations, learning partners, or visiting lecturers. In any case, encouraging the development of these skills requires that the graduate instructor go beyond lecturing into the coaching function.

Needed Facilitation Skills

What are the tutor or facilitator skills necessary to support the development of these goals in the typical face-to-face setting? Certainly, the tutor needs to have good presentation or lecture skills, as almost every course will have some element of information transfer, and this transfer will require oral or written presentations to be given. But current thinking indicates that a wider repertoire of skills is needed. The tutor must be able to set and communicate the intellectual climate of the course or seminar; model the qualities of a scholar; support, mould, and direct the discussion; design a variety of educational experiences; and comment helpfully on students' work.

There are many models of the functions of the teacher, but since so many of our courses use a group discussion or problem solving format, it is useful to turn to the literature on small human groups. Early in the research on small groups, Robert Bales and Philip Slater (1955) identified two kinds of group functions: those functions related to the task that the group is trying to perform, and those functions related to the group building and maintenance. These categories are developed further in a chapter by Benne and Sheats (1978, pp 54-56). While these roles can, and should be performed by any group member, the group leader needs to see that they are performed and that a balance is maintained between the two sets of functions.

Benne and Sheats describe the group task roles as roles related to the task which the group is deciding to undertake or has undertaken. The purpose of the task roles is to facilitate and coordinate group effort in the selection and definition of a common problem and in the solution of that problem. Some of the individual group task roles might be: initiator; information seeker; opinion seeker; information giver; opinion giver; elaborator; coordinator; orienter; evaluator-critic; energiser; procedural technician; or recorder.

Benne and Sheats describe group building and maintenance roles as those roles which are oriented toward the functioning of the group as a group. They are designed to alter or to maintain the group's way of working, to strengthen, regulate and perpetuate the group as a group. Some of these group maintenance roles might be: encourager; harmoniser; compromiser; gate keeper; standard setter; observer; or follower.

Skill in performing these roles is useful to the tutor or instructor in organising and facilitating group discussion. In any particular discussion, the roles will be shared by members of the group, but it is essential that the tutor be aware of the necessary elements in facilitating group discussion and model roles that are otherwise absent.

DESIGN CONSTRAINTS FOR ON-LINE EDUCATION

Before we can begin to explore ways to meet our educational goals through CMC, we need to look at some characteristics and challenges of the medium. There are a variety of constraints currently present in the CMC medium, yet we must be aware of the rapid development of computer conferencing software. The constraints that I list are my perception, based on my experience with using OISE's Participate system. They may not be present in other systems, and in any case, software designers, such as Murray Turoff, are constantly working to provide new tools for the teacher. As machines become more powerful in the near future, the software will allow for a greater flexibility.

Accessibility

The major constraint at the moment is the limited availability of computers and modems. I will not discuss this limitation to any great degree, except to note that in the North American context, microcomputers continue to drop in price and rise in power. A computer is within the means of most professionals, and indeed most now have or are planning to acquire some form of microcomputer in the near future. Fewer have modems because they do not usually need these devices for their day-to-day work. However, one can purchase a 1200 bits per second modem, and full featured terminal software for less than $300, and this price is within the means of most potential professional conference participants. However, while the problem of accessibility is solving itself within the professions, there is more difficulty in accessibility among the general population, including some potential students.

In the CMC courses offered at OISE during the past four years, the major problem has not been the accessibility of machines. The single most difficult set of problems reported by our students has been the connecting of their modem to the computer and the telephone line, the operation of their terminal software, and the achieving of the communication link with OISE. Since we do not provide a standard computer for every student, these are difficult problems. I do provide consultation to students to help with these problems, but the wide variety of machines and software make my consultation of limited benefit. I generally provide a place within our CMC courses where students can help each other with suggestions. While this, of course, does not help the student make contact in the first place, it is often helpful in understanding the variety of commands and features available in other software. The work being done on the provision of shells, such as the shell program used at the Open University [3] or other programs run on the student's own microcomputer, should help alleviate these problems for many.

The Small-Window Problem

Let us turn to some of the conceptual problems. The first of these is what I call the small-window problem. Most microcomputers display about 25 lines of text at any one time. This limitation makes the reading of long texts difficult. These long texts may either be text provided as a resource by the instructor or tutor, or they may be the comments entered by other students.

In our experience, presenting long papers is very problematical on the microcomputer. It is hard to follow the argument of the paper, and staring at the computer screen for long periods of time adds to eyestrain. I deal with this limitation by either presenting long texts in printed form distributed with the course materials, or suggest that students download the longer papers, and either read them at their leisure or print them out in hard copy. [4]

For student contributions, I try to train the students to limit their contributions to one or two screens of material. In addition to helping the reader, this suggestion has several other advantages which I will discuss in the section on editing the transcript.

Keeping Track

The small window problem also leads students (and tutors) to the problem of keeping track of where they are. A computer conference with a complex structure helps organise the vast amount of material in the conference, but at the same time, makes it difficult for the new user to keep track of where within the complex structure he or she is, and makes it difficult to remember how to move among levels. This problem is more or less difficult depending on the computer conferencing software. Some systems make it easier and some make it more difficult, but the problem exists on all systems to some extent.

Disjointed Transactions

Another major problem is the disjointed nature of the transactions. Lynn Davie calls up the conference, reads the preceding notes, composes and leaves a note and logs off. Jane Smith calls up the conference, reads the preceding notes, composes a response to Lynn's note, adds another thought or two and logs off.

Jack Higgins calls up the conference, comments on Lynn's note, and logs off. Pretty soon the linear transcript contains numerous topics being developed in a leap-frog manner and the new reader has difficulty in following any particular topic. Computer conference systems with some sort of threading feature, which links notes that refer to each other, help immensely with this problem, but even there individuals make mistakes when specifying the parent note and the argument can be disjointed. Participate is particularly bad in this respect as it does not have an automatic threading feature.

Problematic Metaphors

Those of us using a computer conference system to offer courses, generally structure the conference with some kind of educational metaphor. I may call the main discussion the seminar room; provide a faculty office for advising; provide a small meeting room for informal interactions or help; provide an in-basket for student assignments; or provide workspaces for small group projects, subtopics, etc. To the extent that our metaphors have an obvious structure and one that is familiar to the students, these metaphors can help the student learn to navigate around in the conference. To the extent that we have been overly cute, or too complex, the metaphor itself can obscure the structure of the conference. We need to examine closely the advantages and disadvantages of different metaphors.

Procedural Decisions

In my face-to-face classes, I often assign projects to be completed by small groups of students. In order to complete the projects, the students often have to deal with numerous procedural questions, such as when to meet, what topic to choose, how to organise themselves to accomplish the tasks and the like. I have found when attempting to replicate this experience in a computer conference that these procedural decisions are problematical. Since students log on at different times, and there may be a lapse of several days between log-ons, it seems to take forever for students to negotiate interests and come to a decision. Even when we use electronic mail to make an appointment with another faculty member there can be difficulties if one or both do not log onto the computer regularly.

Socio-emotional Issues

Another area of problems lies in the emotional reactions of conferencing participants. Issues such as the response to attempted jokes, dealing with anger, etc. can be very difficult. Indeed, this problem is prevalent enough in computer conferencing experience that it has been given the name 'flaming'. Since discussions and debate can be very intense, attention needs to be paid to how to manage emotional reactions.

Fear of Publication or How to Get Them to Leave a Note

There are two kinds of participation in a CMC course. One is passive reading of the notes of others and the other is the composing and leaving notes for others to read. McCreary and Van Duren (1987, p 111) say:

> Getting students to come on-line is only the first of the teacher's hurdles – similar to earlier programs of educational outreach that had to actively enlist reticent populations. Once on-line, the student may act as a read-only participant, never venturing a comment. To some extent, individual participation is determined by the personality, degree of confidence and level of interest in the subject matter of each student, much as in the classroom situation. However, observations reported on nearly 20 academic conferences indicate that student conferencing behaviour in general may be influenced by academic level, curriculum area and relative status of conference participants...

While this area definitely needs more research, I think that for graduate students, the problem seems to lie in the perception that leaving a note in the conference is an act of publishing, rather than an act of speech. As a student confronts the issue for the first time (or maybe at any time) life scripts relating to significant other's reactions to one's written work are activated. We become overly concerned about how others will view our writing. Will they think we are unscholarly? Will our writing make sense? In a face-to-face conversation, we can monitor how the other person is receiving our contribution through the feedback of body language, gestures, and short verbal expressions. In the computer conference, we wonder if anyone has read our note, and if so, how did they receive it? Without feedback our fears are magnified, and we become resistant to continuing our contribution.

Typing Ability

Finally, we should take note that all or most of the material entered into a conference is entered through a keyboard. Students and tutors have widely varying levels of typing skills. In addition, they often have word processing and terminal programs of varying levels of sophistication. In one recent conference, a student used a computer that could only send upper case (it looked as if she was shouting at us!); several students had difficulty with backspacing, and produced notes with many errors, and one student's skill and software allowed him to send every note perfectly typed, spell checked, and with the margins right justified. The range and visual impact of the notes in different conferences can vary enormously.

FACILITATION TECHNIQUES

Climate Setting

This final section looks at a variety of facilitation techniques. We begin with the function of climate setting. In a face-to-face group, it is the function of the instructor to create the initial climate of the learning experience. Usually this function is facilitated by helping the student feel welcome and attempting to decrease the anxiety felt upon first entering a new situation. Typical techniques might involve introductions to other students as well as to the instructor. Some face-to-face experiences might also involve the serving of food or beverages to call up feelings of comfort, and to provide an opportunity for the participants to put aside their concerns from outside the classroom. The time spent in climate setting provides a respite and allows the participant to focus on the matter at hand.

In addition, the facilitator generally wants to set the intellectual climate of the course by letting the student know what to expect. What will be the requirements for the course? What activities will it involve? What will be the schedule?

The problem for climate setting in the computer conference is that the individual often needs to be introduced to both the medium of computer conferencing and to the climate of the course. In our courses we handle each of these needs separately. We begin by an introduction to the milieu of the course.

I decided to begin my courses with a face-to-face workshop, conducted on the Saturday immediately preceding the course. It is a matter of debate as to whether a face-to-face meeting is necessary for successful computer conferencing. Certainly, in many distance education settings it would either be impossible or impractical. However, in our settings the off-campus students often travel to distant locations for courses with fly-in instructors, so one meeting at the beginning is seen as a small price to pay for being able to take most of their course in the comfort of their own homes. The face-to-face meeting allows us to introduce ourselves to each other. Often, we take photographs of the students and reproduce a set for each class member so that they can recall what their classmates look like.

I introduce the course materials and requirements, and answer student questions. Through a variety of exercises I help the students find a learning partner for their first on-line task. I serve refreshments so that the students may eat together and get to know one another socially. The face-to-face workshop's goal is to enable the students to view the computer conferences as a human experience mediated, but not controlled by, the technology.

After lunch there is a two hour period set aside to provide training on the Participate system. We have enough terminals available for the class to be all trained at the same time, although they do share machines. I set up Participate accounts for each student beforehand and I link them to the main course conference. This prestructuring of accounts has three advantages. First, it means that a new student does not have to go through the account creation sequence. Second, it ensures that everyone's Participate name conforms to our practice of full first and last names. [5] Finally, since the accounts have been set up beforehand, I have been able to leave an individually addressed message for each student, welcoming him or her to the course.

The facilitator needs to pay careful attention to welcoming each student to the electronic course, and reinforcing early attempts to communicate. In the first few weeks, I make sure that my notes in the conference specifically reference prior student notes. I send many individual messages to students commenting on their contribution, suggesting links to other students, suggesting resources, and generally reaching out to students. The coaching function is key to easing the students' transition to computer-mediated communication.

In addition to attempts to make students welcome, I make sure that I model expected behaviour in the main conference. I make my contributions short (one or two screens), I try to avoid fancy formatting of my responses, and I have even been known to deliberately misspell a word or two. I try to ease the publishing anxiety by providing direct feedback to other contributors, ignoring questions of grammar, spelling, or format.

I explain to students that the expectations for individual notes are that they are seen as similar to verbal communication and as a group, we should not expect perfection. I see these notes as quite different from the on-line term papers, where I expect the same standards of scholarship as for any academic paper.

Managing Group Discussion

During the course, the functions of the facilitator are similar to the functions of any moderator in a discussion. The task and maintenance roles described by Benne and Sheats above are critical in shaping and encouraging the discussion. In terms of the task roles, I try to keep the discussion on track by providing leading questions, or by refocussing the discussion on the main topic if it tends to get off track.

I like Andrew Feenberg's notion of the weaving comment. [6] When he summarises a conversation, he not only draws together the main themes, but he also provides a reference to the notes containing the original thoughts. My notes will often point to other materials or reference other notes in the conference, and I provide some ongoing commentary to the developing topic. However, it is possible to be so enthusiastic that my notes overshadow by their very number the other contributions, so as in a face-to-face group, I need to limit consciously the number of notes that I write.

In a similar fashion I attempt to perform the group maintenance roles. I encourage, help to show how some notes can fit into others, mediate differences between participants, suggest ways in which the conversation might go deeper, and comment on group process. In my face-to-face classes, these functions are often managed with a variety of different types of humour. In the CMC course, however, it is necessary to be very careful of humour. In a face-to-face situation, we know when someone is being humorous by their tone of voice or their facial expressions. Without the nonverbal cues of smiling faces, it is often hard to properly detect attempts at humour, especially sarcasm. If we want to use humour in a computer conference, it is important that we provide the necessary cues, such as putting the word 'smile' in parentheses, or using a special symbol which has been defined as denoting humour, such as [:-)]

If a topic comes up which appears to be a distraction from the main discussion, but which is interesting in its own right, a branch of the main course can be created, and the beginning notes moved into the branch. This allows those participants who are interested to continue that discussion at any length they wish without disrupting the main discussion. Try that in a face-to-face group!

Joint Writing Projects

My objectives for graduate education, discussed in this paper's opening comments, place much emphasis on students creating logical arguments and submitting their arguments for comment and critique from other students and the instructor. I have used two different methods to facilitate the achievement of these objectives (Davie, 1987, 1988). I begin by discussing assignments, by asking students to work in a small group, presenting a group paper. Although I always include an individual requirement for grading purposes in the course, I believe the joint writing project has several advantages. In the necessary discussion and debate leading to a cooperative statement, the students must examine and analyse the material deeply. In addition, they have the advantage of other students' perceptions as they wrestle with the analysis. To facilitate this, I open a workspace (actually a branch conference) for each group, with the members of the group and myself as members. By being a member I can monitor the discussion, provide some assistance from time to time and communicate privately with the group. It is as if each small group has the instructor as a member.

Most of the time I do not participate, but I can if it seems appropriate or if the group asks me a specific question. Of course, the group has a separate channel available so, if they wish, they can write private messages to each other.

I have found that it works better to assign two group writing projects in a course rather than only one. The first project is generally short and the groups contain only two members. These electronic learning partnerships are formed at the face-to-face meeting at the beginning of the course. By working with only one other person, the number of procedural decisions is reduced and the students can become used to working together in a simple environment. If a particular group does not work well together, changes can be made without major damage.

For the second assignment, I combine pairs of learning partners into groups of four or six. This arrangement makes sure that each individual has at least one other partner with whom they are familiar.

For the group writing projects, I have found that it is helpful to be fairly explicit about the nature of the task. For example, in one course I asked the small groups to choose a case study amongst those in a course text, and to write a case analysis using a framework developed earlier in the course. Limiting the major procedural variable to the choosing of which case to analyse meant that the group had to solve only one procedural question before attacking the main task.

Students report that they like the experience of writing together. Over the years, students have developed two major strategies for dealing with the on-line writing assignment and I pass these suggestions on to new students. First, groups find it helpful to be on the computer at the same time. They make appointments with each other such as "Let's all sign on Sunday afternoon." Even though Participate is an asynchronous system and only has a rudimentary feature for real-time communication, by being on at the same time there is a momentum built when the notes are quickly passed back and forth, and the students feel that they can get on with the task without waiting weeks for a reply.

The second major strategy is to pass drafts of the paper back and forth. After some preliminary discussion one student will usually create an outline of the paper and ask for comments from other students. At that time, the group will often decide who is responsible for creating the draft of individual sections. Then each student prepares a draft of his or her section and puts it on-line for comment or editing by the other students. Typically, a student will download the paper, provide editing or additional comments and upload the revised draft. This process continues until the draft suits everyone and it is formally submitted to me. It is even possible in this process for the instructor to suggest revisions or extensions to the paper in time for the suggestions to have some meaning, rather than leaving it for marginal comments on the final paper.

The papers are formally submitted to the instructor and I make the text available for everyone in the course to read. This is done by creating a branch conference containing the text of the papers which students can read at their leisure, either on-line or by downloading the papers to their own computers.

Individual Papers

It is possible to extend the same concepts to individual term projects or papers. By requesting that students upload their seminar papers, the instructor can present them one at a time to the other students, thereby conducting a seminar on each paper, or if the papers are not to be the focus of a seminar, the individual papers can be put in a branch conference for reading by other students (something that is not often possible in a face-to-face course using typescripts). Obviously, in any particular course, not all of the described writing techniques are used. The course might be designed with two group papers or with an individual paper and a group paper.

Editing the Transcript

One of the obvious features of computer conferencing is the existence of a transcript of the course. Every student, and the instructor, have a word by word record of the entire course. I know that some scholars use computer conferencing to write papers, editing the transcript of their contributions for the final paper, and I have begun to explore this idea as an educational tool. For example, it might be possible, for students in a research course, to set the following assignment near the end:

"Search the transcript of the course for all notes relating to the concept of reliability. Organise the found notes into categories and write a commentary on each category."

Furthermore, the problems caused by the disjointed nature of the transcript can be alleviated by editing. The instructor/moderator is able to move, delete, or edit notes. If the instructor identifies ten notes pertinent to a particular course topic that are interfiled with other notes, he or she can move the ten notes into a branch conference. In addition, the instructor might add editorial comments to some of the notes, indicating references to other materials. The student contributions would then be indexed in a beginning note for the branch conference. In this way, students could return to an earlier concept and find the related notes in an appropriate order with instructor annotations. If the branch conferences were left open, the student could add his or her own observations to the end of the conferences. This kind of recursive interaction with conference notes could add greatly to the comprehensibility of the resulting transcript.

SUMMARY

This paper has discussed a number of facilitation roles, reviewed a number of design considerations for CMC education, and discussed various facilitation techniques for the instructor or tutor to meet the specific needs of graduate education. These techniques have been developed in the context of small on-line graduate classes, but they may have some applicability to any course designed to support student to student interaction, rather than the one way flow of interaction from instructor to student.

NOTES

[1] I would like to add a special note of thanks to Robin Inskip, whose help in research and editing made a significant contribution to this paper.

[2] See Chapter 4 above. (ed)

[3] The OUCom front-end to CoSy, see Chapter 9.(ed)

[4] See chapter 3 for an opposing view on the practicability and desirability of reading lengthy text materials on screen. (ed)

[5] One of the features of Participate, that was a major factor in our decision to purchase it, is that the Participant name was separate from the computer account name. Being able to write to Lynn Davie is much preferable to writing to L_DAVIE when one is trying to enhance human to human communication.

[6] See Chapter 2, and the section on 'Meta-Communication and the Art of Weaving'. (ed)

CHAPTER 7

THE THOUGHT BOX:
A COMPUTER-BASED COMMUNICATION SYSTEM
TO SUPPORT DISTANCE LEARNING

Gary Alexander and Ches Lincoln
The Open University
Milton Keynes, UK

INTRODUCTION

The Thought Box project is developing a set of computer-based tools to support the needs of distance education. It is an attempt to transcend the limitations of current CMC software, and at the same time to combine the advantages of remote communication with the use of local computer-based learning resources. The Thought Box will provide a flexible communications system offering easy contact and discussion, together with libraries of educational materials and a richly expressive medium for their presentation. The overall project includes a communications network, a user environment in which communications are integrated with teaching and presentation tools, and a special purpose workstation, optimised for the needs of distance learners and tutors. This chapter describes the current state of the project, with emphasis on the structure and user interface of the communication system. [1]

The Thought Box is aimed specifically to fit the needs of home-based students (eg Open University students) as well as other students and trainees involved in a variety of open and distance learning programmes mounted by government and commercial organisations. Such programmes aim to enable education to fit in with people's everyday lives, with study taking place in home or workplace. Computer support for distance learners in such programmes has two main applications: for communication, and for presentation of teaching material.

Computer-mediated communication can offer access to tutors and other students for discussion and help, without requiring travel or the simultaneous presence of two or more people. Flexibility in communication is the key to its effectiveness. It also can provide libraries of educational materials for direct teaching or background information and a channel for handling educational administration.

A computer screen, using graphics and animations, can also offer a powerful alternative medium for presenting teaching material. It has the potential for presenting abstract concepts, and especially, dynamic concepts, visually, in a way equalled by no other medium. This is especially important for technical material: technology, science and mathematics. However, for this potential to be achieved, it needs software tools which enable teaching material to be created easily.

There are a number of essential requirements for a learner workstation for home-based students, especially given the fact that such students will have little help learning to use any computer-based tools. Moreover, they may be using a variety of learning packages for short periods of time each. Thus learning to use the system must be particularly easy.

Students may not have a large space in which the computer can be left permanently. Thus it must be compact and easy to set up and put away. Finally, educational users of computers typically have far less money available to spend on it than do businesses. The facilities must be cheap.

The research being carried out in the development of the Thought Box is based on earlier experience at the Open University. [2] The principal question we are addressing in this work is not "How can we adapt business computers to the needs of distance education?" but "What kind of computer support system is really needed for distance education?"

SPECIFICATION

The Thought Box project is developing a range of facilities to satisfy the needs described above. These include a communication system, a teaching support system, an integrated user interface, and a workstation. During the past year a variety of models and prototypes have been developed in an attempt to specify the system overall.

The Communication System

The communication system includes electronic mail, computer conferences, libraries and storage. A lively, graphic-oriented user interface is being developed, with good facilities for off-line working (to keep costs down) and easy navigation, as will be described more fully below.

The Teaching Support System

The teaching support system includes facilities for creating flexible user interfaces for interactive work, and computer-generated visuals and animations for presenting ideas. It will also include an audio cassette player, with an interface to enable recorded speech (or other sounds) to be synchronised with the computer-generated visuals.

The combination of speech plus visuals is likely to be the most powerful computer-based teaching medium for the short to medium term. For distance education, it is a way of bringing the lecturer to the student. A lecturer can point to parts of a diagram and can build it up as he describes it. Similarly, diagrams can be built up on the computer screen, and parts can flash to bring them to the student's attention. Moreover, animation can add a dimension that no lecturer can copy. The combination of voice and computer-generated graphics is particularly suited for topics which are inherently dynamic and abstract, and which are awkward to describe in print. It could be used to present short segments of material (with no user interaction) alternating with interactive segments (with no tape accompaniment) in which the learner tries out the ideas just presented. This combines the best features of lecturing (but at a distance) with computer-based learning.

For such a system to be of any practical use it must be easy for an educator to prepare the material. Conventional computer-based training material takes around 150-300 hours to develop for each hour of material presented. We hope to improve on that in two ways:
- the integrated user environment will provide the tools for easily creating and modifying graphics, animations and models
- the network will offer access to subject-specific libraries of images and existing learning material which can be customised to the needs of the course developer.

Thus the network will be as important to the course developer as it is to the student and tutor.

The Integrated User Environment

The purposes of the integrated user environment are twofold. Firstly, it will provide users with a lively, easy to use interface to all the facilities of the system, including the communications, teaching support system and productivity tools (for writing, drawing, calculating, filing, etc). All these will appear as aspects of a single system so that switching from one to another is simple and so that there is no need to learn a new style of interface and commands when switching from one to another. Secondly, the user environment will provide high-level software support for developers of learning materials on the system.

Working models of various aspects of the integrated environment have been developed using HyperCard on an Apple Macintosh as a prototyping tool.

The Thought Box Workstation

No existing personal or business computer today includes full support for the facilities we consider to be necessary, although fair approximations could be achieved with substantial add-ons. Several design studies have thus been carried out to develop the Thought Box workstation, which is optimised to the needs of the project. [3] The specification for the Thought Box workstation, based on the various physical and ergonomic design studies, and on a planned working prototype, is described in the final section of this chapter.

A Public Domain System for Education

If the system is marketed only as a commercial product of the Open University, its usefulness will be very limited. For it to be most effective, it should be deployed as a public domain system under the control of its user community. The existence of easy and convenient communications will enable the user community to organise itself for the production of both software and hardware in a way which is impossible today.

An organised user community can create a synergy which permits the rapid and efficient development of a large software base, libraries, user support services and flexible hardware. It can commission and buy software which will then be freely available to members through libraries. Updates and backups will thus not be a problem. The integrated environment would provide a high level starting point, greatly reducing programmer effort. Source code would also be public, enabling programmers to build on existing work. Obviously, copy protection would be unnecessary.

Hardware would be in the public domain in the sense of public specifications and designs, available to anyone who wished to produce and market them. Educational institutions could also use these designs to commission manufacturers, as the Open University did with its previous computers, thus obtaining them at manufactured cost. The relationship is similar to that between a publisher and a printer.

This form of control by organised users would enable the educational community to control its own computer support systems, outside of the commercial wars of the business computing market.

THE USER ENVIRONMENT

In addition to the network, the user environment is the key to the success of the project. The system is being designed to cater for both students and teachers/trainers who are not likely to know much about computers, or to want to know much. Their efforts must be concentrated on what they are learning, not on the machine. Thus the user environment must be lively and enjoyable to use. Learning to use it will be largely by exploration.

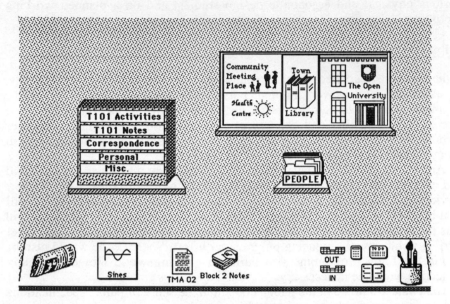

(a) Opening Screen

(b) The Conference System – Overall

Figure 7.1 The Thought Box: Prototype Screens

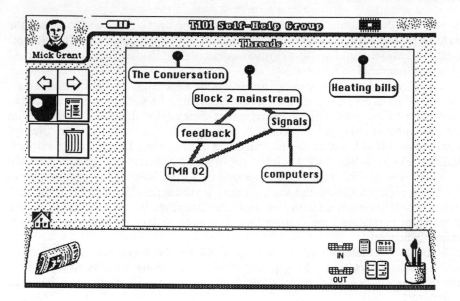

(c) A Conference Overview

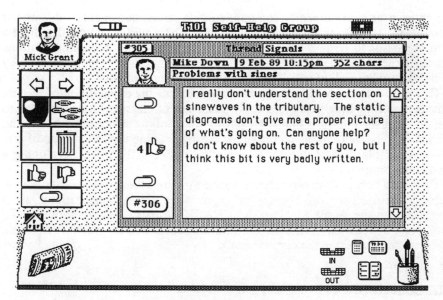

(d) Conference Messages

Figure 7.1 The Thought Box: Prototype Screens

The Set of Facilities

Figure 7.1a shows a preliminary design for the opening screen, and indicates the style of presentation. Everything is functional and is designed to offer the user metaphors which build on his intuitive understanding. Most objects are 'buttons' which are operated using a mouse.

The screen displays the range of available activities. For communication, there are distant organisations the users can contact (the window upper right) and a box of 'people cards' with information on their personal contacts. Connection occurs automatically by clicking on the appropriate buttons. The files of information stored within the machine are represented by the filing cabinet, which works as an associative filing system, set up according to the user's needs.

The lower part of the screen is what we call the 'sill'. That area is always available, no matter what else the user may be doing, and is used for rapid task switching. It includes an array of tools for drawing, writing, calculating and personal organisation, and is used for temporary storage of whatever files are currently needed.

Educational material will be displayed in the same graphic-oriented style, with student interaction taking place by either pressing buttons or by typing information in defined fields as required. Simple animations will be used extensively.

Software Structure

The entire user environment – communications, tools, documents, educational material, etc. – will form part of a single unit. There will be no need to load a word processor to write a message, then close it and open a communications package to send the message. Instead, different functions will be performed by specialised toolkits, all of which mix smoothly with one another.

The basic software will form an integrated, extensible object-oriented system in the sense of the Smalltalk system. [4] Basic sets of classes will be provided to operate the user interface and for each of the toolkits. Creating educational software will be more in the nature of extending existing toolkits, or modifying classes available through the libraries on the network than like developing a stand-alone program.

There will be a built-in high-level language giving access to all the toolkits to enable users to customise the system or to write simple applications, as in HyperCard on the Apple Macintosh, or BASIC in early home computers. To build larger applications, standard programming tools will be available to create the desired extensions to the core system.

THE COMMUNICATION SYSTEM

The communication system is the central feature of the Thought Box, with both hardware and software optimised to support it. Its purposes are:

- to give students easy access to each other and their tutors/trainers for discussion and mutual help, to libraries of educational and reference materials, and to bulletin boards
- to assist with the preparation of learning materials by providing access to libraries of graphics and prototype learning materials, as well as to people who can offer advice.

The communication system is designed to overcome or reduce several of the main problems we and others have encountered when using conventional computer conference systems. These problems include the following:

- Time spent on-line is expensive and should be kept to a minimum without making the system awkward to use.
- Users are often faced with information overload. There can be too many messages coming in for them to keep up-to-date. What is worse, many of the messages are of no interest to them. If the uninteresting messages could be weeded out, the residue might be manageable.
- Discussions tend to ramble all over the place, regardless of any nominal 'topics'. This creates problems in knowing where to find information of interest and where to put new contributions.
- New users often have difficulties in becoming oriented, ie finding out where the discussions of interest to them are located. Experienced, but fairly casual users have similar problems.

Overall Strategy

We are developing a number of strategies to help with the problems identified above.

Distributed operation
The overall structure of the system should be distributed, with larger master nodes and smaller user nodes. The master copy of a conference will normally be on a large node. Each user will keep copies of limited subsets of each conference of interest to them, tailored to their needs and interests. The users will normally interact with their own copies off-line. The activity of bringing the local copies and the master copy up-to-date will normally be an automatic facility provided by the system, and will not require intervention by the user.

Updating mechanism: the electronic newspaper
Use of a distributed system means that there is a need for a mechanism which collects information from all central nodes and brings it to the attention of the user. For this we propose the metaphor of the electronic newspaper. The electronic newspaper, however, is a two-way information system. All users are active contributors, and so the same mechanism is used both to collect and deliver contributions. Users set up their electronic newspapers to their own needs. Collection would normally be automatic and overnight, either daily or at intervals the user specifies. However, it could be used for on-line usage if desired. Material to be collected would be specified in a 'shopping list'. For

different categories (ie certain conferences, mail, etc) the user would have the choice of receiving material either in full or as headlines only. Some material would be specified by category (ie all new messages in such and such conferences) while other material would be searched for by keywords.

Dynamic conference structure
To help users cope with the rambling nature of human conversation we are developing the concept of dynamic 'threads'. Each conference will maintain a list of active topics or threads specified by keywords or phrases. When a user creates a new message, he will be asked to specify the thread(s) to which it should be connected. This will be done either by selecting from the existing list or by adding a new one. When a new thread is created, it will be added to the list when the user next updates, and subsequently sent to all other users, when they next update. Threads to which nothing is added for a specified period will be dropped from the active list.

By using a strategy in which users normally work off-line, connection time is kept to a minimum. With no on-line thinking time, the benefits of high speed modems are maximised. Also, the task of the central node is changed somewhat from current practice. It will no longer be necessary for the central node to provide the user interface, enabling sophisticated graphical interfaces to be generated on the user's workstation. All that needs to be transmitted are the contents of the various fields of the messages. Moreover connection protocols can be shortened as no user prompts are needed. The principal function of the central nodes will be to offer efficient search, up- and down-load facilities.

The User Interface

Three basic views of the conference system are envisaged, as shown in Figure 7.1 b, c and d. [5] They represent the conference system overall, an overview of a particular conference, and the messages within that conference. Users move easily from one view to another by pressing appropriate screen 'buttons'.

The conference system overall (7.1b)
This shows a customised view of the facilities which the user wishes to have readily available, including the set of conferences to which he is currently joined. These are shown as a map of a metaphorical electronic campus, with conferences grouped into 'buildings' to facilitate rapid browsing. A possible alternative to the representation shown is to let the list of conferences in each building appear as a pop-up menu. Selecting a conference from this view takes the user to the next view.

A conference overview (7.1c)
In this view, the threads (currently active topics) are shown as a concept map. If the user presses the button for a given topic, the list of new messages received (sender's name plus headline) appears as a pop-up menu. This view offers facilities for gathering messages for viewing, deleting or filing. The face in the

corner is that of the conference moderator. The control panel includes buttons linking to the conference system overall or to the detailed view of conference messages.

Conference messages (7.1d)
This view retains the overall look of the previous one, to show that it is an alternative view of the same conference. Control panel buttons link back to the previous two views. The header includes the thread, and optionally, the 'electronic face' of the sender (stored locally). If this message is a comment on an earlier message, that is indicated by a button which links to that message. The body of the message is shown in a scrolling field. Adjacent to the body of the message is a field for 'marginal comments'. These can take several forms. The paper clips indicate very short comments, which pop-up when the paper clip is pressed. Longer comments, meriting a full-scale message are indicated by buttons with their number. Thus it is easy to move back and forth between linked messages, and moreover, very minor comments are given a reduced status and so do not clutter up the conference overview. Finally, the 'thumbs up or down' icons can be used to indicate agreement and disagreement, thus offering a simple voting facility.

THE THOUGHT BOX WORKSTATION

Physical Design

The principal physical features of the Thought Box workstation are illustrated in Figure 7.2. It is meant to offer maximum physical convenience in an educational environment.

The display
The starting point of the design is the display. Ideally, the machine should have a flat screen, and be fully portable. However, as we investigated flat-screen technology, it soon became apparent that flat screens with the resolution and performance we require would add several hundred pounds to the cost. Moreover, the prices of flat screens are coming down quite slowly. Thus the initial version will be based around a CRT.

The size and resolution of the screen we have chosen is also the subject of various compromises. The paramount consideration is for a crisp, clear display able to show detail and animation. As a presentation medium, it will include text mixed with graphics, with text as the principal carrier of detailed information. Thus it must be able to offer well-formed characters in a variety of fonts, sizes and styles. A large screen offers greater information content, but also increases the overall bulk of the workstation.

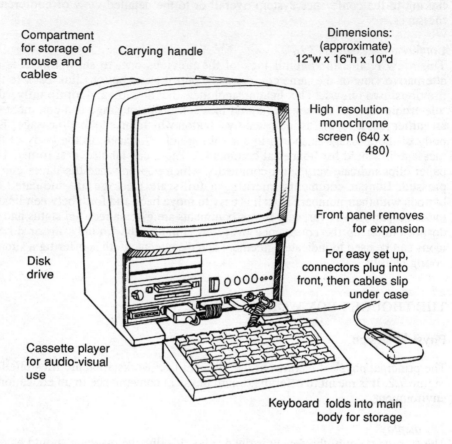

Compartment for storage of mouse and cables

Carrying handle

Dimensions: (approximate) 12"w x 16"h x 10"d

High resolution monochrome screen (640 x 480)

Front panel removes for expansion

For easy set up, connectors plug into front, then cables slip under case

Disk drive

Cassette player for audio-visual use

Keyboard folds into main body for storage

Figure 7. 2 The Thought Box Workstation

We have settled for a 12 inch monochrome monitor with a resolution of 640 x 480 pixels. This will display the equivalent of half an A4 sheet of paper with detailed diagrams and text as small as 10 point. The resolution chosen is the same as used in VGA and extended EGA monitors and the Apple Macintosh II. We are thus beginning to find suitable screens at low cost. This resolution gives 75% more pixels than a standard Apple Macintosh.

The electronic design supports the use of colour, but, after many agonising discussions, we decided that the basic version of the machine should be monochrome. A colour monitor of VGA standard would add several hundred pounds to the price. Moreover, the presence of the colour mask would reduce the crispness of the display. Text would be especially affected, with small sizes less easily readable. Colour brings additional penalties as well. The screen memory required for monochrome is 37 Kbytes, but for colour it is 150 Kbytes. Aside from the additional cost, this carries a considerable performance penalty, especially for animations. For a given cost and graphics processing power the choice is between high resolution monochrome or medium resolution colour. When used imaginatively, the additional detail and crispness of the former can more than offset the appeal of colour, especially in an educational context.

The physical shape

For educational use, a large desk space devoted permanently to the workstation will often be lacking. We needed a compact design which can be easily set up and put away. Thus, the keyboard folds away into the body of the machine for storage, so that even if left on a desk, it takes up minimum space.

We felt that cable control is especially important. To this end, there is a compartment in the rear of the machine which opens for storage of the mouse and cables. If the machine is to be set up and put away often it is important that cables are easy to plug in for minimum wear. Thus connections are on the front where their orientation can be seen, but cables can then be slipped between the legs of the machine to the rear so they are not obtrusive. The only exception to this is the mains lead, which, for safety, is on the side together with the power switch.

Part of the front panel opens to enable expansion cards to be added and removed. The design includes an integral carrying handle.

Initial versions of the case will be produced using vacuum injection molding which allows small runs to be manufactured with a low tooling cost to enable pilot studies of the workstation software to be tested.

Electronic Design

An outline of the electronic design of the workstation is shown in Figure 7.3, which is based on the current state of the Functional Prototype. The Functional Prototype includes low-level software support for the graphics subsystem (described below) and a real-time, multi-tasking kernel to handle I/O. Our guiding principle in the design was to get maximum performance from low-cost components.

The main processor

The main processor to be used is the MC68000 running at 12 MHz. A 68000 series processor was chosen for its large, unsegmented address space, good register and command set and because of the good development tools and wide experience available for it. This point in the range is the highest obtainable using low-cost versions of the processor, memory and support devices. Instead of using more powerful or exotic processors, the performance of the workstation will be improved in other ways, as described below.

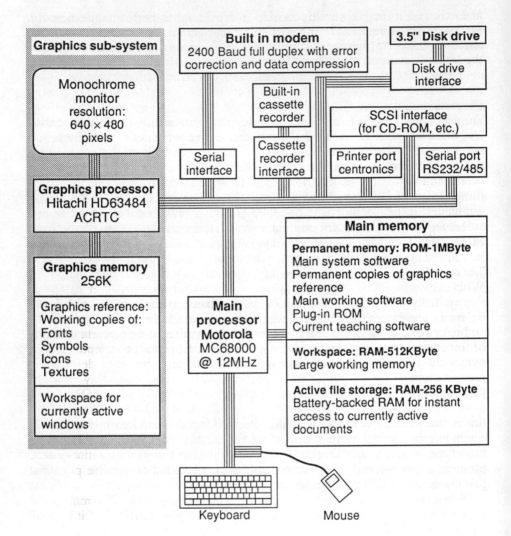

Figure 7.3 Outline Design of Functional Prototype

The graphics subsystem
The display is controlled by a graphics processor with its own memory. This device includes the logic necessary to handle screen memory access, arbitration, refresh and video display, replacing the discrete logic which would otherwise be required to accomplish the same functions at very little extra cost.

In addition to the basic display handling, the graphics processor performs graphics operations concurrently with the main processor. The main processor sends the graphics processor high-level commands which are stored in a buffer and executed at the graphics processor's speed. This greatly reduces the graphics load on the main processor. The screen memory used is dual ported video RAM, and the graphics processor is fast enough so that the video RAM bandwidth is the limiting factor on graphics performance.

The graphics processor offers high-level commands for the bit and block moves necessary for windowing and animation. On top of this there is a set of graphics primitives which can be used to construct objects on or off screen. The graphics primitives include lines, rectangles, polygons, polylines, circles, ellipses, arcs, patterns and fills. There is also a hardware control for a moveable window. 256 Kbytes of video RAM will normally be used to store working copies of a library of fonts, symbols, icons and textures, plus the currently active screen and workspace for additional screens and parts of screens. Not only does this solution provide very good graphics performance at little extra cost, but it eliminates the need to develop low-level graphics routines as part of the system software, which alone might cost more than the design of the entire Functional Prototype.

The use of memory
With conventional business computers, the need for the computer to access floppy disks is a major limitation on performance, often causing significant delays in response. Also, the need to initialise disks, handle system, application and data disks and keep the files on them well organised is an important source of inconvenience and confusion, especially to novices at computing. To overcome these limitations, the Thought Box workstation has been designed to require minimal use of floppy disks, and in fact, for many uses, may not need them at all. All of the main working software will normally be in ROM, and a modest amount of working storage is kept on battery-backed RAM. The result of this is that when the machine is switched on, all facilities are instantly available. Switching between writing and drawing, or to some educational package, are instantaneous. The responsiveness provided by this all-memory operation should produce a machine which is nicer to use than one based on a more powerful processor, and at lower cost, as memory prices fall.

When used in conjunction with a particular course (say, on loan or rental), the course-specific software will either be in the form of plug-in ROM (if it is small enough) or on disk.

The modem
To provide high-speed, error-free communications, the Thought Box workstation will have a built-in 2400 bits per second full-duplex modem, with error-correction and data compression, tentatively using MNP protocols to level 5. This would be expected to give an average throughput of 4800 bits per second. By including a purpose-designed modem we can offer a much higher standard at low cost than would be possible with an add-on modem.

Workstation Costs

The Thought Box workstation has been designed so that any educational or training organisation could commission its manufacture in moderate quantities (as the Open University has already done with its previous educational computers). In this way, machines are obtained at manufacturing cost, but the savings possible with very large production runs are lost. The result is generally very high performance for the cost, and that is the case here. However, the workstation is certainly also suitable for speculative commercial manufacture.

Current estimates for overall unit costs of the workstation, based on a 2000 production run, with tooling costs amortised over a run of 10,000, work out at around £600 sterling.

To obtain comparable specifications starting with any current commercially produced microcomputer would be difficult. None in this price range come anywhere near it. For example, none are designed to operate with all working software in ROM, and RAM extensions to 2 Mbytes would be necessary to simulate this mode of operation. Additional electronics would be required for the high-speed modem, for the cassette interface and probably for the high-resolution graphics. Graphics monitors of this resolution are very expensive. The cost of such additions are unlikely to be lower than the total cost of the Thought Box workstation. No CRT based machine has the physical convenience of the Thought Box and low and moderately-priced portables have much lower screen resolutions.

NOTES

[1] Many of the ideas developed in the Thought Box concerning the user interface and the structure of the communications system reflect the comments made in earlier chapters concerning the need for improved user tools – both for learners and tutors – in CMC systems. (ed)
[2] To support some of our electronics and computing courses, we have developed a variety of special-purpose microcomputers. The first of these was the OPUS, sent to students in 1975, years before Apples and PETs were available.
[3] The design studies are aided by a grant from The Training Agency (formerly the Manpower Services Commission), and we gratefully acknowledge their support for this work.
[4] See Goldberg, A. (1984) 'Smalltalk-80, The Interactive Programming Environment', Addison-Wesley.
[5] The screen designs in Figure 7.1. are a snapshot of the state of work on the Project in October 1988.

CHAPTER 8

COMPUTER-MEDIATED COMMUNICATION AND ORGANISATIONAL CULTURE

Elaine McCreary [1]
University of Guelph
Ontario, Canada

INTRODUCTION

The gradual metamorphosis of our traditional campus into an on-line community, five years after the introduction of CoSy at the University of Guelph, is providing us with a living case-study of knowledge-producing corporate work in the information age.

Those of us who are attracted to CMC and find great potential in its effect on corporate life, act I think on three premises:

- in the information society described by Masuda (1980), quaternary production, or economic activity based on knowledge-producing industries, will predominate; this condition already pertains and would seem to have no foreseeable limit
- virtually all types of productivity are improved through synergy – the value added by working in interaction; people come together in organisations to accomplish tasks that will not yield to the sum of their separate efforts
- synergy in turn derives from successful communication, hence our acute interest in communication patterns and our association of overall organisational vitality with ease and comprehensiveness of communication.

Enthusiastic users of CoSy at Guelph would like to see virtually every one of our 13,000 students, 2500 staff, 770 faculty and 65 executives on the system because we believe – or rather, we conclude from direct experience – that it improves corporate life.

Some people consider that two conditions would be necessary to guarantee universal CoSy adoption throughout our organisation: the first would be to make it universally possible; the second to make it universally mandatory.

The first condition has been achieved through completely rewiring the campus with a digital phone system which can accommodate two voice lines,

101

bridgeable for teleconferencing, and a data line flowing through the same sender/receiver concurrently.

However, not every phone line terminates with a personal computer or terminal. While the wiring decision was of necessity taken at the organisational level, equipment decisions take place at sub-organisational levels. And because we have not made it mandatory for every employee and student to be reachable through CMC, there has been uneven investment in communication equipment.

So for us, organisational impact is conditioned by the fact that adoption of CMC has not been pervasive. There continue to be three constituencies of people: those you can always reach on CoSy; those who use it sporadically, and those who have yet to be touched by it.

With that caveat, we can now turn to five points of impact that have been affected, like dependent variables, by the introduction of CoSy. These are hierarchical isolation, role requirements, managerial functions, the extent of networking, and measures of organisational vitality. Each will be addressed in turn in the remainder of this chapter.

HIERARCHICAL ISOLATION

The information gap that results from status differences is often referred to in terms of hierarchical isolation. In our first flush of enthusiasm some four years ago we expected a dramatic levelling of status. Such has not been the case. But neither has our hierarchy remained as it was before CoSy. Evidence on this point is quite mixed.

Some senior management do participate in open conferences of the 'social interest' or 'outside issues' type. In these settings they mix with staff and students, occasionally asking questions and receiving tips, information, or opinions in an apparently equal status manner, because the respondent is often not aware of the former's institutional role. Other people with seniority have expressed the feeling that they should be absent so as not to inhibit conference participants.

Some research conducted elsewhere on top executives indicates that they prefer to exert their influence via the spoken word; that they resent being contacted by plebeians; or that they wish to have more control of the discussion among their inner councils than is possible on-line.

At Guelph, our handful of top executives have IDs on the system and there are some celebrated anecdotes of how the people lower down in the hierarchy made use of those addresses. For example, in one instance a student was able to prompt an invitation from the President for a face-to-face meeting in his office; another involved senior management personnel on a short time frame, unable for days to reach one Vice-President (VP) by phone, phoning the VP's secretary instead to announce a CoSy message outlining the situation, which then received a reply from the VP – by phone – in time for the deadline. One deterrent to adoption by top executives has been the tendency to treat CMC flow as official discourse and to try and file it all, either in hard copy or electronically. This of course counteracts the benefits of spontaneity.

ROLE REQUIREMENTS

Role requirements refer to the set of behaviours which people expect of someone who occupies a particular location in an organisational structure.

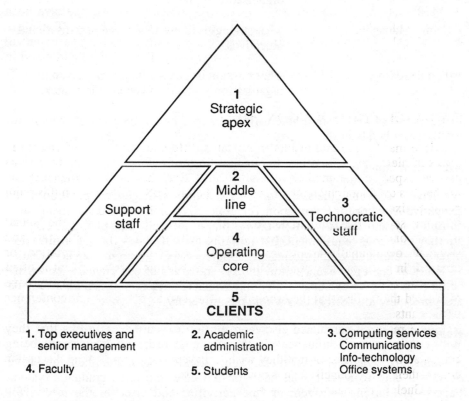

Figure 8.1 Adaptation of Mintzberg's Organisational Roles to the Academic Environment

Borrowing from Mintzberg on organisational roles (Mintzberg, 1979), we have at the university basically six kinds (see Figure 8.1). Each role profile includes certain characteristic decision areas:

- Support Staff: how to maintain the built environment and the
                                    people working in it.

- Students: how to manage their own programs.

- Faculty: how to design and deliver a direct service.

- Technocratic Staff: how to carry out required operations.

- Academic Administration: what tactics to use in implementing sub-
                                    organisational plans.

- Senior Management: what strategies to use to achieve organisational
                                    objectives.

- Top Executives: what mission or goals to undertake given the
                                    organisation's social and economic context.

In the wake of CMC some interesting changes have come about, which are
briefly described below.

Additional Roles

We have discovered the need for a new senior management position titled
Executive Director for Information Technology, to orchestrate the tremendously
complex system transformation taking place. Beneath that planning level is
another new role requirement that remains to be filled – that of a diffusion
manager – although various technical support services are promoting adoption.
    Roles of conference moderator, and several kinds of conference support, are
being picked up by existing faculty and graduate student assistants but they do
amount to new job descriptions within the university.

Role Expansions

Students now seek out faculty more often, provide more mutual help, and have
opened a club to recruit each other on T-CoSy, the undergraduate system.
Faculty are having to invent on-line activities and discover the means for
evaluating or giving credit for contributions made there. Some technocratic staff
have noticeably improved their ability to help and communicate with the
technically illiterate when they are approached and can respond with the
necessary time lag via CMC.

Altered Role Expectations

The most interesting changes are ones which have actually altered expectations
of what a traditional role can or should entail. For example, students exposed to

CMC in one course are cross-fertilising the technique from one professor to another, and not leaving it to the faculty member or advisors to make decisions in their own time about designing and delivering the educational service. Furthermore, students are overtaking faculty in some cases in the function of providing feedback on institutional goals to senior management.

For their part, some faculty are experiencing discomfort with expectations placed on them to adopt technologies when the accountability procedures with their administrators do not adequately acknowledge the new form of invisible work, the time it entails, and inequities in teaching effort.

Technocrats are finding themselves drawn into consultations on management decisions about objectives, time frames and strategies. But management for their part will occasionally exclude technical staff from some advance planning in order to preclude the situations where an eager technocrat, driven by curiosity, may immediately begin work on solving a problem and then feel deflated or abandoned when the organisation takes the decision to head in a different direction.

Academic and other administrative middle line people are discovering that there are now higher expectations of cooperation among working groups. People who need decisions taken within tight deadlines, and have been thwarted by non-cooperative colleagues, are finding that they can carve new, *de facto*, permission pathways around the difficulty by using CMC.

A final example of altered expectations has reached even the senior management level where decisions of consequence are now more visible and more readily discussed publicly. Without disclosing corporate history, it would suffice to say that our university is more sensitive than it was to personnel issues involving due process.

MANAGERIAL FUNCTIONS

Several members of senior management have provided me with examples of how their ways of working have changed irrevocably since the introduction of CoSy.

Even with relatively simple responsibilities for maintenance tasks in the library (such as repairing photocopiers, terminals, and CD-ROM players), what began as a use of CoSy to deploy repair staff by putting their work orders on-line, unintentionally grew into a way of automatically monitoring equipment to see which machines needed to be serviced most often, and whether the rate was excessive.

From the hub of strategic planning (the 4th floor of our University Centre) came the example of how CoSy has enabled more effective use of short-term working groups. CMC makes it possible to mobilise a committee or work group by sounding out potentially interested and suitable people without the need for lengthy background memos. Once assembled, such trouble shooting or problem solving groups have used CoSy to delegate parts of the problem, self-managing the division of labour so that one person takes the responsibility to look into a sub-problem and inform the others. Such groups also illustrate the strategic use of unofficial information systems, because they can consult via CoSy, inviting comment and opinion (more like taking a straw vote than asking people for formal statements of their position).

The most formidable changes in managerial functions at our university have taken place in the library, which is also a leader in information technologies. There, virtually everyone above a supervisory level conducts part of their workday on-line; and there we also find the University's best example of CoSy as a means to augment the regular decision process. It is used as an adjunct to face-to-face meetings to set agendas, negotiate the priority of business, advise people of the need to prepare background materials, and take some advance time to consider options.

Sometimes CoSy has been used to attain closure on a choice of action, which is then simply reviewed in face-to-face meetings; or to confirm what has been decided as a follow-up to the face-to-face meeting.

EXTENT OF INTERNAL NETWORKING

There has been a phenomenal increase in the formation of 'communities of interest' across our institution since the introduction of this technology. People cite an increase in the number of issues addressed, the speed of formation of viable groups, and the ease of interaction once interested parties have identified each other.

Not all interest groups lead to collective action, although such examples do exist – such as a joint statement on smoking policy at the university, or on Canadian copyright policy. Many interest groups support private actions, such as how to make an equipment purchase, or rid one's rose garden of earwigs. Without doubt, CMC has enabled unorthodox connections between people whose traditional enclaves or lines of reporting would never have brought them into contact with each other. This adds vitality to the intellectual life of everyone who finds their way into conferences in ferment. It has also produced some long-term relationships of support and mentoring between exceptional faculty, and sometimes staff, with bright students from other colleges or programs who never would have come under their care before CMC created an invisible, parallel campus. A few such relationships have been formalised, for example, by making faculty from other institutions, who have a telepresence on Guelph's internal network, into official members of a student's thesis supervisory committee.

EXTENT OF EXTERNAL NETWORKING

Networking external to our physical location has also increased remarkably – in several different forms. The first simply entails casual exchanges with guests in some of the open conferences – only to discover that they are coming in from

New Zealand or Malaysia, Finland or the U.S.S.R., Britain or the Netherlands. I cannot explain why it should be thrilling that we have managed to get together despite the distance – but it is.

Then there are some rare guests, like George Thompson in Switzerland, whose telepresence made such a deep impression on everyone who interacted with him. When he disappeared suddenly and permanently from on-going conversations, the emotional gap that opened was so great, a kind of CMC wake was held in which people spoke of the personal loss they felt of someone they had only known via CoSy. That unique tribute is archived at Guelph.

A second form of external networking is provided to locals by associations that are attracted to our host facility. CPPNW (Canadian Physicians for the Prevention of Nuclear War) and their International affiliate both use our system. While they conduct their business through closed conferences, they also host open conferences in which Guelph system members can participate.

A third form of external networking is found in the 'daytrips', taken by a few of our students, staff and faculty onto other exchanges like the 24,000 member BIX. These telecommuters bring back items of interest onto the Guelph system either by paraphrasing what they've read, or importing messages directly from outside conferences.

The most formal kind of external networking is our collaborative overseas tele-work. Examples include:

• The Sulawesi project undertaken by our School of Rural Planning and Development working daily in cooperation with the Jakarta office on development of six rural sites in Indonesia.
• The linkage of 150 Indonesian academics and equal numbers of their Canadian counterparts on several areas of work including biotechnology, medicine, and rural development.
• The project that joined southern and northern scientists working in the area of lignocellulosics (which in translation means 'woodchips').
• The planning of a visit I made to the Universiti Pertanian Malaysia, an institution with an agricultural heritage like Guelph's, that is also eagerly expanding its applications of computers to education, especially in the area of teaching English as a second language.
• Our twinning with the agricultural University of Wageningen in the preparation of a textbook on extension education, and other projects of a rural development nature.
• Rurtel, an EEC longitudinal study of rural change in Western Europe, to which one of our Guelph faculty consults closely.

Historically, Guelph has been disproportionately well connected to the outside world because of our century of work in agriculture, veterinary science and home economics. While these commitments have always given us the reasons for overseas work, CoSy has given us an entirely new means of implementation.

The impact of CMC has not been entirely to replace our physical presence in the outside world by extending telepresence. In fact, by making it possible for senior management to be in daily contact with Guelph from many parts of the world, it has enabled some to increase their travel and still keep their jobs. The travels of our Chief Librarian, John Black, are legendary and his recent appointment as Honorary Chief Librarian of the Agricultural University of Beijing has been accomplished with rarely a day's absence from on-line management at home.

EVALUATION MEASURES OF ORGANISATIONAL VITALITY

After five years, how can we evaluate the organisational impact of the cultural sea changes reviewed above? Several indicators of overall organisational vitality come to mind.

Productivity and Effectiveness

The first course is productivity. Is the organisation measurably more 'fruitful' because of CMC?

Guelph is not a distance-mode institution like the British Open University, or Athabasca University. We do not sport their economies of scale in our teaching. But we can point to some increased teaching efficiency by operating in a 'mixed mode', joining some students at a distance of several thousand miles to our on-campus graduate classes for an exercise in shared learning. There are also some examples of increased efficiency with our research, for example in co-authoring a book with Wageningen, and a more recent project comparing agricultural computing in Europe with Canadian videotex experience. There are also cases of administrative advantage in negotiating international contracts, making travel arrangements, and screening personnel.

A second indicator is effectiveness: if an improvement in the quality of education means that deeper or more significant changes are brought about in the people we serve, then CMC has made its contribution. A principal benefit is that we can assemble teaching teams from other institutions and countries far less expensively than by physical presence, far less sporadically than by other media. As for teaching and learning in the medium, our students have been given assignments to moderate sub-topics or to assist in servicing some conferences, and therefore have gained not only knowledge about, but competence with, the medium. We expect this will enable some at least to continue to use it later for independent, self-conducted learning.

Internal Self-Governance

We have had a conference called 'chairs' which was a private commiseration among the chairpeople of university departments. In it they discussed such things as tenure and promotion procedures, operating guidelines within the university, salary policy, and their difficulties with the higher-ups to whom they in turn report.

Other discussions have flared up among employees in general and we have seen that the airing of grievances does not necessarily diffuse the situation. In fact, like the 'fishbowl technique' of face-to-face human relation labs, a large number of on-lookers may amplify any ill-feeling.

While our ideal would be to use CMC to determine consensus among the main players on some decisions, and among all employees affected by policies on smoking, parking, early retirement and so forth, our experience is that the medium has not yet been tamed to serve this purpose. We do not fully understand the impact of CMC on self-governance.

Occupational Hazards

With every really new set of working conditions there is an unavoidable time-lag before its effects are felt and safety standards are established. Factories, mines, submarines and space stations all involve work environments which put special demands and constraints on the worker. CMC is a new work environment with some detrimental physical effects on the eyes and spine of workers. It can also affect mental state through fatigue, over-exposure and information overload. Some people have trouble resigning from conferences, and feel guilty if they don't participate. They complain that discussions are trivial, instead of simply withdrawing in favour of ones that are meaningful to them. They express frustration with the lack of closure in some discussions, instead of learning the skills of precipitating and testing closure. We do not need to deny that CMC may entail hazards to the physical and mental hygiene of workers deeply immersed in it. We can however, redesign hardware and software, and train people appropriately to use the medium without detrimental effects.

Organisational Allegiance

Despite these qualifying remarks, people usually thrive on CMC. Like any polity, a university can only flourish with the voluntary cooperation of its members. Their conscientiousness and extra effort will be forthcoming if they have established a sense of identification between their personal or career satisfaction, and the well-being of their cooperation. For academics a large part of career satisfaction comes from finding peers with whom they can continue to satisfy the kind of curiosity and intellectual appetite that made them academics in the first place. Many people have reported to me that CMC has enriched their academic life by selectively bringing them people to enjoy. This makes them more content with their place of work and more likely to find themselves doing something extra to assist their colleagues.

Creativity, Adaptability, and Innovation

Prior to CMC the wheels of innovation seemed to grind rather slowly for us, particularly in the difficult area of cross-disciplinary centres, several of which never got past the planning stage whilst others operated for a short while and disappeared. One successful example is our Centre for Gerontology Research. It may have been just a product of the time, or it may have been that the degree of cross-departmental, cross-college communication that would have been required to keep the funding and faculty credit systems working just didn't happen when people had to arrange real time meetings several blocks across campus.

Recently a new Centre for Environmental Stewardship has been established, resulting from a task force of Senate cutting across physical, life and social sciences, and the humanities. One of its first activities has been to initiate with a member of my department a conference on 'Our Common Future', named after the final report of the World Commission on Environment and Development. While already successful as a think task such institutionalisation is necessary.

External Credibility

A final measure by which an organisation may judge its vitality is the external credibility of its people – its alumni or its faculty in the case of a university. Do its various departments produce people who are respected as a resource, valued by their peers? At home we look for leading academics who are not only competent but who consistently know how to interact well, people who have developed the receptivity to learn from others and the compatibility to help others advance their learning.

We think that any organisation adopting CMC will be developing more of those people within its ranks and thereby increasing its value, serviceability and credibility with its external connections.

DIFFERENTIAL IMPACTS

While impacts have been felt on the hierarchy, role relations, the performance of managerial functions, internal and external networking and the level of organisational vitality, they have been felt unevenly across the university. This may be due to the modifying effects of at least three intervening variables present in any given group of people: the previous technologies in use, the diffusion strategy of their sub-organisation, and the formality of discourse which they attempt.

Previous Technologies In Use

There seems to be a compatibility between certain technologies and CMC that predicts a likelihood to adopt, while familiarity with other forms of technology tends to predict non-adoption.

The information technologists who helped develop Guelph's on-line catalogue, our external database search methods, and our CD-ROM catalogue, invest much of their professional creativity in anticipating the needs and behaviours of their users. The instructional technology staff in my department or the Office of Educational Practice spend their time on the structuring and sequencing of ideas in anticipation of the learner's information processing behaviour. Communication Services staff try to solve point-to-point communication problems; and some of the Fine Art people have made very successful transitions into computer graphics. All of these areas have had large percentages of their people (staff, faculty or students) adopt the interactive technologies.

In contrast, the physical science and maths people (including most of the Institute of Computing and Information Science) have followed a path in the last five years from mainframe use for statistical analysis to mini to micro usage. Their point-to-point communication levels may even be less than before. People accustomed to high tech chemistry and microbiology laboratories work in a self-contained manner; and the majority of arts and humanities faculty who tend to view scholarly work as a solitary activity also shun interactive communication.

While there are personal exceptions to both groupings, the generalisations hold.

Sub-Organisational Diffusion Strategy

The predictive power of 'prior technology' may be confounded by another variable, that of sub-organisational objectives which in turn influences the likelihood of there being an intentional diffusion strategy.

Sub-organisations of the university that have objectives related to serving people (such as the Library, the Department of Rural Extension Studies, the Office of Educational Practice, and Student Counselling and Resources) have all moved in some way to promote near comprehensive adoption. And in 1988 the student newspaper 'The Ontarian' put its writers and editors in on-line contact with its student readership for reaction and rebuttal.

Other sub-organisations that do not see a direct connection between their academic research product and interactive communication also tend to miss the point – we think – about the value of re-integrating academic life from the deplorable fragmentation into which it has sunk. The benefits we stand to gain await us at both intellectual and pragmatic levels. When C.P. Snow wrote in the 1950s about the schism of intellectual life in 'The Two Cultures', there was no such technology as CMC to open a leisurely dialogue of reconciliation.

At a more applied level is the necessity for us to educate people with very specialised skills to function in the multi-disciplinary teams that are required to redress environmental problems and help us establish a pattern of sustainable development. At the most pragmatic and mundane level are the issues of self-management and workplace democracy that show universities to be among the most backward of present-day organisations.

Like the historic effort to unify nation states a century ago, we are currently engaged in an effort within the university as a large scale organisation to convince quite autonomous units that we will all benefit if they join us in a unifying invisible campus.

Formality of Discourse

Finally, it is necessary to mention the effect of formality of discourse on rates of adoption and consequently on organisational impact.

'Formality of discourse' refers to the consequences attached to messages in a conference which may be relatively serious and weighty, or relatively light. The most formal or consequential conferences are those that support official committee work or academic courses for credit. These formal administrative or student conferences are the least frequently used on our system. Somewhat less weighty are the 'issues' conferences: those that address controversies internal to the university, and those that belong to the outside world. There are more people meeting by telepresence in these conferences than in the formal ones. Most popular of all are the least weighty 'social interest' conferences such as 'micros', 'networks', 'fixit', 'cars', 'never-ending-story', 'gourmet goodies' and 'genealogy'.

These kinds of discourse have been allowed to develop spontaneously. Any system member may initiate a conference. After five years of such undirected growth, system activity shows a near-normal distribution of telepresence based on formality of discourse. What this means to anyone within the university who would like to promote adoption of CMC, is that the least comfortable and last place to begin is with credit courses or management committees. It makes more sense for new users to start with informal and social discourse, and then to move on to more structured and formal applications once they are at ease with the medium.

CONCLUSION

After five years of exposure to the medium we do not feel we have mastered it, or even fully harnessed it. It continues to surprise us. In a non-directive way CMC is giving us a stimulating new experience of ourselves as an organisation. Its impact on overall organisational vitality has been positive but not unequivocal. This Fall (1988) we are beginning a new era with a new President, and that will undoubtedly mean a new world view and sense of our institution's place in the scheme of things. As that becomes clearer we will be able to take a fresh look at what CMC can do to advance the work we undertake together.

To this moment, we can draw one conclusion about the impact of CMC on organisational vitality: the only way human beings can individually or collectively be 'more vital or alive' than 'just alive' is to be more conscious, and for better or worse CMC has made us that.

NOTES

[1] I would like to thank the many colleagues throughout the University of Guelph whom I consulted when carrying out the research on which this chapter is based.

PART 2

COMPUTER CONFERENCING AND MASS DISTANCE EDUCATION

The following three chapters look from different perspectives at the first large-scale application of CMC in education, namely, one of the British Open University's high population, undergraduate courses. Each author provides important pieces in the complex jig-saw of how computer communications has been grafted onto a well established, mass distance education institution. The extent to which any of the conclusions are generalisable or transferable to other situations depends on several key questions:

• How many students will study each course?
• How much of the delivery of the course will be carried out electronically?
• How much hardware support will be offered by the institution?

In the case of the Open University, very little overt teaching was carried out on-line in the first year, although a great deal of learning occurred. To transfer significant amounts of the course delivery from the medium of print to the electronic environment would not be impossible, but would have profound consequences for the whole cost structure of mass distance education. Drawing from the three analyses of the OU application, one can see that using CMC as a major teaching medium for low-population courses has economic as well as educational benefits. With very large numbers, the value of CMC for support, information exchange, and tutorial provision is undeniable. However, unless CMC replaces other media, the costs involved are additional to the already major investment of a distance education institution in the preparation and production of printed and broadcast material, and the organisation of face-to-face tutorials throughout the country.

To use CMC as the primary delivery medium on large population courses would change the focus of distance education institutions from product to process, from written materials to on-line teaching. The resulting cost structure would then more closely resemble that of a traditional, face-to-face teaching institution. The less entrenched in the print/production model the institution has become, the easier the transition would be. For those in the fortunate position of creating an electronic, mass education institution from scratch, the possibilities are wide open (Mason and Kaye, 1989). The flexibility of distance education can then be combined with the interactivity of face-to-face education and compounded by the advantages of electronic communication to produce an institution offering top quality, mass education.

The level of hardware support offered to students by the OU, in the first year at least, was laudable, and reflects the institution's degree of concern for students and its commitment to the importance of discussion and interaction. Even its development of a user-friendly front-end to CoSy, though welcomed and applauded by other CoSy sites internationally, has not been tackled before by the many educational institutions which use CoSy. If the perceptive reader of Chapter 10 (on the cost of CMC at the OU) deducts all these 'paternalistic' provisions, the license fee for purchasing CoSy, a portion of the communications network charges and the staff time on-line are together the actual rock-bottom cost of introducing CMC.

To those involved with the use of CMC at the OU, the first year has raised as many more questions as it has answered. Already new initiatives for the second year are planned – primarily in the direction of exploiting the teaching potential of the medium: small groups of self-selected students in discussion with an invited speaker, short term teaching by central academics, and better use made of the part-time tutors' input. By the last year of presentation, CMC may well be meeting more of the educational needs of more of the 1300 students.

Does CMC work in mass distance education? Despite all the difficulties and uncertainties, there hasn't been a single suggestion that the attempt should be abandoned. Indeed, even its detractors say that conferencing should be used more, or better, or differently, but everyone recognises that it can work.

CHAPTER 9

AN EVALUATION OF COSY ON AN OPEN UNIVERSITY COURSE

Robin Mason
Open University
Milton Keynes, UK

INTRODUCTION

Following small-scale trials of the use of electronic mail on two courses (Henry, 1986; Emms and McConnell, 1988), and after an evaluation of a range of conferencing systems (Kaye, 1985, 1986), the Open University purchased the CoSy system from the University of Guelph, Ontario, in 1986. Its principal use was for the proposed course *An Introduction to Information Technology: Social and Technological Issues*. This chapter gives an account of the experience of using CoSy on this course in its first year of presentation, 1988.

The largest portion of this course, as with all major Open University courses to date, is the print component of seven 'blocks' of material. These are enhanced by a Course Reader, audio and broadcast media and supplementary materials.

However, in addition to these standard presentation media, this course is one of the first to require all students and tutors to have an IBM compatible micro computer in order to gain practical experience of the social and technological issues discussed in the written material. Four software packages are introduced on the course, some commercial, some specially developed at the OU: word processing, database management, spreadsheet analysis and communications. Altogether, this practical component of the course comprises 20% of the work, and the communications element is, therefore, a very small part of the whole.

THE INTEGRATION OF THE COMMUNICATIONS MEDIUM

A number of steps were taken to prevent this small communications element from being perceived by students as an added extra, which could be ignored if necessary. Open University students resemble many other students in tending to be 'assignment driven'. Moreover, OU students have the additional motivation that their course work assignments, in contrast to the usual practice in British universities, count for 50% of their final mark on the course and that working at a distance as they do, their written assignments form their main means of contact with direct personal teaching. They tend, therefore, to be highly conscious of what their tutor requires in assignments. Furthermore, many of them feel isolated as distance learners from an academic environment, especially in courses such as this which have no summer school. These considerations helped in integrating computer communications into the course as a vital and exciting component.

In the first place, the communications package is used not only as a piece of IT software to be understood, experienced and mastered like the word-processor, database and spreadsheet software, but it is also exploited as part of the tutorial support on the course. The 14 hours of tutor contact allocated to the course were divided approximately in half, with 3 face-to-face meetings during the course, and tutor support on CoSy throughout the course, especially before the due dates of each of the 7 assignments.

The second integrating feature of the communications element in the course was the design of the project, in effect a double weighted essay which would assess all the practical elements of the course. The subject of the project is an evaluation of computer-mediated communication, based on the student's experience of it during the course, the textual material presented in the units and readings, and the reactions of fellow students. The latter information can be gathered directly from conferencing messages, but is mainly drawn from a database formed by all students uploading answers to two detailed questionnaires concerning their reactions and use of the conferencing system during the course, supplemented by questions on their own personal and educational backgrounds. Students are expected to download data and combinations of data from this remote database, present it in graphs and tables using the various software packages and write an assessment of some aspect – social, educational or technological – of computer-mediated communications.

THE CONFERENCING ENVIRONMENT

One of the initial difficulties in conveying the potential of computer conferencing is that it combines elements from a number of communication modes in such a way as to form a unique medium which doesn't replace or directly compare with any other single medium. Consequently, students were presented with a metaphor of an Electronic Campus, as a mental model on which to base the facilities and design of the conferencing provision for the course.

The conferencing system, CoSy, provides three areas for different kinds of communication, as shown in Figure 9.1, the Electronic Campus Map, which was used in the course teaching material. The electronic mail facility is immediately obvious as a one-to-one, personal mode. The conversation area is pictured as an unstructured, informal grouping for discussions amongst a few colleagues. The conference area is has many more facilities to allow interchange among any number of participants. The student, with a communications notepad in hand, can partake in many kinds of interactions from the personal to the public, from the social to the academic, from the interactive to the purely informative.

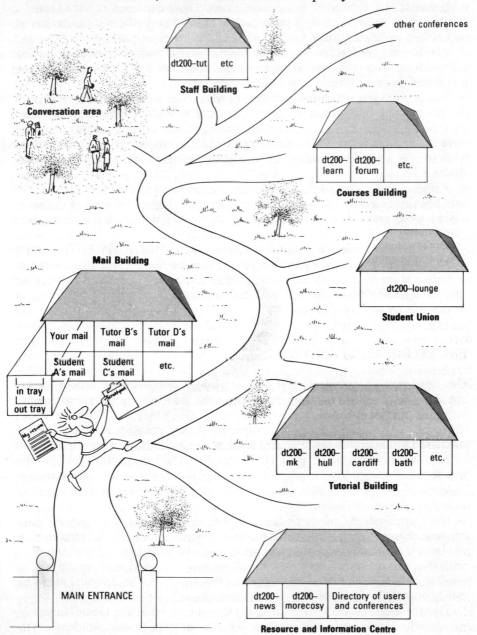

Figure 9.1 Electronic Campus Map (from Open University course DT200)

Each tutor on the course was moderator of a conference for his or her tutorial group of up to 25 students, thus forming an on-line classroom to discuss the assignments, practical work and course issues. These conferences were closed to other users in order to create a contained discussion area where students, having met at face-to-face tutorials, would feel confident to participate.

A read-only conference was set up for the course team to provide up-to-date information, stop press announcements and fixes for software bugs. Students could read these messages but not add comments.

Tutors were given a closed conference, which was a private space for them to discuss tutoring issues amongst themselves and provide feedback to the course team on the course generally and conferencing in particular. Students, likewise, were given a conference for socialising, a place to 'meet' others on the course with similar interests, to moan about course problems and to chat with other students.

Rather at the last moment, a forum conference was added where course issues could be discussed by all students, tutors and staff. Topics for each of the seven blocks were created, as well as for the project, practical work, errata and gremlins.

Although the conferences for the course were all prefixed with DT200, which is the number designated by the administration for the course, all of the open conferences on the system were available to students. The university does not operate separate systems for staff and students, so all staff with IDs on CoSy are contactable by students.

THE INTERFACE TO COSY

The conferencing system CoSy, was originally designed for access by on-campus terminals, with no connect charges for students – a different situation from the distance learning environment of OU students. With the Open University's launch of the Home Computing Policy, students were expected to purchase (at favourable rates) or rent an IBM compatible PC with printer to use in their own homes (see Chapter 10 for details). The course team felt that this remote access by students required an interface which would provide automated log-on facilities and an off-line editor for the preparation of messages and reduction of connect charges.

Most applications of computer conferencing to date have placed great importance on an initial face-to-face meeting where users can be introduced to the basics of electronic communication and the structure of the particular conferencing software. As this kind of hands-on experience would not be possible, a third facility was introduced to the interface – an optional menu bar to help new users remember the commands and available activities.

This front-end to CoSy was designed and produced at the Open University for use with the Pace Linnet Modem, which was sent to each student for the duration of the course. The interface consisted of an automatic dial-up and connection through to CoSy with a few key strokes, an off-line editor and an optional menu bar when on-line.

THE STUDENT PROFILE

The number of students who finally registered for the course was 1364. About 100 of these dropped out almost immediately and a further 250 did not sit the final exam. This was slightly higher than the normal drop-out rate for second level OU courses. Disappointingly few students were female: 1006 males to 358 females. About half the students were aged between 30 and 40, and all were over 21. This distribution is roughly typical of OU students generally.

The educational and occupational background of the student population was biased toward the technical, clerical and managerial, despite the fact that this course was developed jointly by the Social Sciences and Technology Faculties, with a major contribution from the Institute of Educational Technology. [1] However, the range of educational and occupational backgrounds is very wide, with over 5% having no educational qualifications at all prior to their OU study, and over 12% already having considerable experience with electronic communications.

In terms of the computer communications for the course, there were very regrettable levels of disadvantage built in to the system. The OU operates a network of 17 dial-up modem bureaux throughout the country, providing local call rates for students living near these areas. Despite considerable efforts to provide similar rates for all students, one third of the students were required to pay long distance charges for all electronic communications (b or b1 band). In fact, only half of the students were within local call distance of the nearest dial-up node and an intermediate charge (a band) applied to just under a quarter of them. Those living in the most remote areas of the country, who, it could be assumed, would most benefit from increased access to communications, were most disadvantaged. The map in Figure 9.2 shows the different charge bands applicable over the whole country.

Fortunately more than two thirds of the students had the facilities to have their computer workstation permanently set up, but that leaves a significant number who either had to pack up the machine after each use, or did not have free access to their machine at all times.

The computer literacy of the student population on the course ranged from about 20% with *no* experience with micros, to half with word processing skills. Many were games players or business package users.

Although at the start of the course by far the majority of students felt positive about using computer-mediated communications to increase the amount of communication they had with other students on the course, nearly one third of them at that stage felt nervous or lacking in confidence about taking part.

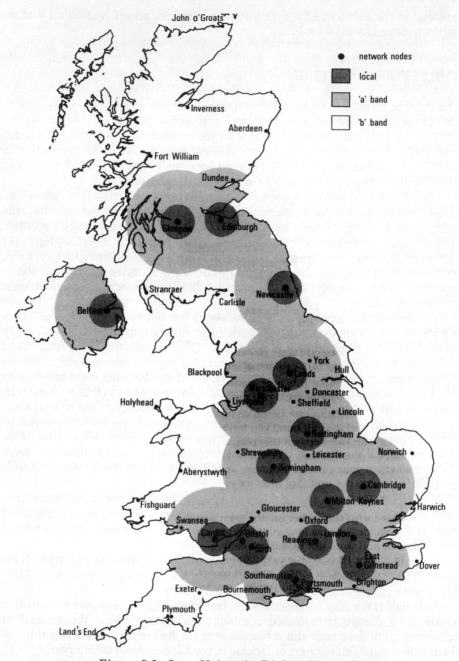

Figure 9.2 Open University Dial-up Network

Figures 9.1 and 9.2 are reprinted from Block 2, Part D of DT200 Introduction to Information
Technology: Social and Technological Issues, © Open University 1988.

THE TUTORS

The 65 tutors hired part-time to provide support, mark assignments, take face-to-face tutorials and moderate the on-line tutorials were drawn from social science and technology backgrounds. In fact, the majority had computer experience of one kind or another, but about half a dozen were not 'computer literate'. Almost all of them came to a briefing weekend held a few months before the start of the course, where they were introduced to all the software, the assessment strategy and the course content. Although two or three of them were experienced computer conferencers, most were complete novices. Hands-on experience was offered at the meeting as well as discussions about the possible uses of educational computer conferencing on this course.

It was discovered through interviews, [2] that a good many tutors had volunteered for this course expressly because of the conferencing element. Indeed, interest in this new teaching medium was encouraging right from the beginning. A number of tutors were eager to explore the potential of computer conferencing for greater discussion, for cooperative work, and even for peer assessment.

Suggestions were made that tutors with varying areas of expertise join forces through electronic communication to provide support for each other in covering the wide range of the course. Tutors were also briefed on the importance of good moderation of their tutor conference – putting up introductory messages, providing lots of encouragement and giving direction to discussions. The 'senior common room' conference, 'dt200-tut', set up for tutors on CoSy continued the exchange about moderating and later on, provided a vent for a number of tutors to express their frustrations with the course and with conferencing.

ASSUMPTIONS ABOUT THE OPEN UNIVERSITY USE OF CMC

When asked to anticipate the outcome of the first year of this unique undertaking before it had even begun, the following eight assumptions (Table 9.1) were recorded and described by the author, in consultation with the main proponent and champion of computer conferencing for the course, Tony Kaye (Kaye, 1986, 1987). One year later, they form an excellent framework from which to build an analysis of the actual use made of CoSy by the first intake of students.

Table 9.1 Assumptions about the Use of CMC

1   Convenience

Students would find conferencing much more convenient than travelling to face-to-face tutorials to meet their tutor and fellow students.

They might find conferencing, or email, more convenient than telephoning their tutor who could be busy or out when called.

Tutors might find they could answer a common query once in a conference which all their students could read, rather than many times to individual students.

2   Increased Access to Help

It would provide greatly increased access to help and expertise than was previously available to students as distance learners.

3   Equality

Many students would welcome the equal status of the conferencing environment and the opportunity to contribute from their previous experience as adult students.

4   New Learning Medium

Some distance learners would respond enthusiastically to the potential of this medium for thoughtful expression of ideas and active participation in the learning process.

This medium might positively encourage some students to develop greater autonomy and self-direction in their learning.

5   Social Needs

The 'networking' aspect of conferencing, the ability to contact other students on the course and to participate in the unpackaged, serendipitous nature of the medium, could fulfil some of the social needs of distance learners.

6   The Conceptual Model of Conferencing

The mail facility, because it so resembles postal communication, would be very successful, but fewer students would become confident contributors to conferences, as this is a less familiar conceptual model.

7   Technical Difficulties

A significant percentage of the students would experience so many technical difficulties, whether with the telephone lines, the work station or the conferencing system that they would abandon further attempts to use the facility.

A smaller percentage would drop out because they could not adapt their learning style to this medium.

8   Variations in Moderating Styles

The wide range of teaching styles of the 65 tutors moderating conferences would considerably advance the available research on the relation between moderator styles and successful learning outcomes.

ACTUAL USE OF CMC: THE FIRST YEAR

The nature and amount of use made of CoSy in the first year will be examined in the light of these eight expectations. Quantitative data used in the analysis are from three sources: systems-generated statistics for time on-line and amount of character input, the database of 55 questions answered by 75% of the initial number of students, and background information collected by the administrative arm of the university. Qualitative data come primarily from the messages sent to conferences themselves, but also from extensive interviews with students, tutors and OU staff at various points throughout the first year. Despite this plethora of data, many of the conclusions drawn in the following analysis are derived from the personal involvement and perspective of the author. [3]

1 Convenience

"I see nobody on the road," said Alice. "I only wish I had such eyes," the King remarked in a fretful tone, "to be able to see nobody! And at a distance too!" [4]

A series of questions about the convenience of electronic communications was included in the questionnaire for the course database. These show that about 60 to 70% of students returning questionnaires found conferencing *less* effective for contacting their tutor, getting help, socialising and saving time and money in travelling. Although this may appear to be an indictment of the convenience of electronic communication, a number of factors mitigate against this conclusion.

First of all, these questions had to be answered by students, not at the end of the course as originally conceived, but in the middle of it. As any experienced conferencer knows, the start-up time in turning new users into confident and contributing members of a conference is notoriously longer than anticipated. With an opening date of March 25th, some students were logging on for the first time in July (see Figure 9.3). With this in mind, it is remarkable that nearly 350 students of the 875 who uploaded the questionnaire found conferencing as good or better a means of getting help or moral support as telephoning their tutor. Even more remarkable is that, at this point in the course with such a small proportion of the total presentation being on-line, nearly 375 students could say that conferencing was as good or better a medium for intellectual exchange as a face-to-face tutorial.

As might be expected, there is an association between use of CMC and attitudes about its effectiveness. The survey showed that use, as measured by number of successful log-ons, was positively correlated with the proportion of students who found conferencing effective for getting help, socialising, saving time and money etc. Whether the the amount of use affected the attitude, or whether the attitude affected the amount of use, is open to debate.

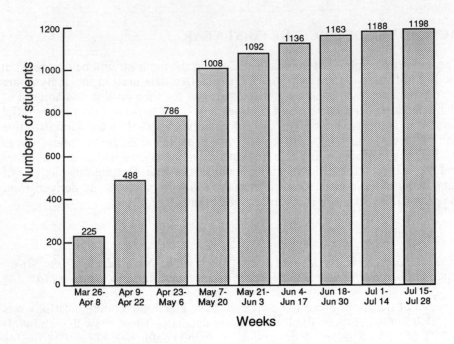

Figure 9.3 Replies to the Coco 'Welcome' Message

Secondly, it must be stressed that the range of student use of CMC on this course was very wide, with significant samples in all categories from total non-use, to minimal use, to more than the course requirements through to exceptionally heavy use (see Table 9.2). There is considerable qualitative data to show that students in the latter two categories certainly found the medium convenient. [5] The following are a few illustrative examples among many.

CoSy message in a tutor group conference:

```
DT200-luton block,#4, pa-starling, 12-Jul-88 21:15
--------------------------------------------------------
I've never been one to contact my tutor because I find it
very difficult to disturb someone at home or at work with
what might be a trivial point. I know they have elected
to do the job but I still feel I might be inconveniencing
them. Telephoning fellow students is even worse because
(i) they are not paid and might not want to be bothered,
and (ii) they might not be able to help. As a result I
have studied previous post foundation units in relative
isolation.....If I have problems I can log onto a
conference and leave a message knowing that I am not
inconveniencing anyone. Those who want to respond will
```

respond and at a time that suits them. Further I may get
several responses and hence a variety of views to my
question.

Interview with Abdul Parker, June, 1988: [6]

Q What difference has electronic communication made to you as a student this year?

A One of the things about conferencing is that you can describe your problem on the day
you are having it, rather than storing it until you have a day school or tutorial. You
have it out of your system, bang in an instant – throw it out at somebody or into the
system.

The convenience of electronic communication applies particularly to the mail
facility, which has been used both as a substitute for other forms of
communication and as an additional medium to increase the 'friendliness' of
distance education. Unfortunately the major shortcoming in the statistical data is
the lack of any computer-generated statistics on the number of mail messages
sent on the course. However there are indications both in conference messages
and from interviews that many students have taken full advantage of this new
ability to contact their tutor or other students.

Interview with Howard Webber, June 1988:

Q When I talked with you before the course started you said that you would be very
careful in how much time you would devote to CoSy...

A But I do use it a lot – from the mail point of view, and that I find very useful, much
more so than the telephone.

....

Q You keep saying you find email useful...

A Mainly because it keeps conversation short and to the point. It is also direct to the
person concerned – no telephone tag. It really is efficient – you get good feedback
from it.

Table 9.2 Total Student Hours on CoSy on DT200

hours	students	hours	students
none	115	10 - 20 hours	259
up to 1 hour	72	20 - 30 hours	39
1 - 2 hours	94	30 - 40 hours	24
2 - 3 hours	124	40 - 50 hours	5
3 - 5 hours	213	50 - 100 hours	12
5 - 10 hours	380	100 - 200 hours	5
		> 200 hours	2

Note: There were 1364 students in all.

Discussion with DT200 tutor Bob Peacock, August 1988:

A I have a student in Her Majesty's Prison who sends me a mail message nearly every
day.
Q About what?
A Oh anything really – little queries, comments on how he is getting on...

2 Increased Access to Help

"We can talk," said the Tiger-lily, "when there's anybody worth talking to."

There is considerable evidence to show that for those students who made any
significant use of the conferencing system, the increased help available was
highly valued. The database answers confirm that of all possible sources of help
(tutor, fellow students, spouse, Academic Computing Help service, other people)
the messages on CoSy were rated as the most valuable (see Table 9.3). The
'gremlins' topic, where students were to report practical problems was the first
conference to take off, with over 500 messages generated in the first 3 months. A
number of students and tutors took a very active part in supplying 'fixes' for the
many difficulties reported there. Indeed, these active participants were in most
cases considerably ahead of the course team in providing useful advice and
support to students. This topic was outstanding as a vehicle for those with
expertise to become known on the system and to offer the benefit of their
experience to the course team and students alike.

Exchanges about practical, computing matters are a popular and useful topic
on most electronic bulletin boards and conferencing systems. Helpful exchanges
about more theoretical subjects are another matter altogether. This issue of the
quality and degree of help available through electronic communication is a
critical one and will be analysed from a number of angles.

First of all, the direct availability of members of the course team to answer
queries, to provide advice on practical difficulties, and to initiate and participate
in discussions about the course material is unprecedented in the history of the
Open University. At least 9 staff members involved in the design and writing of
the course were active participants in conferences and responded to direct mail
from tutors and students. A systems ID, called 'coco', was set up to which
students could direct their queries. During the first 3 months of the course, coco
was handling 20 to 30 messages a day and replying to queries usually within 24
hours. Contrary to initial fears that students might 'take advantage' of this
unique access to the course designers, there were frequent expressions of
gratitude and appreciation, but no abuse or unjustifiable use made of the facility.

Table 9.3 Difficulties and Sources of Help

The following information is taken from the database created by students for their use in the course project. Permission has been obtained from the course team and from students to reproduce parts of it here.

Q 46   If you had difficulties with the computer-mediated communication part of the course that you could not resolve on your own, did you turn to any of the following for help (enter as many codes as apply)?

Q 47   If you used any of the above sources of help which was the most helpful?

	Person	Q46	Q47
A	Tutor	230	84
B	Fellow student	262	160
C	Spouse or partner	103	55
D	Your children	27	14
E	Non-course friend	50	10
F	ACS help service	225	121
G	Colleague at work	86	35
H	On-line help*	376	179
I	Other people	33	14
J	None of these	194	201

*Although this choice was accompanied in brackets by the words (ie typing the code 'holp' or '?'), it would seem reasonable to assume by its position as the most often consulted and the most helpful, that the term 'on-line help messages' was understood by students to include the content of messages in the topics like 'gremlins'.

Other course team members contributed extensively to Forum topics, extending and developing areas of the course, and explaining and interweaving parts of the course material.

```
dt200-forum/4, 180, aw_bates, 7-jul-88 10:32
-------------------------------------------------
Good - Pat and Richard are forcing me more and more on to
the defensive. But Richard, what is it exactly that
tutors provide in the OU system that could not be done by
an intelligent machine? Let's suppose for instance that
you had a large mainframe, with a huge data-base, that
stored responses to all known points raised by students,
with a small team of central staff to pick up new points
raised. Would that not do the job? And how do you know
that I'm not a machine?
```

The indefatigable moderator of the Forum, Ray Thomas, made numerous attempts to stimulate debate on the technological issues of the course.

---
dt200-forum/tma 215, r_thomas, 22-Sep-88 13:50

TITLE: TECHNOLOGICAL ISSUES

It may be some consolation to dt200 students to reflect
that it is not only within the course that there is a
neglect of 'technological issues'. The problem seems to
be that technologists think in terms of clients' problems
and technological solutions. Technologists are not
interested in discussing technological issues with
clients.

The current disk space crisis on CoSy is a case in point.
The technological problem, in so far as it has been
identified, is that CoSy is all on one file and that file
has been put on a relatively small disk which also
contains other files. That was last year's technological
solution. This year a shortage of space for CoSy becomes
apparent. But the problem is presented as belonging to
users. The conferences are wasteful of space. There is a
need for tidying up. Moderators should be more ruthless
with deletions. And of course there is a lot of
discussion of a 'sociological' nature.

But there is no discussion of the technological issue of
the problems of dealing with last year's technological
solution. There is no shortage of disk space on the VAX
system - only with the CoSy file.

Secondly, the contributions of various tutors also added considerably to the expertise and advice available in the Forum conference. Furthermore, the sheer number of students on the system meant there was a very good chance that someone would answer any query.

---
dt200-forum proj, 227, cm-johnston, 2-sep-88 20:23

I have gained confidence as the year went on because, if
I got stuck, it was highly likely that someone else had
already entered comments which were relevant. This has
been the greatest bonus for me and I can fully understand
why so many browse or lurk in the system. The information
is so readily available for all. I've spent a fortune in
phone bills but it has been worth every penny! We really
cannot assess just how effective CoSy is but there are
absolutely no doubts in my mind.

With the notable exception of a few discussions initiated by staff members, the help and expertise available on the system were of the 'one or two message' variety. There was very little extended discussion of relevant course issues. It was certainly envisioned that students with a social science background would provide help and support through CoSy to more technology oriented students and vice-versa. Although there was considerable discussion on various Forum topics about the alleged social science bias of the course and the difficulties which technology students were experiencing with writing the assignments, there is little evidence that CoSy did more than offer a space for students to moan about these problems. The hope that students would pick up 'the language of the discipline' or deepen their understanding through discussion of areas in which they had little background seemed to go largely unrealised.

3 Equality

"I don't know what you mean by your way," said the Queen; "all the ways about here belong to me."

Inequalities in the cost of accessing Cosy and technical difficulties preventing access are acknowledged and regretted by all those involved. Furthermore, for whatever reasons, students made very unequal use of the system as is shown in Table 9.4. In certain other respects, however, the use of CoSy increased students' ability to participate equally. For instance, the status and personal appearance of users are not evident on the system, so students who work unsocial hours or are housebound, were suddenly able to take as much advantage of what was offered as other students. Disabled students were not identifiable as such and tutors were not distinguishable from students by their ID. The peculiarly personal yet detached atmosphere of conferencing obviously encouraged many students to express their opinions, whether positive or negative, and to contribute information from their previous experience, with all the hallmarks of equal members of a group. The feeling shared by some students and tutors of being involved and even influential participants, rather than passive recipients of a course, has played its part in sparking real enthusiasm for the course. CoSy has also been a vehicle for open criticism of course material, and vigorous complaints and outright condemnations have appeared in conferences for all to read. The impact of this direct feedback to the course team has perhaps not had tangible effects as yet, but the feeling of real accountability is much stronger amongst those of the course team who participated in the electronic communication than those who did not.

Statistics from the database confirm the fact that students did appreciate conferencing as an 'equal opportunity' medium. Nearly 500 of the 875 who answered the question agreed with the statement that "individuals can participate more equally in electronic than in face-to-face communication."

Table 9.4 Use of the Forum Conference

1364	students initially registered
110	students never logged on at all
162	students never entered the Forum conference
728	read but never contributed to the Forum conference
364	were individual contributors of at least one message

Statistics contributed by Richard Turner, Academic Computing Service.

topic	# of contributors	topic	# of contributors
00	121	digest	69
1	69	errata	33
2	67	exam	35
3	67	gen	99
4	72	gremlins	156
5	55	guidelines	34
6	6	prac(tical)	92
7	7	proj(ect)	86
		tma	82

4 New Learning Medium

"You may call it 'nonsense' if you like," said the Red Queen, "but I've heard nonsense compared with which that would be as sensible as a dictionary."

By far the most significant and unexpected outcome of the use of CoSy in the first year was the lack of significant activity in the 65 tutor conferences and the nature and amount of activity in the 'national' conference, Forum.

Table 9.5 shows the total number of messages by the end of the year in the course conferences. The mean and standard deviation given for the 65 tutor conferences shows a very wide variation in usage. Those with the highest activity are in most cases the result of Herculean efforts on the part of the tutor to stimulate discussion or to copy messages from other conferences. Despite these efforts, the content of messages has been on the level of information exchange, rather than of discussion, opinions, comments or critiques, and the number of active participants has been only around 5 to 10 students. The table shows that the chat topic in the tutor conferences was the most heavily used.

The first fact which must be made clear about participation in the Forum is that only 26% of all students were contributors and about 53% read or scanned some portion of the messages. Of course there were students who took to the medium immediately; others who grew into it, but undoubtedly many who never used its potential for directing their own learning.

Table 9.5 Messages in CoSy Conferences by Sept 20, 1988

DT200-Forum

block00	263	block6	6	gremlins	715
block1	120	block7	5	guidelines	90
block2	164	digest	13	prac(tical)	235
block3	131	errata	67	proj(ect)	254
block4	291	exam	71	tma	215
block5	166	gen	354		

DT200-Lounge

chat	607	moans	92	newconf	135

Tutor Conferences

block	524	chat	246	practical	764
project	445	tma	709	other	348

Tutor Conferences (n=65)

topic	total messages (all conferences)	mean (per conference)	standard deviation (per conference)
block	524	8.1	8.0
chat	246	38.5	29.8
practical	764	11.9	12.1
project	445	7.0	8.5
tma	709	11.1	9.9
other	348	na	na

```
Mail from tutor Colin Shaw, 17 Aug 88 21:32
----------------------------------------------------
I really don't know about the high level of lurking, yes
its there but I find it slightly irritating, almost as if
the students are using me. I feel that they are being too
passive and that they are like great vacuum cleaners of
knowledge sucking up all the little tip bits. I am
inclined to think that it is because they have adopted a
student stance, have become purely passive learners.
Perhaps the way they use CoSy is as much to do with the
education system as anything but that is one of the
angles that I am working on, trying to challenge their
assumptions about what a student should do and what a
tutor should do......
```

A number of messages from students on CoSy present a different view of the
practice of 'lurking', that is, reading without contributing.

```
dt200-forum proj, 240, d-reeve, 5-Sep-88 23:51
-----------------------------------------------------
CMC has its advantages too - it provides access to a
wider group of people than is possible in local groups. I
personally, though not contributing very much to CoSy,
have found answers to problems with practical work. When
stuck over a problem, I could log on and try to find a
solution. This can be done at any time whereas it may not
be convenient to disturb a fellow student at midnight!
```

The Forum consisted of many topics: there was one for each block of the course,
one for the project, for practical work, for the assignments, for gremlins and
several others added as the course proceeded. In the early stages there were
many messages which were garbled, in the wrong place, completely irrelevant,
or glib. These diminished with time and the topics came to be dominated by
about 100 regular contributors (students, tutors, and staff) with new students
making a first appearance at frequent intervals. A very rough indication of the
level of contribution, lurking and complete withdrawal can be seen in Table
9.4. [7]

The reasons for non-participation in the Forum, which are derived from
interviews and messages on CoSy, are relevant to this analysis primarily as a
focus for understanding the nature of the use that was made of it:

• Lack of time is a constant cry from OU students about their non-use of many
  course facilities. There are indications that this course – a full credit course
  specifying 12 to 15 hours of work per week for 34 weeks – was 'overloaded'
  with readings, and new software to learn at regular intervals. By far the
  majority of students on the course were in full time employment and most
  were married and had children.
• Although students were instructed in the use of CoSy in the second block of
  the course, there were no specific requirements to log on after that. The
  project, which was to be handed in near the end of the course, could in theory
  be completed with a minimum of actual use of the system. Indeed, frequent
  logging on by students was never envisioned by the course team and regular
  contributions from all 1300 users would, if it didn't crash the system,
  certainly have overloaded the conferences by producing more messages than
  anyone could handle.
• As it was, the volume of messages in the Forum conference for all but the
  very frequent and regular users was very difficult to manage. The tools within
  CoSy to manage large conferences – the skip command and the list headers
  command, read by reference and so on – really do not address the problem of
  the infrequent user wanting to get information efficiently, let alone contribute
  to a discussion.

- The nature of the messages in Forum on the whole offers a broader rather than a deeper understanding of the course issues. Students with considerable expertise in certain areas of Information Technology contributed sometimes long and complex messages which gave a wider perspective on many areas of the subject, but very few messages tackled specific course issues.
- The sense of addressing a large public audience certainly prevented a number of students from contributing to the Forum. The intimacy of the tutor conference, where the other participants were often known from face-to-face tutorials, had more appeal to those who shied away from this degree of exposure. Related to this shyness, was often a sense that such public utterances should be polished pieces of work, or at least that some of the messages already in the Forum were above their level.

The following comments from interviews illustrate these points from the student perspective. [8]

John Kemp – "I would like to have gone into it a lot more – look at a lot more of the conferences. But partly it is lack of time and partly if you join a conference with hundreds of messages it is hard to find out what has happened and what has been said before. I was looking for something on modems in Forum/gremlins and after 3 weeks there were 200 messages! I did a search on 'modems' and there were still 60 messages! If people would get rid of outdated stuff it would help."

Deanne Seymour – "There seem a lot of people with axes to grind, particular things which interest them which they put into the conference which aren't really relevant to the course at all. Sometimes they are interesting to read. But it is pretty much pot luck – you don't know what you will get out of them."

Linda How – "I found the early messages in Forum a bit high-flown. I wasn't really sure what they were getting at and what relevance it was. It was in the category of 'nice to know'. It might be quite useful to pick something off there and include it in your assignment. I don't know – to get the full picture you need the comments on the message because that is where the discussion takes place. It can actually take quite a while to get the complete picture and put things in perspective."

Sarah Bamford – "There is an awful lot packed in, so if you don't move on you get behind. I like the facility of CoSy; I enjoy doing it. I quite like it as an entertainment factor. I like putting in a message and getting a response very quickly. But it is not really helping me get on with the course."

John Gouff – "I know you can skip backwards and forwards – but you are making the decisions blind. Quite often I jump to the last 10 messages, but I don't know what I have missed. There might have been something really important or really interesting. Really the person who puts things in, or the person who is managing it, is in the best position to extract things that are no longer important."

Iain Robertson – "It is like coming into a dinner party right in the middle. You can see people have been talking about something and you feel, 'What am I doing here?'"

Comments from student assignments submitted to tutor Dave McConnell:

"I have a reluctance to join in conferences other than DT200-Cotswold, I'm not sure of the reasons but I think it may be a combination of not being able to put names to faces and the content of some of the conferences is either too highbrow or inconsequential rubbish."

"Before we started I had naive visions of vast amounts of stimulating conversations going on, unrestricted by geographical distance or by only having occasional tutorials at which to meet. By and large this has not happened and I have learnt that electronic communication is both hard work and time consuming. There is also concern about social isolation produced by the new technology, the electronic communicator can spend a large part of his or her time physically alone, neglecting the family and perhaps having little time left over for face to face social interaction."

5 Social Needs

"Have you invented a plan for keeping the hair being blown off?" Alice enquired. "Not yet," said the Knight, "but I've got a plan for keeping it from falling off."

The social needs of distance students are composed of a number of different elements. The question in the database on the social aspects of CMC was perhaps too narrow to encompass this range and this may explain why the statistical data from it are not confirmed by the qualitative data. Only 157 of the 847 students said that conferencing was as good or better a means of 'socialising' as a face-to-face tutorial. However, evidence from CoSy messages and from interviews shows that conferencing met many social needs of students – even of those who were infrequent users.

The psychological effect of having the facility to contact the tutor or get help electronically was strong for many students, particularly those who made minimal use of CoSy:

Interview with Arthur Haynes, June 1988:

Q Has the ability to contact other students, your tutor or the central staff made any difference to you as an OU student this year?

A Oh yes. I don't feel anywhere near as isolated. I did T301 last year and was very very much on my own. I don't feel anywhere near as isolated this year. I could have done with conferencing last year.

Q A psychological feeling or an actual fact that you can and do contact other people?

A Both, though possibly more that I could if I needed to.

Students who 'lurked' in rather than contributed to conferences felt re-assured on one of the most frequently cited drawbacks of distance learners – not being able to assess their progress in relation to other students.

Interview with Deanne Seymour, June 1988:

Q Would you like to see more academic discussion in the tutor conference? or do you
   find that the social function is beneficial in itself?

A In itself yes, I think it is beneficial. I have never felt so comfortable doing an OU
   course before. But yes, we should be discussing more of the course I'm sure. I think
   we are wasting the opportunity.

Q To what extent is your comfortableness due to CoSy?

A Quite a lot. You see you can struggle on your own in a course and think you are the
   only person who doesn't understand. Summer school is usually the time when you
   realise everyone is in the same boat. Here you realise that very early on – that people
   are struggling over certain parts of it.

The most common social need which conferencing fulfilled for students was the
desire to be 'in touch' with others on the course. Being part of what is going on,
feeling in contact with the 'people who designed the course' and alleviating the
sense of isolation are all mentioned by students in interviews and CoSy
messages.

```
DT200-forum/4,139, h-gibson, 4-jul-88 19:49
-------------------------------------------------
CMC has allowed me to share the experiences and to
'listen to' the views of many more students and tutors
than I would ordinarily meet at course tutorials. I would
think that at this point on the course - just over half
way - the CoSy Experience adds up to much more than the
TOTAL of all tutorials that I have attended on four
previous courses. Despite the medium's inability to
transmit the smiles (and glares) and other non-verbal
speech parts enjoyed in face - face, I still feel more
involved and a part of things than I have done on other
courses. CMC, as implemented on this course, is one giant
step toward removing that feeling of being 'on your own'
suffered by OU students, certainly by me.
```

The conversation facility was also used by students to chat more informally.
Fifty-two conversations were set up containing anywhere from 2 to nearly 1000
messages.

6   The Conceptual Model of Conferencing

*"Now here you see, it takes all the running you can do, to keep in the same
place. If you want to get somewhere else, you must run at least twice as fast as
that!" said the Queen.*

Two questions in the database (Table 9.6) deal specifically with the ability and
speed with which students mastered the concepts of mail and conferencing. The

responses prove the initial assumptions that conferencing is much more difficult to master than electronic mail.

Table 9.6 Confidence in Using CoSy

Q 49 Do you feel comfortable yet about:

Logging on?	yes	843	no	28
Sending mail?	yes	691	no	175
Participating in a conference?	yes	396	no	479

Q 50 If yes, about how many times did you have to use the system before gaining this confidence?

# of times logged on	1-5	6-10	11-20	21+
Logging on	678	157	23	14
Sending mail	527	165	25	25
Adding to conference	329	123	64	56

Note: A careful look at these statistics shows that 572 respondents feel *confident* about participating in a conference – that is 65% of the total number of respondents, but 396 or 45% feel *comfortable* about contributing to a conference. So it seems that 20% feel confident but not comfortable about contributing. It may be that respondents have interpreted 'comfortable' at a cultural level and 'confident' at a technical level.

During interviews, it became apparent that some very infrequent users had a hazy idea of the structure of CoSy, that of a number of separate conferences made up of topics, and of the difference between the local tutor conferences and national conferences, and a confused notion of the nature of the communication appropriate for conferences.

Interview with John Franklin, June 1988.

Q   How do you feel about contributing to your tutor group conference?
A   I suppose first of all I think, let's see what everybody else has done....then it is a problem – I am so used to working on my own, I'd have to really think, what could I contribute. It is not a fear of giving away information............
Q   You mean it is a matter of figuring out where to come in from?
A   Yes, and what amount of effort to put into it.

This student's lack of certainty is a reflection to some extent of the ambiguity of the status of conferencing on the course. Strictly speaking, Cosy was a piece of software for students to experience, plus a half-time substitute for face-to-face tutorial support – in short, no more than 5% of the course. Nowhere was it specifically spelled out as a teaching medium or a vehicle for course presentation. Its use was 'built into' the course through the project and yet its major potential as an educational tool was never exploited. Had it been conceived as a teaching tool, the whole environment would have had to be structured differently. As it was, a number of staff enthused by the response in Forum did gradually begin to exploit its educational potential, but this was more of an afterthought than a pre-planned activity (Table 9.7 gives a content analysis of one topic on the national Forum conference). Those students, tutors and staff who took an active part in the Forum conference engaged in it considerably above and beyond the 'call of duty'. This ambiguous, changing nature of the national conference did not help the weaker student cement a firm concept of the value and appropriate content of messages.

The structure and purpose of the tutor conferences, however, were laid out more specifically, and yet they suffered greatly from lack of contributions. The database questionnaire shows that 80% of students felt comfortable about sending mail but only 45% felt comfortable about contributing to conferences at the time of the survey. Each of the 15 students interviewed, was asked why they hadn't contributed more to their tutor conference. Despite a wide range of actual time spent on CoSy by the sample, all students blamed lack of time as the reason for lurking rather than contributing. Some admitted that they felt guilty about reading without writing messages and others referred to a sense of disappointment at finding no new messages in the conference. This constant refrain begins to sound like noise generated to cover a more basic cause – the lack of a clear model on which to base their conception of how to participate. [9]

In any group of 25 students, about 5 were regular contributors and this was insufficient to generate discussion. Whether the tutor has a direct teaching role or merely a supportive, facilitating role is another ambiguity within the OU. However, to suggest that this in any way contributed to the almost complete lack of academic discussion in the 65 tutor groups would be missing the point. For the average student on this course logging on relatively infrequently, the effort of remembering how to operate CoSy and the difficulty of coping with the large backlog of unread messages, meant that the 'return' on their time was simply not high enough to justify or encourage further exploration or contribution to the medium.

Conferencing did not have a high enough profile on the course to be a medium for discussing course issues in depth. The fact that interesting and worthwhile interchanges did take place on the Forum is a tribute to the medium and to the people who took part.

7 Technical Difficulties

"It's a poor sort of memory that only works backwards," the Queen remarked.

As with other aspects of this study, the range of student experiences was wide. Some students experienced no difficulties with their workstation, had no trouble making the connection to CoSy and worked through the teaching material about electronic communications without a hitch.

Table 9.7 Analysis of Topic 4 of Forum: Information Technology in Education

Total number of messages sent: 291

Contributed by: 8 members of staff, 9 tutors and 52 students

Roughly 9 identifiably different topics were discussed at length:

Topic 1   Late mailing   *71 messages*

The late mailing of written material, partly due to the postal strike was discussed most frequently. At times the interchanges became very heated with accusations and justifications for the delay.

Topic 2   Teachers v. machines   *53 messages*

Tony Bates initiated a discussion asking students to make a case for or against replacing teachers with machines. The debate developed into more general issues of teachers and Information Technology.

Topic 3   Interactive video   *23 messages*

This was a lively discussion about the merits of interactive video, sparked off by one of the course TV programmes.

Topic 4   Computers in schools   *21 messages*

The use of computers in schools and secondarily of computer communications in schools was initiated by one of the students.

Topic 5   Compact discs   *15 messages*

The subject of compact discs, topical at the time, received a number of very long and detailed messages from one particular student knowledgeable in the area.

Topic 6   Quiz   *12 messages*

The moderator of the Forum introduced a quiz whereby students were asked to identify the author of a particular quotation.

Topic 7   Concept Keyboard   *9 messages*

The 'Concept Keyboard' was discussed by a number of students who had experience with it.

Topic 8   Satellite TV   *9 messages*

The subject of satellite broadcasting for education was initiated by Tony Bates and developed into a discussion of satellite TV.

Topic 9   User feedback   *8 messages*

Tony Kaye requested feedback from users on their attitudes so far, to computer-mediated communication for education.

In fact, despite bugs, complaints, totally inexplicable technical failures and unforeseen happenings, [10] there were actually fewer technical difficulties than the pessimists anticipated. Table 9.8 shows the number of difficulties experienced by students at the time of the survey on a range of technical areas: the modem, the OU dial-up network, the host machine and the lines through to CoSy. Table 9.3 shows which sources of help students turned to and which they found most useful. The list of possible sources of help was clearly inadequate as the largest source of help was given as 'none of the above'.

Table 9.8 Technical Problems

Q 37 Have you had problems in any of the following in connecting to CoSy?

	never	some	many	total
Modem set up and dialling	576	261	30	867
Dialled but no answer	400	432	26	858
Answered, but no 'connect'	191	608	71	870
Stuck at 'Select service/username'	558	267	30	855
Stuck at DT200	649	186	17	852
No carrier after connected	343	460	46	849

Note: The respondents to this questionnaire, of course, do not include any students who were unable to log on at all, as it was necessary to enter the DT200 environment in order to upload answers into the database.

One of these 'unknown' sources of help was certainly course team members and particularly the chairman, Nick Heap.

Interview with Nick Heap, May 1988:

A   From my point of view, the last time I logged on I had 25 mail messages, accumulated over 10 days. That is an average of 2.5 messages a day......I have been besieged by phone calls at the rate of 5 a day for the last 5 or 6 weeks.

Q   How usual is it for a course chairman to have that level of queries directly from students?

A   Well it is horrendous. They were all queries that everybody else had filtered down because they couldn't answer them! I have only been a maintenance chairman and I have never had this.

Q   Surely most of this is caused by the fact that you are the only person on the course team who can deal with these queries.

A   Sure, but it also gives me a rather distorted view of what is going on. Unless I can say to myself, this is the bottom pile of rock I am getting, then I would have to conclude that the course is in a mess! I don't believe it is, because the level of inquiries that we are getting is far too small for the course to be in a mess.

There is no doubt that the level of difficulties in the first 2 months of student access to CoSy was hard to manage. The gremlins topic in Forum proved invaluable as a place for students to register their problems, as well as for other students and tutors to offer advice. The 'comment' facility within CoSy, whereby a message related to a previous message can be linked directly to it, was particularly useful in this context. The return on temporary contract of the original programmer of the communications software, Ben Hawkridge, to work through the 500 messages in gremlins helped to relieve the strain on the course chairman. As a result, messages were put into the read-only news conference offering the best fixes for a number of the software bugs.

Although students continued to experience technical difficulties, some of which seemed invulnerable to solution, the level of queries subsided and many were 'handled' by other students on Cosy.

The Academic Computing Service has for many years provided a telephone help desk on weekdays and Saturday mornings for courses with a computing element. This service offers diagnostic assistance on the physical use of equipment and the operation of software. A trial extension to the service was added for courses under the Home Computing Policy to include coverage on the 7 weekends before the course began – primarily to answer questions about setting up machines and preparing disks. In total the Service registered 1396 calls from students of which about 300 were related to CoSy. Feedback from students, on CoSy and in interviews, indicates that the service was invariably courteous, though not always able to address the problem.

Inability to access the host computer at Milton Keynes, was one of the persistent problems which frustrated students. Faults on the network account for some of these, as the 17 dial-up nodes are not monitored on weekends and holidays – when of course students are most likely to want access. Poor telephone lines also account for some of the problems. Perhaps most frustrating of all were those which could not be traced or explained.

Though not within their remit, tutors also received calls for help from students. OU students often feel more comfortable about contacting their tutor than other 'faceless' people at the centre. The database shows that of the 80% percent who turned to the tutor for help, only 45% percent found the tutor most helpful. Indeed many tutors were as unfamiliar with the workstation and with CoSy as the students.

A most useful statistic on the issue of technical difficulties would be the number of students who 'gave up' because of technical problems – either in the sense of abandoning the course entirely or attempting to pass with little or no access to CoSy. These statistics will be difficult or impossible to obtain without considerable follow-up investigation and interviewing. Most students who abandon their OU studies say that they do so for private, personal reasons – lack of time, rather than an inability to cope with the course material (Woodley et al., 1987). The drop-out rate on this course was about 25% and on this basis one could guess that about 5% might have given up the course because of technical difficulties. However, Table 9.2 shows that two thirds of all students spent less than the suggested 10 hours on-line over the whole 6 months.

8 Variations in Moderating Styles

"If you only spoke when you were spoken to, and the other person always waited for you to begin, you see nobody would ever say anything," said Alice.

Though the major disappointment of the use of CoSy was the lack of success of the tutor group conferences, a number of interesting results have emerged (see Table 9.5 for number of messages in the tutor conferences).

First of all, tutors who continued to input messages – cajoling, informative, chatty or substantial – produced the largest number of messages. Tutors who put in opening messages in each topic and then expected students to carry the ball were disappointed.

```
dt200-tut eval, 32, b-lucas, 2-jul-88 15:41
-------------------------------------------------
......I have a topical-reading topic, which contains a
number of gleanings from the computer freebies, of
possible interest and occasional amusement, but not
essential for the course. I was hoping this and other
topics such as chat would encourage students to try CoSy
among their town group before having courage to try the
national conferences.

I believe this has had moderate success, since those few
of my students who are now contributing nationally
started on the town conference, and are still more fluent
there. I have tried to make it fun as well, by my initial
messages such as on the electronic massaging misprint,
and "DT200 students do IT with a modem", but it was all
left to me at first.
```

Secondly, as the pattern of 'quiet' tutor conferences and 'active' national topics became established, the local conferences became the place for information specific to the tutor group – dates of next tutorials or self-help group meetings, friendly chat messages like birth announcements, but most usefully, information about assignments. During the two postal strikes which occurred in June and September of the first year, CoSy proved a vital medium of exchange amongst students, tutors and the course team. Many tutors provided a service much appreciated by students of summarising the good and bad points found in each batch of assignments and giving the range of marks for the whole group. Individual students were emailed with their own results. Some tutors joined students from completely dead tutor group conferences to their own conferences and other tutors provided a real time- and cost-saving service to their students by copying the most important messages from the national conferences into the tutor group conference. Students in these tutor groups, therefore, did not need to go beyond their local conference to access all vital information.

Thirdly, the idea of an intermediate area between the local and national levels developed as a result of the under-use of the one and the over-use of the other. Providing a regionally based conference of approximately 150 students, it was hoped, would catch enough frequent users and attract a few of those who were daunted by the enormity of the national conference to produce a lively but not overwhelming discussion area for course issues. After consulting students and tutors about this idea via CoSy, it was discovered that the regional conference should not replace the local tutor conference but merely supplement it. This pattern is now to be adopted for future presentations of the course.

```
dt200-tut eval, 59, b-sanderson, 11-Sep-88 21:06
--------------------------------------------------------
TITLE: FEEDBACK

We in Cumbria had our last face-to-face tutorial Sat. 3rd
and I would like to report on a few points which were
brought up.

CONFERENCES - General feeling that a local conference was
still a good idea as it was VERY much less intimidating
to start on, but probably only need one or two topics -
TMA and chat.

I too have found this restricted conference great for
giving rapid feedback on TMAs (assignments). I send
individual email messages for marks and a detailed
general conference message for comments.
```

Apart from confirming research findings from many sources [11] that moderators need to provide continual support – either in encouraging users to participate or in directing a well established conference, little in the way of new findings about moderating styles has resulted from this very large application of computer conferencing. The reasons for the disappointing quantity and quality of tutor conference messages, however, are related to the nature and place of CoSy on the course, rather than the moderating styles of the tutors.

CONCLUSIONS

Four categories have been chosen in which to present a final evaluation of the many findings detailed above. These four are: the value of computer-mediated communications for students, the implications of its use for tutors, the integration of this medium into the OU's distance learning package, and finally, the impact of CMC on the organisation of the university.

The Students' Viewpoint

The fact that so many students were exposed to this rapidly expanding field of communications technology, and that so many were able to jump over the hurdles of its use, is justification enough for its place on this course. The value of computer conferencing as a tutorial support has also been established in this first year, and were the costs involved in supporting all students in this manner less problematic, it could certainly be recommended as an ideal supplement to the telephone and face-to-face tutorial. Its benefit to students as a life-line to help, information, contact and exchange has been proven, though the cost of access for both students and tutors is a significant deterrent to its further development.

The educational exploitation, while never specifically part of the original intention for its use on this course, developed through the enthusiasm of a few members of staff and a minority of the students. The potential of the medium for presenting course material, and particularly for student interaction with course issues, was demonstrated sufficiently to warrant further investigation by other course teams. It is to be regretted that the graduates of this course have no other options within the OU to continue and expand their new expertise in computer communications.

Implications for Tutors

The combination of a new course, covering at least two disciplines, with an MS-DOS workstation as well as a new medium for interacting with students has led to a considerable amount of work for tutors in the first year. Many tutors have given unflaggingly of their time and energy in contributing to the success of the communications package and to supporting students through it. The arrangement of regional conferences in subsequent years is intended to relieve the burden on tutors in addition to its anticipated benefits for students. Although the various regional groups may devise their own sharing of the workload, it is envisioned that tutors will take turns in supporting the academic content of the regional conference and that through the benefit of this larger grouping, students will develop effective self-help mechanisms as was in evidence in the first year in the national help topic.

The range of tutor use of CoSy was as varied as that of the students, namely, from virtually none to almost daily logging on. Some tutors had free access to CoSy through their place of work, but the reimbursement for 20 hours of connect telephone time did not nearly compensate a number of tutors for their out-of-pocket expenses, let alone for their time. However, it was clear that many tutors did enjoy the medium, both as a communications tool and as a new piece of educational technology.

Media Integration

The place and purpose of computer conferencing on this course is understandable and justifiable. However, this model of a very small exploitation of the medium amongst a plethora of other teaching tools can not be recommended for other applications and indeed, was responsible in great part for the little use made of it by the majority of students. Some of the frustrations experienced by tutors and students alike would be considerably reduced if conferencing formed a more significant role in the teaching and delivery of a course. Tutors would have to receive proper recognition for their role in the presentation of the course and all students would be obliged to log on frequently to take the course. The life-blood of a conferencing system is the contributions and interactions of its users. It can integrate with and enhance other teaching media, particularly print, but not when relegated to a 5% stake in a course.

Organisational Implications

The impact of CMC on the organisational structures of the OU has been marginal to date – partly because the full potential of electronic communication has not been exploited in this application. The delivery and management of courses at the OU relies heavily on sending print through the postal system. Although technically possible for students on this course to submit their assignments electronically, this innovation was considered too difficult to manage administratively. [12] Similarly, although some information to students was available on CoSy earlier than in print through the post, this was a duplication rather than a replacement of the print-based system.

The development of the CoSy environment and the design of the OUCom front-end were joint ventures of The Technology Faculty, The Academic Computing Service and The Institute of Educational Technology. However, the continued support of the course needs a considerably higher staff allocation than the normal, very small, maintenance team. The range of queries and difficulties which arise from 1300 students using communications technology requires an equally wide range of skills to respond adequately. For instance, if students are expecting to find relevant, up-to-date information about the course on the system, then at least one member of the maintenance team must keep abreast of what is happening on the conferences and must input regular messages as required. If aspects of CoSy cause problems, a different person needs to respond. The support for the database requires yet another person to handle student queries. The conferencing coordinator ID, Coco, needs regular attention by someone knowledgeable in many areas of the course to meet students' needs for quick help and advice. Finally, if the most exciting aspect of the use of conferencing in the first year – the teaching potential – is to continue, then a number of other core members will need to take a leading role in organising and stimulating on-line discussion. In short, when students are 'admitted' to the centre of the university, the centre is obligated to respond! In the first instance, the course team, the maintenance chairman and the computing service help desk are implicated, but as students learn to rely on this new tool, other administrative services – registration information, payments, exam results, counselling, student records and other services could all be available on-line.

The facility with which academics can receive direct feedback, both positive and negative, from students about materials they have written, has great potential impact on the content and writing styles of academics. Instead of receiving written summaries or reports of survey questionnaires some considerable time after the original writing of the material, course teams can now interact with the 'consumers' of their work. On this first year of the course, students were very candid with their praise and their criticism, in both cases unsolicited. However, this new facility was used intentionally to gather feedback from students for the re-write of the practical work on computer conferencing. Students whose response to the initial opening welcome message from Coco showed signs of poor understanding of commands, were mailed individually asking for detailed follow-up of how they had used the teaching material.

A balanced summary of the impact of CMC on this course in the first year would have to conclude that for the majority of students, tutors and course team members, computer conferencing was an interesting but marginal activity. For the committed or 'converted' minority, however, there is little doubt that this medium was an exciting, innovative and satisfying way of participating in distance teaching and learning.

NOTES

[1] See Table 11.1 in Chapter 11 by Thomas for a breakdown of students by occupation and previous educational qualifications.

[2] 15 tutors from all over the country were interviewed before the start of the course – some were experienced OU tutors, others were not; some had a stronger social science background, others a stronger technology background.

[3] I joined the course team in September 1986, after the decision to use CoSy on the course had already been taken. I was co-author of the teaching material on computer conferencing and author/coordinator of the project questionnaire. After the course began, my on-line involvement included extensive email exchanges with students, contributions to national and local conferences and sharing responsibility for the Coco ID, which students used to contact the course team collectively. My personal perspective, however, is most strongly coloured by my interviews with tutors and students. I 'monitored' the progress of 15 students from two different tutor groups, by participating in their tutor conference, going to face-to-face tutorials and interviewing the students both prior to the beginning of the course and half-way through it. I also made a special study of the views of students and tutors in the Scottish region, through telephone interviews, specially arranged discussions, tutorials, and interviews with both low and high users.

[4] Quotations for each of the 8 headings are taken from Lewis Carroll, *Alice Through the Looking Glass*.

[5] See also the comments by the enthusiastic users of CoSy in the *Prologue* to this book.

[6] All interviews quoted in this paper were carried out by the author and permission has been granted by those interviewed to quote from them.

[7] Compare these figures with the 6:12:16 ratio on a much smaller course given by Gray in Paper 2 in the Resource File.

[8] See also Paper 3 by Keith Grint, one of the DT200 tutors, for another perspective on students' lack of participation.

[9] See also the section on Time in Paper 3 of the Resource File for further corroboration of this point.

[10] For example, the time-out on one of the important menu bar functions, which was set to work perfectly before the course, became far too short with 1500 new users. Secondly, the number of students (over 150) with hard-disk machines requiring unique software was far greater than anticipated.

[11] Brochet, Madge, "Effective Moderation of Computer Conferences. Notes and Suggestions," Computing Support Services, University of Guelph, 1985; Feenberg, Andrew, "Computer Conferencing and the Humanities", Instructional Science 16 pp 169-186, 1987; Davie, Lynn, Chapter 6 of this book.

[12] Other reasons for dismissing this possibility were the added costs to students and the inequality for those with technical difficulties.

CHAPTER 10

ON-LINE COSTS: INTERACTIVITY AT A PRICE

Greville Rumble
Open University
Milton Keynes, UK

THE COST STRUCTURE OF DISTANCE EDUCATION

The cost structure of media-based mass distance education is well understood. In essence capital, in the form of materials (print, audio-visual and broadcast, computer assisted learning), replaces the traditional labour-intensive approach to education, in which there is a direct relationship between the number of students and teachers. While the development and production of materials requires a high initial investment, once developed they can be used, often for a number of years, to teach any number of students. Provided there are sufficient numbers of students, and the number needed will vary depending upon the choice of media, distance teaching ought to be cheaper than traditional forms of education (Rumble, 1988a pp 92-3). There are, of course, other forms of distance education which involve personal tutoring at a distance (using correspondence, telephone and electronic forms of communication) or which are based on guided reading and textbooks. Such approaches avoid the high fixed costs and capital-intensive nature of mass-media approaches, and have consequently a very different cost structure to mass media-based systems.

The Open University's approach to distance education is based on the use of mass media (print, broadcasting, audio and video cassettes, etc); it substitutes capital for labour, and offers what Wagner (1982, p ix) described as "a mass production alternative to the traditional craft approach" to education. Such an approach can achieve real economies of scale (see Rumble, 1988a). A comparison of Open University and traditional university costs in Britain in 1986 showed that the cost per full time equivalent student at traditional universities was about 2.6 times the cost at the Open University, while the cost per traditional university graduate was 2.4 times the cost of an Open University graduate (Open University, 1987).

Unfortunately, over emphasis on materials can result in excessive packaging in which "conventions of 'good writing' and 'good broadcasting' pre-construct a largely passive student" (Harris, 1987, p 139). The problem for distance educators operating a media-based mass education system is to break free from the tendency to over-emphasise the package and provide students with a learning experience which meets their personal needs. This requires an element of two-way communication between teacher and learner, although it need not involve actual face-to-face contact. In nineteenth century distance teaching systems two-way communication was provided solely through written correspondence. Later on the telephone came to be used, initially for individual conversations but subsequently for group audio-conferencing. More recent developments have involved the use of video-conferencing, TVI-type systems (video-out and audio-back), and electronic mail and computer conferencing systems. In addition, many distance education systems do have an element of face-to-face interaction between students and tutors for teaching, counselling or socialisation purposes. Such meetings may be individualised but more generally occur in groups, and may be for varying periods of time – evening tutorials and seminars, whole day or weekend workshops, or residential courses of a week or more's duration. There is plenty of evidence that such contact is enormously valuable. However, as in traditional forms of education, the cost of such support is closely tied to student numbers. Obviously, as the amount of face-to-face tuition provided increases, so the basic characteristic of distance teaching, the physical separation between teacher and learner, is lost, and with it the potential for economies of scale (Rumble, 1988a, p 97). For this reason, there is considerable interest in the cost of providing non-contiguous two-way communication between students and teachers. The Open University's use of computer-mediated communications (CMC) provides a case study in the costs of such provision for a reasonably large group of students following a single course.

HOME COMPUTING WITHIN THE OPEN UNIVERSITY

In the mid-1980s the University became increasingly concerned at its ability to continue to teach certain subjects, notably computing, unless it could at the same time provide its students with ready access to a computer for significant amounts of time. Throughout the 1970s it provided any necessary computing experience through a mixture of access to the University's Academic Computing Service network at local study centres, one week residential courses in the summer, where these were an integral part of a course, and the loan of a specially designed microcomputer on a returnable basis on certain courses. By the mid-1980s it was clear that none of these options was satisfactory, and the University had, instead, to seek ways of providing its home-based students with better access to microcomputers if it were to continue to teach certain subjects. The cost of providing all its students (70,000 undergraduates as well as many students on other programmes) with a microcomputer was clearly too expensive to contemplate. Estimates suggested that even if provision were restricted only to those students taking courses where access to a computer was regarded as essential, the University would need to have provided 5000 computers in 1988, and 12,500 by 1990, with further increases thereafter. In the past, when the University has required students to have access to a particular piece of equipment which is not (unlike radios and television sets) commonly found in homes, it has bought in the equipment and supplied this to students in the form of a 'home experiment kit'. [1] The kit is lent to students for the duration of a course (normally one year). In essence the University supplies students with equipment and related non-reusable consumables (eg chemicals) which it would not normally expect students to own. In the case of certain consumer goods, the University has supplied students with equipment such as audio-cassette players and calculators for several years following their introduction into the market, until such time as the unit cost began to fall and they became a normal consumer durable which it could reasonably expect students to buy for themselves. This is not currently the case with microcomputers. However, cost projections indicated that supplying microcomputers to students on courses where computing was deemed to be an essential element would be beyond the University's capacity. Accordingly the University sought to meet this provision by:

• encouraging students taking certain courses to buy their own microcomputer, which had to meet an approved specification [2]
• providing a stock of microcomputers which students could rent
• providing a limited number of machines which would act as a back-up service and which would be accessible to students through some of the University's 260 local study centres.

The capital to buy in an initial stock of Amstrad PC1512DD-MM (dual disc drive, monochrome monitor) and 540 Akhter PC machines was made available through special grants of £2.25m from the Department of Trade and Industry and £0.2m from the Department of Education and Science. The second of these grants was given to provide machines to disadvantaged and unemployed students.

The University's policy on media has always been to use media and equipment which is accessible (ie on the market and available to students), relatively cheap, and relatively easy to use. In general this policy means that the University is not in the business of developing technologies, nor does it use state-of-the-art technologies, even where these are available. It therefore tends to lag seven to twelve years behind the leading edge of technological development in its application of new methods to distance teaching. This does not, however, prevent it from undertaking trials where this seems appropriate, in order to position itself to exploit a technology for teaching purposes once it is freely available in the market at a reasonable cost to the consumer.

These criteria dictated the choice of an IBM PC compatible as its approved specification for home computing. Students are given advice on suitable and unsuitable machines which conform to this specification. It was assumed that some students would already have access to a machine. Many, however, would need to arrange access. The University therefore made arrangements for students to buy an approved machine (Amstrad PC1512) and computer supplies through mail order. Students may also rent a computer from a limited stock. Rental is through an agent acting on behalf of the University.

In 1988, the first year in which students on a number of courses were asked to provide themselves with microcomputers, all students on home computing courses were given a discount on their course fees, to bring the cost of rental down to below a figure of £100, and to encourage purchase. This discount is to be phased out over 1989 and 1990.

Part-time tutors, many of whom work at other institutions of higher education in the UK, correct the students' assignments, conduct face-to-face tutorials, and participate in on-line tutorial support and discussion. Tutors were expected to have access to an MSDOS microcomputer which met the University's specification. They could either buy a machine through the University's agent, hire a machine, or use their own equipment to tutor the course. In addition to their normal fees, they are paid an allowance in recognition of the expenses which they incur in respect of line charges and computer consumables. The University has arranged for both tutors and students, should they wish, to take out a bank loan of between £500 and £1000, repayable over five years, at 2% below the normal rate of interest, to help with purchase of equipment.

THE COURSE

DT200 *An Introduction to Information Technology: Social and Technological Issues,* is an introductory undergraduate course which aims to explore some of the major issues arising from the introduction of Information Technology (IT). The course has been planned on the assumption that students will spend about 420 hours on the course. Much of this time will be spent reading course materials, with a small amount set aside for watching or listening to television, radio programmes and audio-cassettes, and doing assignments. However, 20 percent of study time is to be allocated to working with a home-based microcomputer system, developing practical skills in the use of various IT systems, one of which is electronic mail and computer conferencing. Chapter 9 describes the way in which this one aspect, computer communications, is integrated into the main content and delivery of the course. The objectives of the course, and the fact that it was part of the newly established home computing policy, made it possible for the University to approve the introduction of this new medium.

The provisions for acquiring a microcomputer for this course have been described above. Surveys indicated that of the 1403 students initially registered, 537 (38.3%) rented a machine; 382 (27.2%) purchased a machine; and 484 (34.5%) made their own arrangements for access. [3] Students also need a telephone with a new standard British Telecom (BT) socket to use the modem. The University sends students the modem and lead, in the form of a kit which is loaned for the duration of the course. Students also have to meet the incidental costs arising from the communications element of the course – in particular, the phone charges. There are 17 dial up nodes in major cities around the UK at which students can link up to the University's central computer (see Figure 9.1). Table 10.1 shows the proportion of students in the various BT telephone charge bands, and the cost per hour of calls at cheap, standard and peak rates. Over 50% of students can access the network at local call rates. Other materials (including computer software) and services are given to the students registered on the course as part of the course. The 1988 course fee of £166 (excluding the £55 rebate mentioned above) is not expected to meet the full costs of the University's undergraduate teaching, which is largely supported by grant-in-aid from Government. Some students who are financially disadvantaged were helped with the cost of their fees and also loaned a microcomputer.

Table 10.1 DT200 Students by Telephone Charge Bands

Charge band	Distance from network node (miles)	Price per hour (£)			Percentage of students
		Cheap	Standard	Peak	
Local	Variable	0.51	2.02	3.04	54.4
Band A	Up to 35	1.82	5.31	7.09	25.1
Band B*	Over 35	4.04	6.07	7.59	17.9
Band B1*	Over 35	3.04	8.10	10.12	2.6

The B1 rate applies to some frequently used routes.

As Thomas observes in Chapter 11 of this book, the University did not introduce CoSy into DT200 with a view to saving money. Computer conferencing and electronic mail are applications of IT and the University believed that students on the course should gain first hand experience of using them, along with word processing, spreadsheets, and databases. The University also saw the course as an opportunity to assess the potential of electronic communication for educational and administrative purposes.

COSTING METHODOLOGY

There is no absolutely correct method of costing an educational project. Over the years various approaches have been recommended (eg Fielden and Pearson, 1978; Jamison, Klees and Wells, 1978, pp 25-62; Eicher *et al.*, 1982, pp 41-53; Levin, 1983, pp 79-105; Orivel, 1987; Coopers and Lybrand, 1987; Rumble, 1988b, pp 247-82). For this reason, every attempt has been made in this study to make explicit the assumptions underlying the cost study.

The first requirement in any costing study is to determine the purpose and extent of the study. This study is concerned only with the costs of CMC operating within the framework of DT200. It does not provide a full costing of the course. Even so, the costing could have been approached in two ways. One would have been to assume that DT200 was a home computing course (as indeed it is) and that students already had access to microcomputers in a stand alone capacity. The additional costs to the course of introducing CoSy could then have been identified. From an internal Open University point of view, this approach makes sense. However, such an analysis would have been of limited use to readers interested in introducing CMC into a course *where the existing computing infrastructure did not exist*. For this reason, this study also costs the equipment elements of the course to provide an idea of the full economic cost of CMC on DT200. Nevertheless, the final section looks at the marginal costs of adopting CoSy on top of the home computing element.

While the study may be of interest to those considering introducing CMC into a course, a word of caution is needed. The specific costs of the Open University's system will not transfer to other institutions because local costs (salaries, distribution costs, telephone costs) will always differ from the UK and Open University experience, and because local management will take decisions which affect the costs of computer-mediated communications. For instance, the fee rebate to students, the arrangements made with tutors, and the freedom allowed for staff involvement, not to mention the home-computing provisions, are all significant elements in the overall cost and yet are specific to the Open University. Also, while some costs are real extra costs, others (eg human resource and central mainframe time) were opportunity costs in this particular case. What were opportunity costs to the Open University might be real extra costs in other circumstances.

Once the purpose of the costing has been established, the next step is to identify the elements which need to be costed. Costs are classified by type as:

- human resource costs
- costs of developing, producing and delivering CMC-related course materials
- capital equipment costs
- consumables and expenses
- space or accommodation costs.

This classification broadly agrees with that used in most educational costings except that revenue 'non-staff' costs have been split between course materials (where the costing system may subsume some labour costs within the costs of certain materials) and consumables and expenses. Tutorial labour costs and some labour costs in support areas such as the Academic Computing Service have, for convenience, and because they cannot be easily separated out, been treated as an expense rather than a human resource cost. The context makes it clear where this has happened.

Following Eicher *et al.* (1982, p 51) and Orivel (1988), there is general agreement that the costs of systems using educational media should be analysed on the basis of the following technical classification of costs:

- general administrative costs
- production costs (including costs of development or conception)
- transmission or distribution costs, including duplication costs
- reception costs including teaching costs and costs incurred by the student.

Orivel (1988, p 2) accepts that this classification, while it is well adapted to radio, television and other audio-visual and print media, is less relevant in the case of face-to-face and correspondence tuition. Nevertheless, it has gained considerable acceptance and Tables 10.2-4 and 10.7, which show the identifiable costs of DT200 CMC, follow this classification.

Some of the costs, notably the capital equipment costs and the development costs of the course materials, represent an investment which will be used over the life of the course; others are an expense incurred only once; yet others are annual running costs (recurrent costs) which will recur each year. The distinction between the first two and the third of these kinds of costs is of crucial importance, particularly in distance education systems where investment in teaching materials is substituted to a degree for the recurrent cost of labour. Tables 10.2–4 identify capital and investment costs on the one hand, and recurrent operating costs on the other. Each line of these tables is numbered to aid cross-reference between the text and the tables. This information is then used when an attempt is made in Tables 10.9 and 10.10 to calculate the real economic cost of CMC for this course.

Table 10.2 Summary of DT200 CMC Production Costs (£)

		Unit of measure	Unit cost	Total costs	Dev't cost	Rec't costs	Who pays
1	*Human Resources*						
1a	Course mat'ls	18.5 months	-	37370	37370	—	OU
1b	CoSy FE	22 months	-	39730	39730	—	OU
2	*Course materials*						
2a	Fixed print costs						
	i main text	budget	-	1572	1572	—	OU
	ii supplementary	budget	-	2780	—	2780	OU
2b	Audio-cassette	budget	-	1050	1050	—	OU
2c	CoSy license	budget	-	1359	1359	—	OU
3	*Equipment*						
3a	Micros for dev't	6 micros	600	3600	3600	—	OU
4	*Space*						
		estimate	-	2126	2126	—	OU
TOTALS				**89587**	**86807**	**2780**	

PRODUCTION: GROUPS 1 – 4

This splits into four distinct groups, which are described in the following sections.

Group 1 Human Resources

The University's courses are developed and produced by full-time central academic staff and consultants, supported by editorial, design, educational technology, administrative, computing, broadcasting and other staff. Some of the staff time used in the production of course materials is costed into the materials (eg design, broadcasting), but some of it has to be estimated by asking staff how much time they spent on a particular project. Data on DT200 staff costs for CMC development was collected in staff months (18.5 for course production and 22 for development of the communications software) and costed to take account of the grade of the member of staff, using average full employer costs for each grade (lines 1a - 1b).

The introduction of CMC required the acquisition of considerable technical expertise. Successful implementation was heavily dependent upon the time which various individuals spent learning about electronic mail and conferencing systems, visiting institutions already using them, and experimenting with systems. The human capital represented by this expertise, once acquired, will have a utility far beyond the bounds and life of DT200. The cost of acquiring it was not insignificant (involving probably several years' work). In addition to this human capital, the introduction of CMC involved change and new practices which had to be 'sold' to colleagues and then implemented. DT200 course writers had to be persuaded to adopt the system and try it out on their course, and administrative and operational areas had to be persuaded to take on the additional problems posed by the system. Introduction of the technology threw up a whole range of problems, which had to be solved. For example, course team members and other professional staff spent many hours considering what kind of modem should be adopted, and generally developing policy and systems. This work had to be undertaken because DT200 was the first course to use CoSy, but it can properly be regarded as a general overhead rather than a course specific cost. Accordingly, these staff costs are not taken into account in the course costs. Nevertheless, those embarking on the use of CMC for the first time should not ignore them.

Group 2 Course Materials Costs

Students are sent printed materials, both main text and supplementary materials, as part of their course. The only main text item associated with the CMC aspect of the course is Part D of Block 2 which provides detailed instructions for using the microcomputer in a communications mode. Supplementary materials consist of the block concerned with the PC, printer, and modem, booklets on setting up and testing the modem and on problems which may be encountered by students, a questionnaire and an assignment booklet on the project. All the material was printed to meet only one year's requirements. The fixed print costs (treated as a production cost here) cover typesetting, copyright fees, illustrations, colour printing. Also included here are authors' corrections to typesetting. Variable print costs (treated as a distribution cost) include the cost of machine running, binding and paper. Print production costs are shown in line 2a. Other production costs included the production of a C90 audio-cassette (line 2b) and the initial costs to the University of using CoSy under license from the University of Guelph (line 2c).

Group 3 Capital Equipment

Six microcomputers were purchased for those involved in the initial development of the CoSy front-end system (see Mason, Chapter 9, for details of the CoSy front-end), and for use by those involved in testing the teaching material (line 3a).

Group 4 Space

A full costing of the project requires that the cost of space occupied by staff involved in the development and running of the project should be included (line 4). Space costs have been calculated using the proxy measure of rental value.

Table 10.3 Summary of DT200 CMC Distribution Costs (£)

	Unit of measure	Unit cost	Total costs	Dev't cost	Rec't cost	Who pays
5 Human resources						
5a Modem service	budget	-	4600	—	4600	OU
6 Course materials						
6a Variable print (all)	budget	-	1999	—	1999	OU
6b Audio-cassette						
copying	1450 cassettes	0.27	391	—	391	OU
6c Postage						
(allowance)	1430 packages	0.46	658	—	658	OU
6d CoSy						
i annual license	budget	-	567	—	567	OU
ii disc	1450 discs	0.27	391	—	391	OU
6e Modem packaging						
i inner	1900 packages	-	3000	3000	—	OU
ii outer	1500 covers	-	600	—	600	OU
7 Expenses						
7a Modem						
i Storage/handling						
	budget	-	1000	—	1000	OU
ii Despatch/return						
	1470 budget	-	6000	—	6000	OU
TOTALS			**19206**	**3000**	**16206**	

Table 10.4 Summary of DT200 CMC Reception Costs (£)

		Unit of measure	Unit cost	Total costs	Dev't cost	Rec't cost	Who pays?
8	*Human resources*						
8a	Time on CoSy	10.2 months	-	20720	—	20720	OU
9	*Equipment*						
9a	Micro rental	600 micros	600	360000	360000	—	DTI/DES
9b	Students' micros						
	i own	445 micros	630	280350	280350	—	Student
	ii purchase	382 micros	630	240660	240660	—	Student
9c	Tutors' micros						
	i own equipment	10 micros	630	6300	6300	—	Tutor
	ii buy (av cost)	7 micros	630	4410	4410	—	Tutor
9d	Modem	1900 modems	83.95	159505	159505	—	OU
10	*Consumables/expenses*						
10a	Network running costs	estimate	-	74736	—	74736	OU
10b	ACS Help Desk	budget	-	1000	—	1000	OU
10c	fee rebate	1364 students	55	75000	—	75000	OU
	Student costs assoc. with microcomputer						
10d	micro hire	537 students	150	80550	—	80550	Student
10e	micro carriage	351 students	5.50	1930	1930	—	Student
10f	discs/paper	1370 students	10	13700	—	13700	Student
10g	GEM buy	217 students	14	3038	3038	—	Student
10h	insurance	1364 students	3	4092	—	4092	Student
10i	maintenance	40 students	50	2000	—	2000	Student
10j	BT line charges	12491 hours	1.95	24357	—	24357	Student
10k	BT socket	630 students	29	18270	18270	—	Student
10l	calls to ACS	300 calls	0.33	100	—	100	Student
	Tutor costs						
10m	micro buy aid	7 tutors	150	1050	1050	—	OU
10n	micro hire fee	48 tutors	150	7200	—	7200	OU
10o	insurance	65 tutors	3	195	—	195	Tutor
10p	line charges	65 tutors	10.12	658	—	658	OU
10q	BT line charges not paid by OU	estimate	-	2827	—	2827	Tutor
10r	BT socket	20 tutors	29	580	580	—	Tutor
	Tuition costs						
10s	CoSy tuition fee	65 tutors	138.64	9012	—	9012	OU
10t	TMAs						
	i TMA 06	957 TMAs	8.85	8470	—	8470	OU
	ii 0.6 x others	4000 TMAs	5.31	21240	—	21240	OU
11	*Space*						
11a	OU staff on CoSy	estimate	—	535	—	535	OU
Total				1422485	1076093	346392	

DISTRIBUTION: GROUPS 5 – 7

The human resource costs of servicing the modem (line 5a) and the expenses of storage and handling, and despatch and return by road carrier (line 7a) are identified in Table 10.3. Other distribution costs all fall under the course materials head, and are shown in lines 6a to 6e. All these costs are recurrent, with the exception of the polystyrene box used for packing the modem, which should last the life of the course.

RECEPTION: GROUPS 8 – 11

Group 8 Human Resources

Members of central academic staff involved on the course were asked how much time they spent using or supporting CoSy during the first teaching year. In all, they were active on CoSy-related work for about 10.2 months (line 8a).

Group 9 Capital Equipment

The capital equipment used on the course consisted of the microcomputer and the modem:
- **Microcomputers**: For the purposes of this exercise it is assumed that the rental stock for DT200 is 600 machines. The capital cost of this rental pool is shown in line 9a. 445 students made their own arrangements and 382 students purchased a computer through the mail order facility (line 9bi-ii). So far as tutors are concerned, 10 tutors made their own arrangements and 7 purchased a machine (line 9ci-ii). The cost of purchase, whether through the University's agents or elsewhere, is assumed to be £630 per machine (the weighted average cost of student purchases under the home computing scheme).
- **Modems**: The kit comprises a modem and a lead. The kit should last the planned life of the course (6 years), but to take care of breakages and losses, the University bought a 25% float. The total purchase (line 9d) was 1900 kits, of which 1500 represent the annual usable amount and 400 the float.

Table 10.5 Network and Central Computer Costs (£)

Item	# of units	Unit cost	Total cost
Network cost/connect hour	15000 hrs	3.00	45000
Computer cost/connect hour	15000 hrs	1.00	15000
Processor cost/cpu minute	6000 mins	2.40	14400
Storage charge/Megabyte	12 Mb	28.00	336
Total			**74736**

Group 10 Consumables and Expenses

Table 10.5 shows the estimated network and central computer costs, and level of usage, associated with DT200's CMC. The costs take account of both the recurrent cost of the service and the annualised capital costs of the equipment used. The unit costs cited are those which are reasonably incurred by the University in the operation of its own services, and bear no relation to commercial rates, which would be considerably higher. These costs are shown in line 10a of Table 10.4. Other central costs include the costs of manning the 'Help Desk'. The University's Academic Computing Service has for many years operated a weekday and Saturday morning help line for all courses with a computing element. During 1988, DT200 students made approximately 1400 calls to this service of which about 300 were related to the communications aspects of the course. A reasonable estimate suggests that the apportioned cost of this service to DT200 was £1000 (line 10b).

In introducing the home computing scheme, the University decided to reduce the fees for all home computing course students in 1988. This subsidy will gradually be withdrawn over the three years 1988-90. The fee reduction on DT200 of £55 cost the University about £75,000 in lost fee income (line 10c).

The introduction of home computing and CMC into DT200 involved students in additional expenses. One of the biggest of these was the rental charge for the machine. 537 students rented a machine at a cost of £150 each (line 10d). The charge covers the handling and maintenance costs of the rental scheme, which is managed by a commercial firm acting on behalf of the University.

Students incurred a variety of costs associated with their use of computing. Some of these (eg. maintenance, line 10i) were incurred by only some of the students. Lines 10c through to 10l show the nature of costs incurred, and the number of students incurring them. So far as line charges are concerned (line 10j), the course team estimated that students would have to be on-line for 10 hours during the course. Table 10.1 shows the proportion of students falling within the various BT charge bands, and the cost per hour of telephone calls at cheap, standard and peak rates. The weighted average cost per hour to students for cheap rate calls is £1.55; for standard rate calls, £3.97; and for peak rate calls, £5.48. 86% of student connect time was at cheap rate, 10% at standard rate, and 4% at peak rate, so the weighted average cost to students of connect time by charge band and charge rate was £1.95 per hour. The total student connect time is shown in Table 10.6.

Table 10.6 Student and Tutor Connect Time on CoSy

	Time on-line (hrs)	Estimated cost (£/hr)	Total cost (£)
Students	12491	1.95	24357
Tutors	1325	2.63	3485

In addition to student-related costs, there were tutor-related costs. One of the tutor-marked assignments was entirely related to the use of CMC, and the cost of this assignment is therefore a reasonable charge to the CMC costs of the course (lines 10t-i). 957 assignments (a 70% rate of return) were marked. Four other assignments have a small CMC element and the cost of this is shown in line 10t-ii. The University also recognised that tutors would incur some costs in respect of the computing element of the course. Tutors were paid for 8 equivalent-hours face-to-face contact time for their work on CoSy, at a cost of £17.33 an hour (line 10s). Contact time here relates to the time spent reading messages on the system, preparing messages and responses, and in-putting them to the system.

The seven tutors who purchased an approved machine were able to claim reimbursement of one year's rental charge (£150) from the University (line 10m), while the 48 who borrowed a machine did so at an annual cost to the University of £150 each (line 10n). Interestingly, the annualised and discounted cost of giving each tutor a microcomputer would have been £128, assuming the tutors worked the full six year course life. The University chose the more expensive option of paying an annual rental fee for the majority of its tutors because it could not be seen to give the tutors equipment bought with public money.

The cost of line charges to the tutor was estimated to be £10.12, and this was the allowance paid to tutors. This cost was based on the assumption that all tutors would be able to access the system at local call rates and that they would use 20 hours of connect time. Where tutors lived more than a local call distance away from a network node, their allowances were adjusted to reflect this. On average tutors spent just over 20 hours on-line. For the purposes of this study it has been assumed that the weighted charge band cost per hour of calls was the same as for students (£1.55), although some tutors would have managed to call toll-free, to them, through the University's internal exchange or the JANET network which links universities. Only 67% of tutor connect time was at cheap rate, with 21% at standard and 12% at peak rate. The weighted average cost per hour was therefore £2.63.

More significantly, nobody knows at present how much time tutors spent off-line preparing and reading messages, whether value for money was achieved, or whether tutors were grossly underpaid for the hours they actually spent on the course. Line 10p shows the cost of line charges accepted by the University; line 10q gives an estimate of the additional costs of line charges over and above the University allowance which tutors may have incurred themselves. (The University paid tutors £30 for expenses such as discs, paper, ribbons and line charges, of which only the line charges related to the CMC aspects of the course.) Arbitrarily it has been assumed that a third (20) of the tutors (compared to 45% of the students) incurred costs in converting their telephone systems to new style socket (line 10r).

Group 11: Space

The total time identified as spent by central staff during the presentation phase was 10.2 months, which on the assumptions spelt out above in respect of space costs (see commentary on Group 4 above) would have had a rental cost of £535.

Table 10.7 Summary of DT200 CMC Administrative Costs (£)

	Unit of measure	Unit cost	Total costs	Dev't cost	Rec't cost	Who pays?
12 *Overheads*						
12a Modem: Admin.						
costs in warehouse	budget	-	2500	—	2500	OU
Total			**2500**	—	**2500**	

ADMINISTRATION: GROUP 12

Most of the overhead administrative costs of the scheme are difficult to ascertain and were, in any case, related more to the costs of either home computing in general, or the course as an entity. The only overhead cost specifically identified as arising from the computer-mediated communications aspects of DT200 arose in the warehouse (line 12a).

ANALYSING THE COSTS

Having identified the costs, the next step is to analyse the costs of CMC within DT200. Levin (1983, p 82) argues the need to apportion costs among the different constituencies incurring costs. This is particularly important in the present case where costs have been met by Government in the form of special grants, the University, students and tutors, and where the various constituencies provide cash contributions and payments that subsidise the purchase of ingredients by other constituencies. Thus for example, the University rebates tuition fees to subsidise the costs of home computing to the students. Tables 10.2 to 10.4, and 10.7, indicated the constituency bearing each cost element. Table 10.8 summarises the costs of the scheme to the various constituencies.

The next question is the treatment of materials and systems development and production costs. These costs are in their nature an investment the benefit of which will be derived over the life of the course and hence need to be spread over an appropriate period of years. The most appropriate course of action is to annualise the costs over the planned life of the course (six years) or some other appropriate period. In the case of stocks of materials where these are purchased to meet several years' requirements, they should, in line with the accountancy convention on accruals, be set against the year in which they are used.

Table 10.8 Summarised Costs (£) of DT200 CMC by Constituency

	Total cost from Tbl's 2,3,4,7	OU cost	Student cost	Tutor cost	DTI/ DES
Production					
Development costs	86807	86807	—	—	—
Recurrent costs	2780	2780	—	—	—
Distribution					
Development	3000	3000	—	—	—
Recurrent	16206	16206	—	—	—
Reception					
Development	1076093	160555	544248	11290	360000
Recurrent	346392	218571	124799	3022	—
Administration					
Development	—	—	—	—	—
Recurrent	2500	2500	—	—	—
Total					
Development	1165900	250362	544248	11290	360000
Recurrent	367878	240057	124799	3022	—
Grand Total	**1533778**	**490419**	**669047**	**14312**	**360000**

In other words, there is a difference between the year of payment of an expense (broadly when the course is developed and produced) and the year of the expense (when the materials so bought are actually used, which may be several years later).

What constitutes a useful life varies. Buildings may have a useful life of 50 years or more. Microcomputers have a useful life of 4 years to the University, but rather longer to individual students. For the purposes of this exercise, this is taken to be six years, which would cover most students' period of study with the University as an undergraduate (Open University undergraduates study part-time). Course materials and the staff time spent on its development may be useful over the whole life of a course, or, as in the case of the fixed print costs of supplementary material, have a useful life of only one year, in which case it is treated as a recurrent cost. In this study various annualisation factors are assumed. However, the capital value of buildings has been subsumed under the proxy measure of rental costs per square metre. The annualisation factors adopted in this study are shown in Table 10.9.

The next question is whether or not to discount the capital and investment costs of the course. Economists hold that it is not enough to annualise the costs of capital over their life. They argue that one must take account of the opportunity cost of the capital investment, that is, the income foregone when money is invested in capital goods rather than being put to work to earn income. Moreover, if one wants to compare the costs of a capital-intensive form of education with one that is labour-intensive, one must take account of the real cost of capital decisions and not treat capital as a sunk cost (ie one in which the impact of the cost ceases to matter once the cash expenditure is incurred). Unless this is taken into account, the costs of a project will be seriously underestimated.

Table 10.9 Discounted Capital and Development Costs (£) of DT200 CMC

		Total costs (£)	# of years annual'd	Annual-isation factor	Annual-ised cost (£)
Production costs					
1	Human resources	77100	6	0.213	16422
2	Course materials				
2a	Print fixed cost main text	1572	6	0.213	335
2b	Audio-cassette	1050	6	0.213	224
2c	Cosy license	1359	6	0.213	289
3	Equipment	3600	4	0.299	1076
4	Space	2126	6	0.299	636
Sub-total					**18982**
Distribution					
	Modem inner packaging	3000	6	0.213	639
Sub-total					**639**
Reception					
	Equipment				
9a	Micro rental stock	360000	4	0.299	107640
9b	Students' micros				
	- own equipment	280350	6	0.213	59715
	- purchase	240660	6	0.213	51261
9c	Tutors' micros				
	- own equipment	6300	6	0.213	1342
	- buy (av cost)	4410	6	0.213	939
9d	Modem (equipment)	159505	6	0.213	33974
	Consumables/expenses				
	Student costs				
10e	Carriage on purchased micro	1930	6	0.213	411
10g	GEM purchase	3038	6	0.213	647
10j	BT socket conversion	18270	10	0.146	2667
	Tutor costs				
10m	Allowance to purchasers	1050	6	0.213	224
10r	BT socket conversion	580	10	0.146	85
Sub-total					**258905**
GRAND TOTAL					**278526**

It nevertheless remains a fact, certainly in the Open University, that State funding separates capital from revenue costs, thus the opportunity to use capital is severely restricted. As with most costing exercises in education, the actual financial value of various proposals is often a theoretical issue because freedom to act on the information is not always available.

To take account of opportunity costs one takes the prevailing rate of interest and applies it to the annualised cost using the formula

$$a\,(r, n) = \frac{r\,(1 + r)^n}{(1 + r)^n - 1}$$

where $a(r, n)$ is the annualisation factor, n is the lifetime of the capital in years, and r is the prevailing interest rate. Table 10.9 takes the information in Tables 10.2 to 10.4 and annualises and discounts the cost of capital equipment and the investment in course materials to provide a truer reflection of the real costs of the project.

In approaching the question of discounting, the issue of the rate of interest to be applied is crucial. Most studies on educational technologies calculate the cost on various hypothetical discount rates, ranging from a minimum of 0% to a maximum of 15%. In this study a rate of 7.5% has been adopted. The initial cost of the capital is then multiplied by the annualisation factor $[a\,(r, n)]$ to obtain the discounted value.

Table 10.10 shows the annualised cost of capital (derived from Table 10.9) for each constituency. The figures in this table can, when added to the recurrent costs falling on each constituency, be usefully compared with those in Table 10.8, which showed the development and recurrent costs by constituency prior to annualisation.

Table 10.10 Summarised Annualised Costs (£) of DT200 CMC by Constituency

	Total cost from Table 10.9	OU cost	Student cost	Tutor cost	DTI/ DES
Discounted capital costs					
Production	18982	18982	—	—	—
Distribution	639	639	—	—	—
Reception	258905	34198	114701	2366	107640
Administration	—	—	—	—	—
Sub-total	**278526**	**53819**	**114701**	**2366**	**107640**
Recurrent costs					
Sub-total (Table 8)	367878	240057	124799	3022	—
Total	**646404**	**293876**	**239500**	**5388**	**107640**

CONCLUSIONS

The Costs of the Open University Scheme

Analysis shows that the total cost of using CMC for DT200 was £1.534m. Development cost totalled £1.166m; the 1988 operating costs for 1364 students (and 65 tutors) was £368,000 (Table 10.8). The annualised and discounted cost of the course is £646,404 (Table 10.10). On this basis the average cost per student (assuming the present population of 1364 students) is £474.

However, from another point of view, CMC was introduced into DT200 on the back of the home computing element of the course. Analysis of Tables 10.2 to 10.4 and 10.7 suggest that the marginal capital and development costs of adding CoSy to the course were £226,044 (covering the items in lines 1b, 2c, 3a, 6e-i, 9d, 10k and 10r), with an annualised value of £47,192, while the recurrent costs were £138,956 (lines 5a, 6d, 6e-ii, 7a, 8a, 10a, 10j, 10p, 10q and 12a). Table 10.11 breaks these costs down by constituency.

Table 10.11 Marginal Annualised Costs of CoSy by Constituency

	Total	OU	Student	Tutor	DTI/DES
Development costs (£)	47192	44440	2667	85	—
Recurrent costs (£)	138956	111144	24357	3485	—
Total (£)	186148	155554	27024	3570	—

Both the full (Table 10.10) and the marginal (Table 10.11) costs of the scheme are shared between a number of constituencies. Table 10.12 shows the average discounted cost per student of the various contributions made, assuming a population of 1364 students. It is impossible to know how many hours off-line students spent on the CMC elements of the course, but they spent a total of 12,491 hours on-line. The course team expected students to spend about 20 hours on the CMC aspects of the course. Table 10.12 shows the cost per student hour on-line, by constituency, and the cost per planned student hour on CMC, by constituency on two bases: full costs and marginal costs.

Obviously the particular arrangements made at the Open University would not be adopted everywhere.

Firstly, the treatment of recurrent costs (for example, the costs of permanent academic and computing staff) which are devoted to the production of a course such as DT200 raises problems. From an economic point of view, when analysing the costs of DT200, such costs represent an investment in the course and should therefore be annualised. From an institutional point they represent the temporary assignment of staff to a particular task. Had the staff not been used on DT200, there would have been a saving to the course, but none to the institution.

Secondly, the distribution of costs between students and the institution depends on the latter's philosophy and objectives.

Table 10.12 Average Discounted Cost per Student of DT200 CMC

	Total cost	OU	Student	Tutor	DTI/DES
Full cost approach					
Average cost/student (£)	474	215	176	4	79
Average cost/hour on-line (£)	52	24	19	*	9
Average cost/hour planned					
Time on CoSy (£)	24	11	9	*	4
Marginal cost approach					
Average cost/student (£)	136	114	20	3	—
Average cost/hour on-line (£)	15	12	2	*	—
Average cost/hour planned					
Time on Cosy (£)	7	6	1	*	—

*insignificant cost

Setting aside the University's wish to explore the use of CMC, and hence use DT200 as a testbed, its underlying philosophy emphasises access and hence tries to mitigate costs which would fall on students as a direct result of their decision to study a particular course.

In particular, the University does not wish to discourage students from studying science, technology and computing based courses where costs tend to be higher, nor does it wish to inhibit potential students from applying by requiring them to purchase expensive equipment. Nevertheless, in many systems students would be expected to supply their own microcomputers and modems. Had the Open University adopted such a scheme then the main changes to the costs shown in Tables 10.2 to 10.4 and 10.7 would have been a saving on the capital costs of buying the microcomputer rental stock, the modem, and the inner packaging for the modem (lines 9a, 9d and 6e inner packaging), and the recurrent costs associated with the modem (lines 6a, 6e outer packaging, 7a, and 12a). The savings amount to £522,505 non-recurrent costs and £14,700 recurrent costs. Had the University also decided not to offer a fee rebate (line 10c), this would have saved another £75,000 (recurrent cost). The discounted saving to the DTI/DES and Open University of all these measures would have amounted to about £157,000 per year, less any costs (say £20,000 per annum) associated with supplying tutors with microcomputers and modems. The saving per student for these constituencies would have been about £100. Conversely, more students would have had to buy a microcomputer, and to this would have been added the cost of a modem. Since the University secured a discount on its bulk purchase of machines, the cost of the equipment to the student would almost certainly have been higher, but discounted over six years, this would probably not have been significant (about £30). However, the cost of equipping oneself to do a course (c. £780) if DT200 were the only computing course one wished to undertake would undoubtedly have put some students off. The University might also have decided not to support students in their use of CoSy to the extent that it did. This would have avoided the costs (c. £40,000) associated with the development of the CoSy front-end and some of the CMC-related printed materials. The discounted saving would have been c. £9000 or a further £7 per student.

Thirdly, there is the question of the attribution of the full costs of CoSy itself to DT200. CoSy was in the process of being introduced into the University to serve other purposes (internal electronic mail and computer conferencing), so that some of the costs of CoSy (for example, the license fee), are not really attributable to DT200. On the other hand, it is unlikely that the significant cost of developing a front-end to CoSy would have been incurred for internal use and it is reasonable to assign this cost to DT200.

Cost/Benefit

CMC was not introduced into DT200 to save money, nor primarily to improve the presentation and delivery of the course, but to teach students about CMC, and also to enable the University to experiment with and understand the potential of this new means of communication. It would not have been introduced unless the course had already adopted home computing for other, academic, reasons. Its introduction has nevertheless had a profound affect on the way the course is taught. It is too early to conclude with confidence that the additional costs of CMC are justifiable in terms of improvements in teaching and learning, although Thomas begins to address these issues in Chapter 11. Any conclusions must have a bearing on whether CMC should be introduced into other Open University courses, and if so, whether it is an add-on to the current media-based mass teaching strategy which the University has, or substitutes for some of the existing media used on courses. On the basis of this study, the latter must be the more likely outcome.

NOTES

[1] The term derives from the original foundation course in science which provided students with chemical glassware, chemicals, a microscope, slides, rock samples, etc.
[2] The basic specification is as follows: 512k RAM, single disk drive (although two are more convenient), 84 key IBM PC compatible or equivalent keyboard, monochrome (or colour) monitor, printer port (parallel or serial), serial port (RS232 or equivalent), mouse (with appropriate firmware or software device driver), printer (80 column, dot-matrix or other, with graphics screen dump capability), MS-DOS Version 2.1 or higher, and capable of running a graphics environment manager GEM, Version 2 or higher. Students who do not have a copy of GEM can buy a copy from the University.
[3] Although 1403 students initially registered, 1364 finally registered, and it is the latter number which is used in the subsequent cost analysis. (ed)

CHAPTER 11

IMPLICATIONS OF ELECTRONIC COMMUNICATION FOR THE OPEN UNIVERSITY

Ray Thomas
Open University
Milton Keynes, UK

CMC AS INTERMEDIATE TECHNOLOGY

The benefits derived from the implementation of new computerised information systems in business organisations are commonly divided into two categories – cost displacement and value added. Cost displacement is the tangible benefit, calculable in financial terms, derived from reduction or abolition of the cost of the comparable 'manual' system. Value added is the benefit derived from the provision of new facilities in the computerised system which were not available in the existing 'manual' system. Value added benefits are often intangible, and they cannot usually be estimated in financial terms.

This distinction between cost displacement and value added is not usually applied to computer-mediated communication (CMC) systems. CMC messages appear to be new and different in nature from face-to-face meetings, telephone, or written messages which might serve the same kinds of function. Studies of the use of CMC in education usually emphasise its new and special qualities. Meeks (1987) refers to a "revolution" and the goal of getting an education without setting foot inside a classroom. Feenberg (1987) emphasises that CMC is a new communications medium "uniquely suited to liberal arts teaching." Hiltz and Turoff (1986) suggest that CMC "provides one of the first opportunities to create a 'virtual classroom'" (quoted in Meeks).

But CMC systems are not new. The first major application, ARPANET (Advanced Research Projects Agency) was developed by the US Department of Defence in the late 1960s. Most major applications of CMC have been organisational rather than educational. Studies of organisational experience where alternative forms of communication compete with CMC do not indicate a record of easy or immediate success. The study 'From Pilots to Contagion in Telecommunications' by the Diebold Group (1983), for example, points to the necessity for building a critical mass of users. Kiesler *et al.* (1984) stress the speed and energy efficiency of CMC, but also stress disadvantages – such as lack of immediate feedback and of any strong etiquette of use.

This chapter examines CMC as a technology which is intermediate rather than new. CMC in the form of electronic mail can be regarded as intermediate between sending a letter and making a phone call, as intermediate between student/teacher conversation on the one hand and reading or writing a lecture handout or essay on the other. CMC in the form of computer conferencing can be regarded as intermediate between face-to-face group discussion and leaving messages on a notice board or putting graffiti on a wall.

Viewing CMC as different from other means of communication focusses attention on the 'value added' by the system. This view leads to proposals for new educational systems (Feenberg, 1987), to suggestions that CMC will have "a penetrating influence on established systems" (Meeks, 1987), and to the suggestion that the new technologies will erode the "geographical monopoly held by many institutions of higher education" (Hiltz and Turoff, 1986). Viewing CMC as an intermediate technology, however, focusses attention on 'cost displacement' and provokes questions about benefits relative to costs.

THE NATURE OF THE BENEFITS AND COSTS

A cost/benefit approach is appropriate for discussion of the Open University experience because CMC has been added to what has already shown itself as an effective educational system for learning and teaching at a distance. About two thirds of students who start an OU course pass the examination about nine months later. The basic medium of instruction is the correspondence text, but this is supplemented by correspondence tuition, local tutorials, audio-cassettes and radio and TV broadcasts.

The CoSy email and conferencing system, as used in the DT200 Introduction to Information Technology course, was an additional component in an otherwise complete system. For most students, tutors, and course team members CMC was a marginal component of a very full course. The time required for study of other components of DT200 limited the use made of CMC (see Chapter 9, especially Sections entitled 'New Learning Medium' and 'Media Integration').

The cost of establishing and running the DT200 CoSy system was shared between students, the Open University, and the Government in ways which are described in more detail in Chapter 10. The introduction of CMC into the DT200 course could be regarded as an experiment. But cost reduction was not part of the experiment. It seems likely that the decision makers within the OU who approved the course were influenced directly or indirectly by some of the studies quoted which emphasise what is new about the use of CMC in education.

The decision makers, in other words, expected value added. What then have been the benefits? This chapter, based on experience of the 1988 presentation suggests that the major easily identifiable value-added components of the conferencing system can be classified under three heads – in facilitating self-help among students and tutors, in enhancing the tutor's teaching role, and in encouraging team teaching involving tutors and course team members.

MUTUAL SUPPORT AMONG STUDENTS AND TUTORS

The communications element of DT200 was not intended for delivery of the teaching material of the course, but 'self-help' messages cannot be clearly distinguished from messages which might be regarded as part of the traditional teaching process. One student/tutor's CMC interaction is another student's opportunity to learn. However the number of messages, the content of many of the messages, and the number of participants taken together suggest that the dominant function of the DT200 conferencing system in 1988 should be characterised as mutual support.

More than 3000 messages were posted, for example, on the national 'forum' conference, and local tutorial conferences generated more than 4,500 messages (see Chapter 9, Table 9.5 for detail). The closed conference for tutors generated 750 messages. Electronic mail messages were running at a rate of about 6,000 a month after students began to come on line in substantial numbers in April. Students also used the 'conversation' facility, but the exact amount of use is unknown.

The national Cosy conferences were also open to the staff of the OU and included many contributions by individuals who were not members of the DT200 course team. Most of the messages on most of the conferences, however, were by students and tutors. Not all of the messages appeared to be related directly to academic matters, and there were frequent complaints about the quality and usefulness of messages posted. But it is not easy to assess the contribution of informal messages to the learning process – as Graddol points out in Paper 15 in the Resource File.

There is no evidence to suggest that the interaction which has occurred among students and tutors of DT200 through use of CMC is substantially different from the formal and informal interaction which occurs among students and tutors on a day-to-day basis outside the lecture theatres of conventional institutions. In the OU situation the introduction of CoSy has enabled students and tutors to help each other in ways which are often taken for granted in conventional teaching institutions which have notice boards for staff and student use, pigeon hole systems for exchange of written messages, and which give convenient opportunities for face-to-face interaction.

ENHANCEMENT OF THE TUTOR'S TEACHING ROLE

The role of the tutor in the typical OU course comprises grading and commenting on assignments, responding to phone calls from students, and conducting tutorials. The CoSy conferencing and email system makes some of these activities easier. CoSy facilitates activities such as provoking and answering questions and giving general feedback to students about assignments already graded and commented on individually.

CMC also makes some kinds of activity practicable which are impracticable via postal mail and telephone calls. These include commenting on drafts of assignments received from individual students, giving advice on problems anticipated with assignments, and giving immediate feedback and grades awarded on assignments to individual students. (For monitoring reasons the graded assignments are routed via the OU headquarters in Milton Keynes before return to the student, which can cause considerable delays.)

The scale of most of these kinds of tutor activity in the 1988 presentation of DT200 was small. But reports from individual tutors (mostly in the form of messages to the closed conference for tutors) indicates that they believed that these activities served valuable teaching purposes. Many of these activities are similar in function to those which might be carried out by lecturers and tutors where there is day-to-day contact between students and staff. This component of the value added by CMC can therefore be regarded as making available to the part-time students and part-time tutors in the OU system the kinds of facilities which are available in conventional institutions of higher education.

TEAM TEACHING BY TUTORS AND COURSE TEAM MEMBERS

CMC facilitated cooperative teaching in three main ways. First, it created provision for members of the course team based at Walton Hall to participate in the teaching of the course. Such participation is not usually practical in the OU system except where the individual course team members also enrol as part time course tutors. Course teams include support staff such as secretaries, course managers, editors and technical assistants as well as the academic staff responsible for the content of the course. CMC made it easy for members of the DT200 course team to participate in the teaching of the course and to communicate with students about any aspect of the administration or presentation of the the course.

Second, CMC has encouraged both tutors and production course team members to contribute to conferences within their field of special expertise. This division of labour evolved informally rather than through course team policy or tacit agreement. But the pattern has meant that individuals have to a certain extent accepted responsibility for dealing with questions which arise in particular areas.

Third, CMC has provided the means to exploit this specialisation through the facility to copy messages from one conference to another. Tutors (and some students) have used this facility to copy messages from local tutorial to regional conferences and the national Forum conference, and for copying messages in the reverse direction. The copying of messages from one part of the system to another indicates how CMC can be used to create structures within the OU system which aim to meet the learning needs of students.

VARIATION IN STUDENT AND TUTOR ACTIVITY

The statistical information given by the computer system, in addition to the content of student messages, has provided feedback to the course team with a speed and immediacy unprecedented in OU experience. A dominant feature revealed by this information is variation in levels of activity. There was wide variation in the extent to which students made use of the CoSy system (see Chapter 9, Table 9.2), in the support provided by tutors, and in the level of activity in local tutorial conferences (see Table 9.5). Perhaps the greatest inequality was evident in the pattern of contributors to the CoSy conferences. Discussion in the national conferences was dominated by a small minority of students, tutors, and course team members (see Table 9.4).

One pattern of inequality has substantive academic importance. In the national conferences there was a balance between 'questioning' messages and 'answering' messages where the subject matter was concerned with practical matters and social science issues. But a major lacuna became evident in the technology area. 'Questioning' messages about technological issues were frequently posted but were largely unrequited. About twice as many students of DT200 came from a technological background as from a social science background. Many students complained that they were unable to use their technological knowledge and that no academic credit was given to study of the Part B Tributaries of the course which were concerned with the technology.

The scant response to questions seeking to identify technological issues is attributable to differences in the outlook of social scientists and technologists, which were reflected in attitudes by members of the course team. Technological issues appear to belong to a kind of no mans land. Social scientists had no difficulty in identifying societal issues associated with use of technology but lack knowledge of the underlying technology. Technologists are habitutated to thinking in terms of technological solutions rather than issues. One of the major roles which could be played by CMC in 1989 and future presentations is the identification and exploration of technological issues. CMC would then be used to remedy what appears to be an omission in the printed and broadcast materials.

The DT200 experience indicating wide variations in usage seems contradictory to that reported by Hiltz and Turoff (1986) and Harasim (Chapter 4) who describe a level of equality of participation in CMC courses in excess of that of face-to-face courses. The difference seems to be attributable to the optional status of CMC as part of the DT200 course. Hiltz and Turoff, and Harasim describe courses in which CMC plays a central role. But the use of CoSy in DT200, as emphasised above, was peripheral to an otherwise fully functional course.

The peripheral status of CMC in the DT200 course seems largely attributable to the strength of the prevailing system of course production in the OU. The use of CMC is not consistent with established planning practices and working practices within the Open University. The manpower available for the maintenance of courses, for example, does not make allowance for time to be spent on CMC.

The terms and conditions of service do not include any clause which envisages that members of the central academic staff would be able to teach at a distance, but allow for this possibility with a general purpose clause which requires members "to undertake such duties.. as may reasonably be required." As a result the time which is given by central academics depends upon the individual academic and the support of his or her Faculty.

Another important example is in the role of part-time tutors. They were required to log on and respond to messages at minimum, seven days before the cut-off date of an assignment and they were reimbursed for 8 hours on-line tutorial time plus a maximum of twenty hours telephone charges for using the CMC system. The training for CMC consisted of a half-day session at the briefing weekend held several months before the course began. This minimal 'training', this minimal logging on requirement, and this reimbursement may have been inadequate for serious use of CMC by many tutors in the 1988 presentation. The terms and conditions of service of tutors indicate first priority to the marking of assignments rather than spending time reading or sending CMC messages. Financial pressures on the OU prevented any significant additional payments which might have encouraged tutors to play a more active role in CMC. [1]

The optional use of computer conferencing on the DT200 course can be described in the language associated with the implementation of computerised information systems as a failure to designate a clear system boundary. It would usually be considered a responsibility of management to take a decision on the nature of the activities which are to be computerised and those which are left for 'manual' operation. The system would then be designed in such a way as to require use of the computerised system within that boundary. But in the application of CMC in DT200 the system boundary has been decided by individual users – and non-users.

The desirability of drawing a systems boundary for CMC raises the question of the nature of the 'manual', or non-CMC, components of OU courses which might be displaced by CMC. Should CMC be regarded primarily as a substitute for the face-to-face tutorial? Or as a substitute for correspondence materials or broadcasts? Or as a substitute for some part of the monitoring and assessment system? Or should CMC be regarded simply as a value added component, supplementing rather than displacing any other component of the OU's teaching system?

VALUE ADDED AND THE CASE FOR SUBSIDY

The argument for extending the use of CMC within the OU system lies in the valued added items described above. CMC enables students to help each other; it can enhance the tutor's teaching role, and it enables course team members to play an active teaching role. Thus CMC would bring to other OU staff and students the electronic equivalent of communication facilities which are already available in conventional teaching institutions. CMC with its asynchronous features is more-or-less what would have to be designed to ensure the possibility of a high level of interactive contact between students and tutors who, because of full-time employment and/or geographical scattering, do not have day-to-day contact and cannot get into the same classroom or lecture theatre at the same time.

Thus it can be argued that use of CMC in the OU system should not be a matter of cost displacement. The support for CMC given to DT200 should be extended so as to encourage other OU courses to use it. This argument would be consistent with the 'Open' principle enshrined in the name of the University. A subsidy for CMC would be justified in terms of maintaining access as improved, albeit more costly, methods of teaching become available.

In support of this argument it can be pointed out that the major element of 'cost displacement' is not within the OU but between the OU and its students. If students are willing to meet these costs, it can be argued, the OU should meet what is in effect an expressed demand. As per capita incomes rise, students can be expected to have access to home computers and telephones in the same way as they have been expected to have video-cassette recorders and calculators. Extension of the use of CMC would be meeting the expectations of a technologically aware population. There seems little doubt that the DT200 course meets many students' needs and that they regarded DT200 as a 'good buy'. Over half of the respondents to the DT200 Survey [2] indicated that the requirement to have a computer did not deter them from deciding to take the course.

It is also true however that the costs imposed on students acted as a hurdle on entry. A maximum quota of 1500 places was imposed on the course but the course was slightly undersubscribed with a final registration figure of 1364 students, and is expected to be undersubscribed in 1989. The costs of the computer and of CMC can also be expected to have influenced the type of student taking DT200. Three quarters of the finally registered students of DT200 in 1988 were male. Most other courses presented by the Social Science Faculty have populations which are more than half female. To what extent is this difference attributable to the subject matter of DT200 and to what extent to the costs of the computer and the CMC component?

A striking feature of the DT200 Survey is that twenty three percent of respondents classified themselves as administrators or managers. But according to the information given when these students first entered the Open University in 1986 or earlier, only seven percent classified themselves as managers. It appears that DT200 has a special appeal for those who have recently become managers.

The difference between the occupational composition of DT200 is dramatised by the contrast, shown in Table 11.1, with another social science course, *Social Problems and Social Welfare* (D211), which was the other new course presented by the Social Science Faculty in 1988. The contrasts shown in Table 11.1 illustrate the importance of considering the influence of the introduction of CMC on the social composition of other courses. To what extent are these contrasts attributable to the subject matter of DT200 and to what extent are they attributable to the costs of the computer and the CMC component? If the cost of the computer system and CMC have been a deciding factor, the implications are important. It would suggest that the adoption of CMC by a course would have a significant influence on the type of student attracted to any course.

Table 11.1 *Occupational Composition and Final Registration Statistics (DT200, D211)*

Occupation	DT200 Survey 1988	Final Reg'n Statistics DT200	D211
	-------in percentages------		
Housewife	3	8	32
Armed forces	2	4	1
Admin and managerial	23	7	2
Education	15	13	6
Medical professions	1	2	12
Social services	1	1	9
Science and engineering	9	4	-
Other professions and arts	5	4	3
Technical	13	23	1
Skilled trades	3	5	1
Other manual work	1	3	2
Communications and transport	4	3	1
Clerical and office	7	12	15
Sales and service	3	6	6
Retired	3	5	7
None of these	6	1	1
Numbers	**873**	**1364**	**1242**

PROSPECTS FOR COURSE PRODUCTION

Most OU courses are 'made to measure' and self-contained. Nearly all materials used by OU students – the correspondence units, audio cassettes and broadcasts – are all specially prepared. There are also set books (which students are required to buy) and recommended books. But not all courses have set or recommended books and such books play only a minor role on many courses.

The introduction of CMC into OU courses could be associated with a reduction in course production costs. Cost reduction could be achieved through greater reliance on existing educational materials and by focus in course production on strategic aims and objectives rather than on comprehensive programmes of study. Tutors and course team members could, complementarily, play an active teaching role through the use of CMC. For courses with small student populations, the balance would change from resources devoted to course production to resources devoted to course presentation. These courses would then resemble the pattern which prevails in conventional teaching institutions.

The complete and self-contained character of OU courses derives largely from the pattern set by the first year foundation courses. As explained by Rumble in Chapter 10, the Open University uses capital investment to realise economies of scale. The cost of producing a course in the OU in terms of academic person-power could be estimated as about 30 person-years per full credit. But this cost is amortised by being spread over a six or eight year course life and, at the foundation level, over several thousands of students every year. At the foundation level where there may be, say, 30,000 students over the life of the course a student to staff ratio of 300:1 may be achieved.

Such economies of scale are not common in second and higher level courses where the number of students per year is typically measured in terms of hundreds rather than thousands. As shown in Figure 11.1, nearly half of OU undergraduate courses have fewer than 300 students. Course production costs could be reduced to the levels achieved by the foundation courses through substituting the use of set books and recommended books for specially prepared correspondence materials and for other costly components such as TV broadcasts. Such a reduction in the detail of course production could be associated with corresponding reductions in the academic resources involved. The additional teaching facilities afforded by CMC should make such changes educationally feasible in these higher level courses.

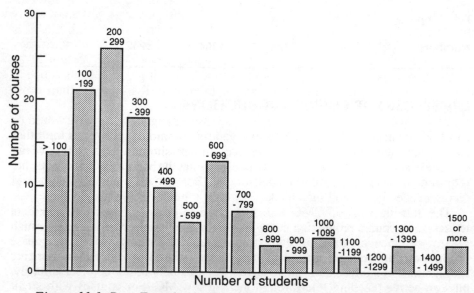

Figure 11.1 Post-Foundation Courses in 1987 by Number of Students

POSSIBILITIES FOR COURSE PRESENTATION

The economies of scale achieved in the production of foundation courses at the Open University do not extend into the presentation stages. It may be possible to achieve student-to-staff ratios of 300:1 in production, but in presentation, these ratios are limited by the need to comment on and assess Tutor Marked Assignments (TMAs) within a relatively short time period. Most observers within the University see the existing student-to-tutor ratios of 25:1 as a maximum – or even as unreasonably high. The introduction of CMC could be associated with assignments which require less time for assessment – such as those involving practical work and group work. The reduction in time required for assessment could be used to enhance the course tutor's teaching role.

One possibility, for example, would be extensive use of two stages in the production of an essay – first a draft introduction/outline and second a full length essay. Two-part assignments of this kind allow tutors to spend more time on teaching and less on assessment. The scope for tuition afforded by assignments of this kind where delivery and comment is subject to postal delays is limited. But the use of word-processors and the email facility of CMC makes such assignments practical and attractive.

Other possibilities are created by the conferencing facilities. Some weight in assessment could be given to the individual student's contributions to the conferencing system. Such assessment would take advantage of the intermediate technology characteristics of CMC. The verbal contribution which students make in face-to-face tutorials in conventional teaching institutions cannot easily be preserved for assessment purposes, but such preservation with CMC is automatic. Conference contributions are written down and students can, if they wish, give just as much attention to them as they would to the content of an essay. An advantage of assessment in this form is that it gives students scope to focus on aspects of a topic which are of interest to them rather than those determined by tightly bounded assignment questions.

CMC also offers new opportunities for setting assignments which would be based on students working cooperatively. It is common practice among other institutions using CMC to expect that a student should send a draft of an assignment to a fellow student for editorial comment before submission to the tutor. This procedure is reported as contributing both to the clarity and presentation of assignments.

The idea of cooperative work could be taken further by setting assignments which require cooperative activity on the part of two or more students and which are assessed by the award of a common grade for all participants. Conventional institutions of higher education in Britain do use cooperative projects of this kind which count for assessment. CMC would make it possible for the OU to follow this pattern, but current OU assessment policy discourages cooperative work for assignments. The Student Handbook states: "there is nothing wrong with discussing assignment questions with fellow-students, or other people, before you tackle your assignment. In fact we expect students to be interested in discussing the course objectives and testing one another's grasp of them...What has to be emphasised however is that when you sit down to tackle your assignment you are expected to work alone and not to send in other people's work, either in its entirety on in part, as if it were your own." [3]

The combination of word processors and email makes it easy for students to exchange ideas and sections of text, and to use sections of text from conference messages. Such facilities push new questions onto the agenda. Where is the dividing line between discussing the course objectives and working on the next assignment? Why such a dividing line? Will it be more realistic to consider the student as responsible for what he or she includes in the assignment, irrespective of the origin of the ideas, or the words used to express them?

EXTENDING THE USE OF CMC WITH 'REGION 14' [4]

At the time of writing this chapter in November 1988 there were no immediate plans for the use of CMC on other courses at the Open University. Members of the newly formed School of Management were actively considering using CMC in courses to be presented in 1991. But within the undergraduate programme the only proposal on the horizon was for the remake of a course in research methods in the social sciences to be presented in 1992.

Part of the problem is the scale of change threatened by electronic communication. The DT200 experience itself suggests that course teams should consider radical changes in course structure in order to make best use of electronic communication. From the student point of view CMC requires substantial investment of time and money which is difficult to justify unless, as on DT200, there are other uses which can be made of the computer system needed and an academic interest in electronic communication.

The scale of change threatened by CMC does not, however, apply to all students. Some OU students are already familiar with computers and are owners of microcomputers. This number seems likely to grow steadily as ownership of home computers increases in the population at large, and as the number of students who have taken courses using computers grows. Some students, for a variety of reasons, have difficulty in making face-to-face contact with their tutor or with other students. There are about 3000 disabled students in the OU system, many of whom fall into both of these categories because their disability limits face-to-face contact, and because they are already familiar with IT devices as an aid to overcoming communication problems. [5]

The use of CMC could be extended to meet the needs of students in these categories through its introduction as an optional component of existing courses. Under the current administrative system tutors are appointed and local tutorials conducted within thirteen geographical regions. It has been suggested (in discussions on the CoSy conferencing system) that the OU could create a 'Region 14' which would be national, or even worldwide, in its scope but which would also constitute a single electronic campus. Region 14 could establish self-help groups and tutorial conferences to function in much the same way, in administrative terms, as geographically based self-help and tutorial groups.

The advantages of electronic self-help groups are given emphasis by the Student Handbook description: "A successful self-help group generally requires someone to take the initiative and to suggest a meeting time and place, and prepare an agenda, topics for discussion, etc." Many self-help groups were set up by students of the DT200 course in 1988 on CoSy. But these groups did not, because of its asynchronous character, require agreement on a time and place of meeting. Neither, because of features of the conferencing system which allow for parallel discussion of a number of different topics, did these self-help groups require preparation of an agenda or list of topics for discussion.

It seems likely that any substantial extension of the use of CMC at the Open University will depend upon the success of the Region 14 idea or something similar. For any course which would not otherwise use a computer, the introduction of electronic communication could be seen, with some justification, as a component which could throw the course awry. But as awareness of computers and CMC becomes more widespread that fear should be lessened. A steady growth in the optional use of CMC on existing courses could make a direct contribution to increasing this awareness.

A POSTSCRIPT

The chapters of this book describe a variety of models for courses using CMC. In some institutions electronic communication is the dominant mode. In some, it is used to extend campus-based courses to students located elsewhere. In the case of the OU, CMC has being introduced as a component of a system geared to mass education at a distance. But it could be used in the OU system in ways which are already common in other institutions.

This chapter has shown that most of the obstacles to the extension of CMC within the OU system are associated with structures devoted to achieving the economies of scale which derive from mass education. The OU should not restrict itself to the mass education model. CMC dramatically increases the opportunities for students to learn from each other. It enables course tutors to fulfil their responsibilities comprehensively and gives the full-time staff of the OU facilities for teaching at a distance. None of these activities depend upon achieving economies of scale.

NOTES

[1] Nevertheless, one third of the tutors spent well over these minimum requirements on-line and contributed substantially to the conferences. (ed)
[2] This is the same survey acknowledged in Chapter 9, table 9.3. (ed)
[3] Student Handbook, The Open University, 1987, p 15.
[4] The Open University has divided the country into 13 geographical regions for administrative purposes. (ed)
[5] See Paper 1 in the Resource File, by Coombs, for a discussion of the use of CMC by disabled students and teachers. (ed)

PART 3

RESOURCE FILE

The documents in this Resource File are summaries of papers presented at the International Conference on Computer-Mediated Communication and Distance Education, held at the Open University in October 1988. We have organised them into two groups:

- papers describing and/or analysing specific examples of the use of CMC in education (nos 1-11)
- papers reflecting, in various ways, on the use of CMC as a medium for education (nos 12-20).

These papers clearly demonstrate the interest and appeal of CMC to those in a wide variety of disciplines, and thus offer very diverse perspectives on the educational use of this technology. Contributors to the Resource File include educational researchers, teachers (of history, poetry, electronics, information technology, sociology, linguistics, and computing), administrators, and writers, from a variety of countries (Canada, Denmark, France, Norway, the USA, and the UK).

Although many of the applications of CMC in education have so far been in areas such as information technology and computing – for the obvious reasons that access to the necessary equipment and software has up to now been easier in these fields – there is no doubt that the picture will change over the next few years as microcomputers and modems become more widely available. The on-line poetry workshop described by Owen in Paper 8, the use of CMC for archeology and arts courses mentioned by Lorentsen in Paper 5, or the use of electronic mail in schools cited by Guihot (Paper 4) and Somekh (Paper 16) are but a few examples of the extension of CMC into curriculum areas that have nothing to do with computers.

APPLICATIONS OF CMC IN EDUCATION

PAPER 1

USING CMC TO OVERCOME PHYSICAL DISABILITIES

Norman Coombs
Rochester Institute of Technology, New York, USA

The Rochester Institute of Technology (RIT) is working to create a barrier-free learning environment for students with disabilities. In the process of implementing computer conferencing to enhance its telecourses, RIT discovered that these same delivery system technologies could be used to transcend some of the learning difficulties experienced by persons with physical handicaps. This realisation fitted in well with the Institute's long concern for the needs of so called 'non-traditional learners'.

Implementing Computer Conferencing

Since 1985 RIT has offered productivity grants to its faculty which focus on developing new strategies for distance learning. For the most part, the target audience live in the greater Rochester area. They work full time, and coming to campus after work creates scheduling problems. The commuting uses much of their valuable 'free' time. Consequently, I submitted a proposal to explore the uses of computer conferencing in education. I am totally blind and have been using a computer and speech synthesiser for the last four or five years. In 1985 I began requiring my students to submit their term papers through electronic mail which permitted me to drastically reduce my need for human readers. Most faculty I knew who used computers did not think of them as a communication tool. They used them for word-processing, calculations and for programming. Realising their potential in communication alerted me to the educational possibilities inherent in computer conferencing.

The RIT Productivity Committee awarded me a grant to adapt the course, Modern American History, to include a teleconference component, and to package it for distance delivery. The course was a College of Liberal Arts lower division core requirement for all students and already included a video component. Some tapes were viewed in class, and others were seen by students independently in the library media centre. As the course content was delivered by videos and texts, the classroom was primarily used for group discussion. This format was easily taken off campus and designed for distance learners.

I ran a pilot study in 1986 with 13 students. The television series is *America: The Second Century*, which RIT broadcasts in the greater Rochester area and there is a textbook which accompanies it. The RIT VAX computer system provides direct contact between class and professor. Electronic mail is used to replace office visits and the conferencing functions in place of the classroom discussion.

The largest portion of the productivity funds was used to purchase a computer conferencing system. After investigation, the Instructional Support and Computing personnel recommended VaxNotes, produced by the Digital Equipment Corporation, to run on one of the Institute's VAX computers. The grant also supported the development of user manuals explaining how to use electronic mail, the Eve editor and the Notes conferencing system. These funds also purchased two dozen modems which could be loaned to students with access to a PC at home or work. The others would have to come on campus to access the VAX from a computer lab, but they would still have the advantage of scheduling flexibility.

What was most widely appreciated about the computer conference was that, while providing many of the elements of a classroom, it permitted scheduling flexibility because of its asynchronous nature. The students themselves evaluated all aspects of the computer more favourably than they did either the videos or the texts. They rated the conference discussion very positively. One student said he doubted whether he would take another telecourse unless it had a computer component. The conference discussion enabled him to evaluate his progress alongside the others in the class. Another said the conference made the telecourse more like a real class and that he enjoyed the computer aspect in spite of the fact that he knew almost nothing about computers prior to enrolling.

One of the other intriguing benefits of the computer conference is that, because of its relative anonymity, many people feel freer to share personal items. Several class members, in a discussion about the impact of the Great Depression, shared amusing and intimate stories from their family history which I have never had students do in the classroom. The grandmother of one made and sold bootleg whiskey, and people still wished they could get her recipe. The mother of another still keeps two freezers in the basement full of food in case of unexpected scarcities. Many found using electronic mail and computer conferencing to be fun, as Mason (1988) has noted.

Computer Conferencing and Physical Disabilities

Before beginning my involvement with computer conferencing and distance learning, I found that a PC with speech synthesiser was a communication aid for the visually impaired. One of the first students to submit a term paper to me on electronic mail was, coincidentally, a hearing impaired computer science major. She was in one of my history classes, and was provided with an interpreter who sat at the front translating my lecture into sign language (signing). After receiving her grade by return mail, she sent another mailing with some questions related to the class. Next, she wrote another mail message filled with amazement and exclamations as she explained that this had been the first time in her life that she had 'talked' with a teacher without needing a human intermediary. What was even more ironic was that the teacher in question, myself, was visually impaired. As gratifying as that event was, the full potential of computer communication for the disabled had not yet occurred to me.

Almost a year later, after concluding the computer conference pilot course, another deaf student came into my office and wanted to enroll in the teleconference version of Modern American History. She had only recently become deaf and therefore had very good English language skills. However, her ability to understand American Sign Language was still poor. A course which involved captioned television, text readings and a written discussion on a CRT was suited to her situation. As the computer version of the course was not scheduled for that quarter, I found a few volunteers from the classroom section who liked the schedule flexibility that it could provide, and created a section to fill her request. She stated at the conclusion of the class that it had been her best learning experience at RIT. She had found it the only place where she could participate in group discussion. Because the group never met in person, her disability was invisible to her classmates. The conference began with a topic where members introduced themselves, and she mentioned her deafness at that time. However, as the discussions progressed, it became irrelevant. Distance learning technology had helped a hearing impaired student participate in class discussions and, at the same time, enabled the visually impaired instructor to handle written materials without a reader.

Early in 1987 I submitted a proposal outlining the concept of utilising computer conferencing, captioned video and text readings as a delivery system for a larger group of hearing impaired students (Coombs and Friedman, 1987). The RIT project in 1986 was designed to facilitate direct communication between the instructor and students and, therefore, not depend on the traditional support services provided by interpreters, notetakers or special tutors. It envisioned the system as only suited to a few courses, interested faculty and some students. The intent was to conduct an experimental course for a few hearing impaired learners. At most, if successful, it would be one system operating within a larger educational context. In no sense was it seen as replacing the human support system. In fact, it was designed to have a computer instructor with signing skills introduce the students to the VaxNotes and VaxMail systems.

The first task was to find a suitable American history telecourse and obtain permission to open caption it. *America: The Second Century* was chosen and captioned. I prepared a set of discussion questions to be posted in the conferences, as VaxNotes displays its material in a window of 15 lines. Rather than having a set of questions that required several screens, one after another, to present the week's content, I restricted each topic to one screen and usually posted 3 to 6 topics per week. This meant that when replying, the questions were still visible at the top of the monitor. This format itself forced me to make my questions brief and to the point. Short direct sentences were congenial to the linguistic skills of most hearing impaired students. In fact, a computer conference tends to encourage a discussion style that is part way between colloquial and formal writing. This was better for the deaf student than long, formal and sophisticated intellectual discourse. Captioning, too, tends to automatically produce a sparse, direct style of presentation. Both formats, without having to make any patronising concessions, helped the hearing impaired student to function more efficiently than in many face-to-face academic settings.

From the beginning, the course was haunted by frustrations. Due to poor promotion of the course, only 4 students enrolled and this was not enough to conduct a lively exchange. The next frustration was that these students did not log on the VAX system often, if at all, during the first weeks of the course. Discussion questions were waiting for their contributions, and personal mail from the instructor, eagerly wanting to be of assistance went unread. Finally, an exam brought about a rude awakening to the students. They were permitted to write an extra paper to improve their grades, which most of them did, and their involvement in the conference began to improve. By the end of the quarter, after much struggle by instructor and students, all four achieved a passing grade. The major lesson drawn from this experience is that any system, to be successful, must take human factors into account and adequately prepare new users.

If captioned videos, text readings and computer conferencing provides an opportunity for personal independence and advancement as the author believes, the nagging question is: why then did so few students select this option? If the problems experienced were not with the technology, what human factors need more careful consideration? It is my opinion that there are two explanations for this phenomenon. First, the widespread computer phobia contributed to the scepticism of both the students and advisors. I believe this played a role in preventing the hearing impaired students from recognising the opportunity before them. Second, while I do not have enough data to be certain, I suspect that some hearing impaired students have become dependent on the human support system and that may have inhibited their developing the degree of self direction demanded by distance learning. As Mason (1988) noted, distance learning techniques usually require a degree of self-directed learning. The one negative comment by a student in the original pilot study said: "I want to say that this course would be excellent for someone who has more self discipline..." Students who have become accustomed to the prompting and encouragement of a support system may not do well in a system requiring self discipline, unless some program of encouragement and support is provided to bridge the early weeks.

Computer conferencing still seems to hold special potential for communication and education for persons with physical disabilities whether that be hearing, seeing or mobility. Computer phobia is a problem to be overcome whether discussing the able-bodied or disabled. Time and familiarity will gradually eliminate that roadblock. The underlying challenge of how to make computer conferencing useful to the physically disabled actually springs from its innermost strength and potential. In a computer conference, participants function on an unusually equal footing. The very anonymity which many find blocking their trying the system, allows the physically handicapped to go unnoticed. The handicapped, once having learned the basic technologies, can participate equally with their disability being invisible.

Therein lies a dilemma. On the one hand, we want to tailor these systems to be of maximum use to persons with physical disabilities. On the other hand, the technology permits genuine mainstreaming because physical appearance, handsome, ugly or handicapped, becomes insignificant. Discussants are judged by their contributions and not by external indications of status or success. Physically disabled persons who are equipped and ready to compete in an educational or social setting may become computer conference participants and be unknown to the system managers. Handicapped persons who are reasonably literate and at home using a PC can use *The Source*, *Compuserve* or other services without special help. Their disability may be invisible both to other users and to the managers. The more such technologies succeed in meeting these special needs, the less will we be aware of their achievements.

Conclusion

Computer conferencing and electronic mail have been used at RIT to lessen some communication barriers for persons with physical disabilities. They have permitted a blind teacher to communicate written material with seeing students and have also facilitated his interactions with the hearing impaired without requiring the services of an interpreter. They have similarly facilitated the communication between a recently-deafened faculty member and his hearing students. Utilising these systems with a phone line and modem could be of benefit to mobility impaired persons as well.

Because this system is a distance education technology, it has the potential to reach persons with physical disabilities far beyond the urban area of Rochester. First, institutions with specialised facilities and trained personnel could share their facilities. Funding specialised resources can be expensive and finding ways to share them would be a step towards cost effectiveness. Secondly, students on campuses with little specialised assistance could also use these resources and transfer credits back to their home school. Finally, there is a potential for adult education reaching individuals who are not located on any campus but who want to study independently.

Although the potential for increased independence and a fuller participation in the community are exciting, our attempts at RIT to expand the use of this system to include many more persons have been halting and slow. In addition to the common fear of computers which is bound to decrease with their increased use, independence itself can be intimidating. If more extensive use of computer communications with the physically disabled is to occur, there will have to be a support system provided to nurture and encourage many of them to overcome their initial resistance. Helping handicapped persons to learn course content is one benefit of these communications systems; another is increasing their independence and self reliance. These distance education technologies contain the possibility of affecting positively the physically disabled person's sense of self confidence. This is their most exciting potential.

PAPER 2

CMC FOR IN-SERVICE TRAINING

Richard Gray
CECOMM, Southampton Institute for Higher Education, UK

Following an experiment in 1987, the Centre for Electronic Communications and Open Support Systems in Education (CECOMM) launched, in the summer term of 1988, a full-scale course aimed at teachers and lecturers who wished to develop an awareness of the use of electronic communication tools in the UK, and to discuss the use of these tools in a manner relevant to their own educational context. In order to provide the most flexible yet interactive working environment possible, as well as to emphasise the potential uses of communications systems, it was decided that the course would be delivered and supported as fully as possible using computer conferencing tools.

A total of 34 participants were recruited, representing a wide spread of geographical locations, educational areas, and specialist curriculum interests. It was particularly pleasing to welcome participants from Sweden and from the Republic of Ireland. The decision was taken to support the course using the CAUCUS computer conferencing system, supplied by The Times Network Systems Ltd. as an additional feature to their normal range of educational services. This offered both convenient access from a familiar educational provider, and a reasonable technical backup and support service.

Participants were required to obtain access to the necessary hardware, and to cover telephone costs. All other access and materials costs were included in the course fee. In order to provide a coherent technical support, participants were requested to use either BBC Microcomputers or IBM PC compatibles as communications terminals.

Course Structure and Working Methodology

Participants were required to attend an initial 'face-to-face' session at the Times Network building in London. This was to introduce them to the concepts and structure of the course, to train them in the basics of using the communications link and the CAUCUS system, and to initiate group relationships. At this meeting, participants were also issued with background text material for use on the course, and a copy of the standard communications software pre-programmed with access codes for many of the services under discussion. Opportunities were given during the course of the day for all members of the group to access the system and to undertake a number of 'icebreaker' exercises to allow them to use the standard commands and to experience the concepts of group-working through the electronic medium.

The introductory day was followed by a two-week induction session in which participants were encouraged to overcome the particular problems of accessing the system from their own remote locations and to gain confidence in the use of the commands and conferencing structures. Exercises undertaken in this session included the building of a 'biography' conference in which course members could record their own interests and experiences, and which could then be used as a reference tool in group working for the remainder of the course, as well as a rather more light-hearted section on the interactive authoring of limericks.

The course itself was divided into six modules, each of two weeks duration. At the beginning of each module, summary text and activities were uploaded by the course tutors into the relevant conference. Participants were then encouraged to download and print the material, read appropriate background references, and attempt as many of the activities as possible. These exercises consisted in the main part of accessing a number of communications services and evaluating their use in particular educational situations. This initial individual component was to be completed within one week; in the second week of the module, participants were encouraged to return to the conference forum to question elements of their experience, to comment on the various systems encountered, and to suggest further uses and applications for these systems of particular relevance to their own interest areas.

Once initiated, a conference module would not be formally closed, thus participants were given the opportunity to continue discussion of topics of particular interest and to incorporate new developments and information as they were encountered. New modules and topics were simply brought in on a 'rolling' basis every two weeks.

A second 'face-to-face' day was held after the fourth module, to review progress, sort out any technical or administrative problems, and to allow demonstrations of systems and material which had been mentioned in the course, but which were not available at each individual location. Some informal course evaluation was also carried out at this stage.

In addition to the module conferences, participants were required to join a number of 'support' conferences for the duration of the course. These included an ADMIN section for course administration, a HELPLINE for technical queries, and a CAFE section for social and non course-related discussions.

Technical Constraints and Difficulties

Most course members coped well with the linear structure and elementary command language of CAUCUS; however, there were some technical constraints which proved difficult, irritating or counter-productive. The largest single difficulty was in overcoming local problems of access through the PSS network, and in using the communications software to download and upload text material.

Within CAUCUS itself, the English specialists were particularly upset by the default setting which caused the system to automatically reformat all text to minimise the number of lines used; although efficient in computer terms, this played havoc with pre-prepared paragraph structures and caused the limericks to scan in a very strange fashion! Although the feature could be disabled with a fairly simple command, it was irritating to have to remember to give this command separately in each of the twelve conferences used by the course.

Another difficulty was caused by the use of null entries on a line as 'end-of-text' markers. With some word-processors, this meant that any blank lines left within the text as, for example, paragraph separators, were treated as marking the end of text entry.

Finally, the early version of CAUCUS used for the course constrained all discussion responses after the initial starter item to a maximum of twenty lines. All of the problems above have hopefully been solved by the introduction of the latest version of CAUCUS, currently being installed by TTNS.

Experiment in Cooperative Working

At the request of a majority of the group, the final module was turned over to an experiment in distance group materials production. Participants were allocated to sub-groups of 6-8 members, split broadly by curriculum area, and invited to produce classroom materials on the use of Electronic Communication Systems. The results from the various groups were extremely variable, with some groups producing nothing at all, and others producing good quality curriculum material. Those who did not enter into productive dialogue were influenced by the positioning of this module at the very end of both the course and of the academic year, and by a lack of preparation time. It is felt, however, that the successful groups established a basis from which further work in this area can be attempted in following courses.

Student Reactions

Although formal evaluation and monitoring of student reactions lay outside the scope of this activity, feedback from the participating educationalists was generally very positive. There were some initial difficulties in adapting to interaction using a text-only medium in which oral expression and non-verbal signals were missing, and also in following the flow of the asynchronous discussion mode enforced by the linear nature of CAUCUS. Those participants

who made best use of the course were the ones who logged on frequently –
sometimes as often as twice a day – to check on new discussion contributions
and offer their own opinions.

Levels of student participation split broadly into three categories; a few
people were unable to cope with the unfamiliar working methods, or failed to
find the time from their usual work to participate, and 'dropped out'. Indications
are that the total number who dropped out at an early stage is probably less than
the average for a comparable traditional distance-taught course, but there may be
a number of factors influencing the motivation of this particular client group. A
further sub-group became 'lurkers', regularly logging on and downloading the
information and comments provided by tutors and peers, but contributing little of
their own. The final sub-group consisted of regular contributors who participated
fully and interacted with each other and with the system to good effect. Although
the boundaries between these groups are difficult to define, the split for
participants in each was approximately 6:12:16.

Those students who did contribute regularly very quickly developed an
informal and 'chatty' style, partly to compensate for the lack of non-verbal
signals. Some satisfaction was expressed at the opportunity afforded by the
system to spend some time in careful preparation of an answer or comment,
without the danger of being 'put on the spot' or missing the chance to insert a
comment at an appropriate point, as can happen with 'live' discussion.

Limited evaluation by means of a post-course questionnaire indicated general
satisfaction with the course and with the modes of working offered by the
system. Several participants were particularly pleased by the fact that they could
enjoy complete flexibility in terms of location and time, and yet still enjoy the
benefits of tutor and peer group support; the sense of isolation which is a familiar
problem with traditional distance learning courses appeared to be minimised.

The most pleasing evaluative factor is the extent to which participants are
continuing to keep in touch and to contribute several months after the end of the
course. Several collaborative relationships forged on the course continue to
produce results, and members of the 'class of 88' have developed plans of their
own to use and exploit the features of computer conferencing in their own
educational contexts.

Conclusions and Action

In terms of student reaction and organisational administration, the use of
computer conferencing in a delivery-and-support role of this kind can be judged
a success. There are wide-ranging implications in developing strategies for both
tutoring and learning within the constraints imposed by the system, but many
lessons learned in the USA and in pilot projects in this country can be applied to
the learning management process. As part of a multi-media package, computer
conferencing can provide the infrastructure for useful teaching and learning.

CECOMM is continuing to develop the use of computer conferencing in the
delivery of INSET courses, and will be repeating the course 'Electronic
Communications in Education' in the spring term of 1989. In addition,

agreement has been reached with the Joint Examining Board to offer a conversion course in Business Studies, leading to a J.E.B. Teachers' Diploma, with all teaching and support provided through a conferencing system. This course will also begin in the spring term of 1989.

PAPER 3

ACCOUNTING FOR FAILURE:
PARTICIPATION AND NON-PARTICIPATION IN CMC

Keith Grint
Brunel University, West London, UK

Since the time of Pericles it has been argued that self-potential can be fulfilled by active participation. Yet participation in discussion and decision making groups tends to be dominated by those embodying institutionalised power, or by the more articulate and less inhibited participants. A critical block to participation seems to be fear of public ridicule (Mansbridge, 1983), and whilst it may be that participation builds confidence, the leap across the ridicule threshold may be too great for some (Sniderman, 1974; Held, 1987; Crittenden, 1988). Computer mediated communication (CMC) provides a whole battery of electronic bridges to enable non-contributors to bypass some of the conventional blocks on participation: no powers of public oratory, interruption or loquaciousness are necessary; rapid exits from unpleasant or threatening encounters are viable: and no physical presence is required. In short, CMC seems to offer an electronic mask to transcend a number of factors that delimit participation. Yet although DT200, the Open University's course on Information Technology, has proved popular, and although the computer conference facilities have been used to a considerable extent, it would seem that only a minority of students actually participate in the debates. How can we best explain the under-utilisation of a medium that, despite its optional use, embodies such great potential? In what follows I discuss the results of a series of semi-structured interviews with twelve DT200 students in one region. The gender division (8 men and 4 women) reflects the course norm, and while I make no claims that this small group is representative of the total student population, their experiences throw up questions about the nature of CMC and distance education that are important in themselves.

Time

Although the asynchronous facilities of CMC are deemed important, and certainly promoted students' use of email, most interviewees regarded the absence of spontaneous and real time exchanges as a disadvantage. Indeed, many only engaged in discussions if they could do so immediately, either by replying on line or constructing messages off-line for immediate uploading. Not only was this procedure extremely expensive in time and money but the awkwardness of dialogue undermined a further prerequisite of successful interaction – the need for continuity. Few students initiated electronic discussions because they felt unable to complete the debate at one session. Time also operated as a constraint in a more material sense: as part-time students many were operating under a very tightly structured time budget that did not provide for casual CMC use, and generally claimed to be too busy to contribute. However, it is noticeable that many spent some considerable time in lurking through the conferences; time that might have been spent in participation but wasn't.

Sensory Overload

Paradoxically, the value of massive storage facilities provided by computer memory acted to undermine the level of participation; anyone logging on to a new conference faced a double barrier to use: first, the amount of information deterred many simply through sensory overload; second, the content of most messages was variably described as 'rhubarb' or 'trivia'. This perceived trivialisation of the conferences was considered especially inappropriate because CMC offered the possibility of avoiding just this form of trivialisation that bespoiled face to face tutorials. In the latter, the norms of social exchange require void filling, so that 'embarrassing' silences are talked out by any possible means. But in CMC the asynchronous aspect and the invisibility of electronic lurkers eliminates such apparent silences. Hence, when the CMC conferences appeared to be full of irrelevant or trivial comments, interest in developing rational and serious discussions was frustrated. [1]

Software Problems

Although most students expected a large number of software bugs, they were surprised to find so few. However, what did inhibit use was the perception, derived from the course team, that problems were more likely to be the result of student errors than hardware or software failures. Furthermore, the very evident limitations of the verbose editor and the absence of scanning or key word facilities in CoSy acted as important deterrents.

Invisible Others

Invisibility and anonymity do not seem to have stimulated the greater level of participation assumed by many (Kiesler *et al.*, 1984; Hiltz *et al.*, 1982). While face to face contributions require some speaking skills and public nerve, the content of the contribution is ephemeral, allowing speakers to deny interpretations or alter ideas spontaneously. But CoSy contributions were, if anything, regarded as more, not less, open to public ridicule. This was related partly to the link between the written word and high levels of expertise – most people occasionally stumble when speaking, but the written word had to be technically correct because the apparent invisibility of the messenger became transposed by the indelibility of the message. It was also related to the issue of technical expertise discussed later.

Status

Some of the most frequently asserted advantages of CMC are the flattening of hierarchies, the consequential expansion of participation, and the channeling of attention away from the messenger and onto the message. The interviewees had some sympathy with this point but generally seemed to have adopted systems for reconstructing statuses. These included searching out personal resumes to confirm assumed status, and systematically ignoring those participants whose comments were considered trivial.

Gender

The irrelevance of gender to technical success within DT200 seems to have been explained by most of the male respondents as a result of the women's atypical expertise – thus confirming, rather than undermining, conventional assumptions about the technical superiority of men. This was buttressed by the common assumption amongst the men that technical messages were by men, while requests for help were from women. But perhaps more interesting was the nature of interaction between men and women. The majority of women interviewed mentioned the rather disquieting experience of inviting unknown males into their home, albeit at one remove and only electronically. Nevertheless, women still found conversing with men electronically easier than in face to face situations, because of the security and anonymity. Where gender was more important in limiting participation was in the response of the spouse; while female spouses of male students tolerated their computer-based activities, male spouses of female students seemed considerably less prepared to cope with the resultant disturbance to domestic routine.

Technical Expertise and Technical Reason

Finally, I want to conclude by considering the delimiting effects of technical reason (Marcuse, 1964; Habermas, 1971) and expertise. Despite the overt determination of the course team to bridge the gap between technology and social science, the majority of students perceived CMC to be a mode of communication configured to transmit technical expertise. It wasn't just that too much information existed within the conferences or that most of this was trivia, but that the criteria for assessing triviality itself reflected unquestioned assumptions about technology. Thus, technical information was usually defined as objective, valid and usually accurate; sociologically informed information was normally perceived as biased, subjective and irrelevant – it was trivia. Since only technical expertise was regarded as sufficiently valuable to form the basis for contributions, and since very few students regarded themselves as possessing that expertise, the conferences were left to self-appointed experts and 'modem sniffers'. It is, then, rather ironic that a major reason for delimited participation is the extent to which technology is perceived as neutral. Since technology is perceived as neutral there can be no philosophy of technology; without a philosophy of technology there can be no debate. If technology never lies why argue with it?

Notes

[1] See Paper 15 for another perspective on this issue. (ed)

PAPER 4

USING TELETEL FOR LEARNING

Patrick Guihot
National Institute for Pedagogical Research (INRP), Paris, France

French distance education institutions are only just beginning to reflect on the integration of educational networking into their activities, and there is little use of CMC in higher education (with the exception of some courses at the University of Paris-Dauphine).

This paper outlines the context of the educational use of the Télétel interactive videotex system, with particular reference to research being undertaken by the Telematics Group at the INRP.

The educational use of telematics in France is both an old and a recent story. It is an old story because the first important experiment carried out by the Telematics Group, involving 21 primary and secondary schools, dates from 1980. The software developed for this trial included 10 CAL packages (in maths, physics, English language, and science), three electronic logical games, and a local database with geographical, historical, and economic information (600 videotex screens with both tree organisation and keyword access).

Two research studies were carried out into this trial, one looking at the specific characteristics of this medium with a view to seeing how it could be combined with other teaching methods, the second analysing the attitudes and behaviour of those involved (pupils, teachers, clerks, administrators).

From our work so far, it is clear that the integration of telematics in the school is difficult – both because of the pedagogical, budgetary, and administrative organisation of the school, and because of the traditional teaching methods used. The majority of teachers have a literary, book-based, culture, and experience difficulty in mastering the new technology. However, the children easily master the Minitel keyboard. As a result the technology disturbs the traditional pedagogical relationship between the teachers, as the sole possessors of knowledge, and the pupils.

Our first attempts at using electronic mail failed; however, the CAL packages and the database were used. This is probably because the use of these latter applications modifies the traditional school practices less than does the use of communication facilities. A second reason appears to be the cost of using network technology, and the rigidity of the school organisation (one hour, one teacher, one classroom, one set). Finally, although our research demonstrated that pupils master the use of the Minitel keyboard very quickly, they were not able to to use the system properly for learning.

I said earlier that the use of telematics in education is also a recent story: this is because, at the end of the trials mentioned above, in the absence of any central national decision, no further developments have occurred, with the exception of some regional initiatives. The latter include:

• the Regional Centres for Pedagogical Documentation (CRDP) in Bordeaux and Lyon, which, in particular, have set up services on Télétel for schools to order and obtain books and other documents

• several experiments carried out by the now defunct CATEN (Regional Centre for Technological Experiments) in Brittany

• some trials of the use of on-line databases run by the Telematics Group at INRP with schools in Picardie and Versailles.

With these few exceptions, during this transitional period, the use of Télétel has been mainly confined to administrative applications in a number of the regional Academies.

1986: The Year of the Starting Point

The real use of telematics in education started in 1986 with two events. The first of these was the sudden development of many private educational services which seem to have taken advantage, firstly, of the weak-minded stance of the Ministry of Education and, secondly, of the interest of French people in education. Although a company called DIDAO had modified some CAL material originally developed at Stanford for use via Télétel as early as 1980, it was the widespread extension of the Télétel network into peoples' homes, from 1986

onwards, that promoted the later developments. Children who access Télétel from home are the users of these educational services, which cost around 60 FF per hour of connect time. The children can, for example:
- use electronic mail to send questions about their homework to anonymous teachers, the answers being obtained either immediately or the next day, depending on the service used
- obtain vocational guidance information
- obtain model answers to questions asked in the main public national examinations.

These private videotex service providers also offer prize-winning electronic games. Their profit levels depend on the number and duration of accesses made to the services they provide – revenue from connect time charges is shared between the service provider and France Telecom.

The second major event which occurred in 1986 was the distribution of a range of telematic equipment to French schools:
- modem cards or modems for the computers which had been distributed under the IPT (*Informatique pour tous*) plan
- 317 local videotex on-line data services; these can only be accessed via telephone links, and the educational applications are developed by the teachers
- 21 more powerful computers with videotex software, accessible only via TRANSPAC (the French national packet switched service), so the cost of their use is the same from any school in the country.

In addition, there has been a swift development of a number of applications in universities, in particular:
- the use of Minitels to improve university management procedures, particularly for initial registration of students in the universities in Paris, which is always a major problem
- the provision of information services on Télétel for future and current students
- the use of CMC, via Télétel, as a learning aid; Professor Marc Guillaume at the University of Paris-Dauphine has recently been involved in the teaching of a course using the French version of the Participate computer conferencing system (*Participe Présent*).

Finally, the Ministry of Education has set up a regularly updated information service on Télétel called EDUTEL, aimed at school staff and parents. It has low access charges (about 7 FF per hour of connect time). Recently, electronic mail software has been added to EDUTEL for use by schools.

Current Research at the INRP

Firstly, I should point out that there are epistemological problems in carrying out research on information and communication technologies, precisely because they are so new. But we do not have time to properly explore the basis of our research, as the technologies are being introduced very rapidly into the schools,

and we have to prepare guidelines as quickly as we can for the teachers and for the Ministry of Education. In France, we are working in two principal directions:
- in what ways can the machines contribute to the learning process?
- what is the real influence of the technology on the learning process?

These are surely two complementary aspects: the main problem is to discover how to use the new technologies to help the thinking process. The INRP Telematics Group is conducting research into the first of the above fields, whereas several different universities are working on the second.

I said earlier that there are two situations in which telematics are used in education: from the home, and from the school. In the first case, use is mainly shaped by the private service providers, together with a few services run by the Ministry of Education. In the second case, we have to take into account a number of factors in determining the best uses of telematics. For example, it is a network technology that allows schools to open themselves to their environment, and can thus be a useful learning aid; but the schools have a variety of technological aids at their disposal, and we need to consider how best to integrate them with each other. We also need to think very clearly about the pupil's abilities in mastering this new technology.

Our current workplan (1988-1991) at the INRP is based on three main orientations:
- adaptation of the supply of telematic services to educational requests
- investigation of the conditions necessary for the integration of telematics with learning activities, and for the adoption of the medium by school users
- the ways in which the various information and communication technologies can complement each other.

To deal successfully with these tasks, we are undertaking three research programmes:

Telematics QCM: this concerns the use of Télétel for students to test themselves with multiple choice questions (QCM). We plan to develop two question banks, in English language and math, with commented answers, and to study their effectiveness and how they are used.

Multi-media approach for vocational guidance: we plan to study access to, and conditions of use of, a variety of information sources in a multi-media environment; we will be looking in particular at the specific contributions of videodiscs and databases, used simultaneously.

Telematic communication: we are going to study the uses made of communications software and networks in schools (including electronic mail, telematic forums, computer conferencing). We will investigate particularly the concepts that pupils develop concerning these technologies, the main rules for using this medium, and its effects on school activities and pedagogy. We are currently working on this project with a group of teachers from the Freinet movement (ICEM) from 75 different school divisions, communicating via electronic mail and conferences on Télétel.

As can be seen, we are beginning to get interested in CMC, but we must be cautious with this new learning method, as its use disturbs many traditional educational practices.

PAPER 5

EVALUATION OF COMPUTER CONFERENCING IN OPEN LEARNING

Annette Lorentsen
University of Aalborg, Denmark

'Picnic' is a new research project at the University of Aalborg, Denmark, the aim of which is to contribute to a clarification of the use and potential of computer conferencing in distance education (Lorentsen *et al.*, 1988). Part of Picnic is an evaluation of computer conferencing used in a concrete context at Jutland Open University. What I will describe are some aspects related to the design of an appropriate evaluation of computer-mediated communication (CMC) in open learning followed by a description of what we have done and of some of our preliminary results.

Evaluation Design

First it is crucial to stress the importance of combining evaluation of CMC with thorough theoretical and methodological studies in order to gain a deeper understanding of what is going on. In Picnic we see these three dimensions as interrelated, whereby evaluation of CMC activities to Picnic becomes a cyclic process of collecting and interpreting data on one hand and refining our theory and methodology on the other hand.

Furthermore it is very important to recognise that much research within fields other than CMC is most relevant for the theoretical foundation of an evaluation of CMC. Many CMC people tend to think that dealing with a new medium means that they have to invent theoretical concepts from scratch. In opposition to this Picnic will be built on ideas, concepts, and results obtained through many years of research within other related fields. Our theory will be divided into two main categories:
• communication and interaction
• learning processes and their pedagogical organisation.
What fascinates us most within the communication part is that CMC in educational contexts today is characterised by a lack of communicative norms. What could such communicative norms look like? (Austin, 1971; Searle, 1969; Wunderlich, 1972.) How will such norms be learned, accepted, and managed by various types of students? To what extent would it be possible to use the concept 'communicative competence' from foreign language didactics as a relevant theoretical communicative framework? (Dietrich, 1979; Habermas, 1981; Dell Hymes, 1972; Piepho, 1974.)

Within the pedagogic part of the project we are interested in whether and how CMC promotes the concept of project pedagogy (including central activities like defining group topics, exchanging experience and knowledge among students and collaboration (Mills, 1963; Negt, 1971; Wagenschein, 1956). We are interested in studying whether the medium, at the same time as it helps overcome certain barriers, in fact creates new barriers to certain groups of students.

Empirical Basis of Picnic

The empirical basis of Picnic consists of an evaluation of CMC within two arts foundation courses and one archaeology course at Jutland Open University (JOU), ie courses where CMC is only a tool and not a study object.

JOU hopes to gain from CMC the following:
- support for education as interactive, dialogue based learning processes
- support for students' activity and responsibility for their own education
- support for social interaction (strengthen student identity)
- support for equality within education.

Evaluation Methodology and Evaluation Data

The methodological framework of Picnic is a Danish version of classroom research called 'classroom methodology', meaning pedagogical research which studies how theories are interpreted and carried out in classrooms with real students. Classroom research in this version means qualitative research.

Our classroom is not a physical, but a simulated one. Therefore we cannot rely on the traditional qualitative methods when studying classroom activities. What we have done is to combine new kinds of data with traditional qualitative data. The new kinds of data consist of statistics from the computer system and from an experimental workshop, where a group of students had to express themselves about CMC and the pedagogical practice in their course.

We have collected four kinds of data from the computer system:
- statistics
- information on student participation in particular conferences
- all texts produced on the system
- students' interaction with the system.

These data are supplemented by questionnaires, small essays on background, family and communication experience and preferences, and interviews.

Preliminary Results

We are now analysing this empirical data, but I will describe some of our preliminary results briefly. Freshmen tend to use the system more than older students, who have established a way of carrying out distance learning without CMC. The use of CMC must be integrated into the course, otherwise students will not use it. However, a fully integrated use of CMC tends to suppress other media, which means that a student will easily drop out if unable to cope with CMC. There is a correlation between the overall pedagogy of the course and the use of CMC. Group work and problem solving tend to gain more from the use of CMC than traditional university pedagogy. Access, introduction to the system, and system design highly influence the use of CMC. We feel that every student must have a PC at home and not in a study centre, as was the case in two of our courses. The introduction to the system ought to stress the communicative potentials and procedures of CMC. This is a field which has been underestimated in all applications so far, in our opinion, and it is a most crucial factor when judging the use of CMC both by students and by teachers. Therefore next year the arts foundation course students will be given a communication manual, where roles, procedures, norms etc. in connection with CMC will be discussed, and training given.

So far our results may be summed up through the statement that extended and fruitful use of CMC calls for:

- description, training, and understanding of communicative roles, procedures, and norms connected with CMC
- appropriate integration of CMC into the pedagogical context
- appropriate system access, introduction, and design.

PAPER 6

EMAIL AND ELECTRONIC TRANSFER OF DATA FILES FOR A DISTANCE EDUCATION COURSE

Jeanette Muzio
University of Victoria, British Columbia, Canada

The Division of University Extension at the University of Victoria (UVic), in conjunction with the British Columbia Systems Corporation, began the certificate program in Computer Based Information Systems (CBIS) for managers and professionals in the fall of 1981. Since 1984, various CBIS courses have been developed for distance education. The first CBIS course to use data communications for both electronic mail and electronic transfer of data files – *Computing Tools for Management* – was offered as a pilot project in January 1988.

The class size was restricted to 24 students, 23 from locations within British Columbia, and one from Ottawa (over 2,500 miles from Victoria). Two factors made this course unique. Firstly, students operated truly at a distance – at no time did they attend class to learn how to operate equipment or to manage the data communications component. Instead, the data communications procedures had been written by the Program Coordinator into a comprehensive manual that comprised part of the course package. Secondly, although other courses have used email, students in this course also uploaded data files (mainly spreadsheets) from their PCs to the UVic mainframe where they were accessed by the instructor for grading.

As this was a first venture for UVic and the CBIS program, a comprehensive evaluation was conducted both during the course and afterwards. Students filled in questionnaires; the instructor, marker, and administrators were interviewed; and complete monitoring of the usage of the system was undertaken.

This paper describes the data communications procedures used, the results of the evaluations, and discusses changes made for future use of this technology in other courses offered by University Extension at UVic.

Data Communications Procedures

Students required access to an IBM PC or compatible with a minimum configuration of two floppy disk drives. To communicate with the UVic IBM 3083 mainframe, each PC had to have either an internal modem or a serial port (RS232C), connector cable, and an external modem. CBIS provided Gandalf Series 24A modems at no charge, if required. Either Lotus 1-2-3 or VP-Planner was used for spreadsheet assignments and Kermit version 2.29b was used to access electronic mail and to upload assignments to the mainframe. Kermit established the telephone connection between the PC and modem, set up the asynchronous communications protocol required for VT100 terminal emulation, and translated the ASCII character code used by the PC to EBCDIC code used by the IBM 3083. On the mainframe, students used MAIL (developed by Rice University, Houston, Texas) for electronic mail and Kermit-CMS to transfer files to and from their PCs in conjunction with Kermit-MS.

To access the UVic mainframe, students used public phone lines. Those living in Victoria dialed the mainframe modem directly, while others used BC Tel's DATAPAC packet switched network by dialing the 1200 bits per second public dial port closest to their location.

Email Usage

Between January 19 and April 22, 571 messages were logged. Of these, the marker and instructor sent 344, the students 183, and the course coordinators 44. The peaks of activity coincided with due dates for assignments, even though 6 out of 8 of the assignments involved the transferring of spreadsheet files directly to the marker's account and did not have an email component. However, students tended to supplement their file transfers with email messages to the marker advising that the assignment had been sent or explaining why it was delayed. The marker and instructor used email to send grades and comments on the assignments to the students.

Although messages were sent between the hours of 06:00 and 03:00, the greatest concentration was during the early evening hours, with another surge occurring near midnight.

There was no significant difference in student usage based on the day of the week.

Very few messages related to the actual course content. Often messages were left for the instructor requesting a phone call to clarify content.

Findings

Students reported that the data communications experience was valuable and they recommended that it be incorporated in all CBIS distance education courses. Most students spent more time mastering and using email and file transfer than they had anticipated. Using data communications did not reduce the time that they would have spent normally in mailing assignments and communicating with the instructor. The course instructor, marker, and the administrators found email to be an excellent tool for communicating more effectively among themselves and with the students although some students did not read or respond promptly to email messages.

The Program Coordinator and the Office Manager had spent approximately 150 hours testing data communications procedures and writing documentation prior to the start of the course. During the first two weeks of the course, about 120 hours were spent by the Program Coordinator and the Program Assistant in troubleshooting. For the remainder of the course, approximately 10 hours per week were spent by the administrator.

The funding for this pilot project covered UVic mainframe and Datapac charges for all students. These costs totalled $3,000 which was considerably higher than anticipated and greater than we could expect students to pay in addition to fees for instructions and materials.

The wide variety of PCs and modems used created some technical problems which were impossible to anticipate. Solving such problems over the phone was complicated by the fact that students could not use their phone lines for both data and voice communications simultaneously.

Some students found the Kermit software inflexible and difficult to use.

Conclusions and Changes

The positive outcomes far outweighed the negative and the decision was made to use data communications in future CBIS distance education courses, beginning with the Office Automation course in September 1988.

Future Datapac charges should be lower than in the pilot study as computing services have increased the packet size for data transmission. The Kermit software has also been rewritten to incorporate an extremely user-friendly configuration program which is run by the student only once. Following this initial start-up procedure, the student merely needs to type 'kermit' and is then shielded from all the intervening communication steps until logged onto the

UVic mainframe. A further refinement has been the inclusion of status messages within Kermit to indicate the progress of the log on procedure. This will help when trouble-shooting student problems.

Our next step will be to introduce full computer conferencing in those courses that do not need to transmit data files electronically but where there is a need for student interaction.

PAPER 7

EKKO: A VIRTUAL SCHOOL

Morten Paulsen
NKI College of Computer Science, Stabekk, Norway

What is a Virtual School?

The NKI College of Computer Science started working on the establishment of a virtual school in the spring of 1986. The Virtual Classroom Project, at the New Jersey Institute of Technology, influenced our definition of a virtual school, but we believe that there are essential differences between a virtual classroom and a virtual school.

Virtual means hypothetical or imaginary. A virtual school needs no physical framework such as a school building with classrooms, offices, reading rooms and libraries. Nevertheless it can be perceived as real because it attends to the functions which we expect a school to perform. A virtual school is an information system which can take care of the functions of a school, without the necessity for a physical existence. As in a physical school, most of the functions will have to be carried out by people. A virtual school should therefore have the fewest possible limitations on communication between people. Communication should be possible without limitations in time and space (an in-depth description of our understanding of a virtual school is given in Paulsen, 1987-88).

Demands on a Virtual School

We make the following demands on a virtual school:
- It should take care of the professional, educational, administrative and social functions of a school.
- It should be accessible from everywhere.
- It should be accessible at all times.

- It should attend to the school's need for communication between people. Necessary forms of communication are: one-to-one, one-to-many and many-to-many.

Technology

We have considered current technology, and our conclusion is that computer conferencing is capable of meeting the demands of a virtual school. However this does not rule out the use of other technologies as a supplement to computer conferencing. We chose to develop our own conferencing system, EKKO in order to put into realisation our virtual school.

EKKO

EKKO is influenced by our knowledge of the conferencing systems PortaCOM, EIES, CoSy, Participate and PC-based bulletin board systems. Development started in the spring of 1986, and the first version of the system came into use in August of the same year. For the first half year EKKO was only used internally at the College of Computer Science. In January 1987 users outside the college were able to use EKKO.

EKKO consists of four main components: user directory, electronic mail, bulletin boards and conferences.

User Directory
The directory contains information on all users (name, address, telephone numbers, etc) and user groups. The information which is stored in the user directory is recorded by the users themselves. It is therefore up to each one to decide how much information he/she wishes to declare.

All user groups are formed by the system operator (SysOp). He is also the only person who can put in or remove users from these groups. SysOp can also close a user group so that only the members know of the group's existence and the identity of each member.

Electronic Mail
The mail system in EKKO is a traditional electronic mail system which enables a user to send private messages to one or more users. After a letter is sent, it is possible to list those users who have received the letter but not yet read it. If the letter is no longer of interest, it can be deleted by the sender. It will then be removed from the recipient's in-basket. It is not possible to store letters in the post system after they have been read. This is done to save storage space in the computer. However it is possible for the recipient to make a copy of the letter on file, or send it straight to the printer, so that the text is not lost.

Bulletin Boards
The bulletin board system in EKKO is organised for one-to-many communication. It is meant to be a one-way information channel for use in

'broadcasting' information. This system was made to meet the needs of a teacher or school to pass on information to one or more classes.

The bulletin boards are made and maintained by SysOp. Nevertheless, users who have written a notice on one of these boards can delete it. If so desired, SysOp can limit the number of people with rights to write on a bulletin board. SysOp can also 'close' bulletin boards so that only some can have access to the information, as in the conferences.

Conferences

The system operator is the only user who can set up conferences. Conferences can be open or closed. All members can have reading and writing access to an open conference, whereas a closed conference is accessible only to selected users.

In a conference we differentiate between contributions and comments. In this context, a contribution is an introductory statement, while a comment always refers to a contribution. Each contribution has a heading which enables users to find the desired information. All comments are organised as a chronological chain under the contribution to which the text refers.

User Interface

EKKO is menu-driven. It is possible to change the extent of menu guidance, if so desired. All new users automatically receive a menu describing all functions. Advanced users can limit this to a short menu without explanation, or remove the menus completely.

A list of all new information will be written out each time a user starts EKKO. This list only contains information from bulletin boards and conferences of which the user is a member. All new information can be obtained with the help of a single command.

Lines of Communication

Up to the present, EKKO has been open to all who wish to use the system. It has been of great help in marketing the school.

In the spring of 1988 we have had 4 telephone lines and 6 packet switch network (Datapak) channels into EKKO. Distance students' use of Datapak has been paid for by the school, so that these students have been able to reach EKKO at local telephone rates.

System Details

EKKO is written in Pascal for an HP-3000 minicomputer with the operating system MPE. For data storage we have used the HP/IMAGE database system together with files. Text for conferences and bulletin boards is stored on files, the remaining information is stored in the database. The text of the letters is stored in the database for greater security.

Using IMAGE as the database system makes it complicated to convert EKKO to another computer or operating system.

On-campus Instruction

EKKO was used for the first time in organised instruction on the course, *Introduction to Computer Science* in the autumn of 1986. EKKO was offered as an optional extra in addition to normal lectures. Since then the system has been used in the same way in a number of subjects at NKI College of Computer Science and NKI College of Engineering. This applies first and foremost to the following subjects: *Introduction to Computer Science*, *Computer Management*, *Computer Applications* and *Data Communication*. To varying degrees EKKO has also been used for administrative announcements at the schools.

Distance Education

Autumn 1987
Our first trial run with distance education in the autumn of 1987 was in *Introduction to Computer Science*. This experiment was completed as pure distance education with no face-to-face sessions. The course was developed around an existing correspondence course with six study units. For each of the units, the four students had to answer a set of exercises, and send their answers to the tutor as a letter in EKKO. The tutor commented on the assignments individually in the form of a letter via EKKO. We also experimented with group assignments.

Spring 1988
In order to gain experience of how this method of instruction works on a larger scale, we ran three courses in the spring of 1988. The courses were: *Introduction to Computer Science*, *Programming I* (Pascal) and *Systems Analysis I*. Together, these courses are equivalent to the first term of the part-time study programme at the College of Computer Science. In all, the courses are worth eight credits.

Organising EKKO

The user's impressions of a conferencing system depend largely on how it is organised. It is important to organise it in such a way that it is possible to direct information to the right target group, and to prevent a user being overloaded with information which is of no interest. This can be achieved by a sensible division of groups, bulletin boards and conferences. We chose to organise it as described below.

First we established a group called FJERN (distant). All prospective distance students who registered in EKKO were placed in this group. This group was sent a welcoming letter in EKKO, which described their rights in the system. They were given reading access to a bulletin board which contained information about the courses and how they could enrol on a course. They were also given reading and writing access to a conference called E-KRO (Electronic Cafe).

E-KRO was established to provide a social meeting place for prospective students, enrolled students, tutors and the administration. All kinds of subjects could be brought up in E-KRO.

We then chose to form three groups (GDB, SYS and PAS), one for each of the three courses in the spring term. As the prospective students enrolled for the courses, they were placed in their respective groups. Each of the groups was given reading access to its own bulletin board, and reading and writing to its own conference.

The bulletin boards were intended for the tutor to enter notice on administrative and subject matters for the class. The purpose of the conferences was to enable the students and the teacher to discuss topics of interest for the subject.

In addition to the groups, bulletin boards and conferences mentioned, the distance students had access to other open conferences and bulletin boards in EKKO.

Requirements Made on Students' Equipment

The school does not require that the students use any special microcomputers, modem or communication programme, as long as they are able to communicate with EKKO. Neither does the school provide any equipment for the students. In this way, we can reduce the school's administrative work.

Course Administration

The work consisted of providing information on and putting into effect applications for enrolment to courses, routines for the despatch of textbooks and arrangements for examinations. General information about this was announced on a bulletin board in EKKO, established for this purpose. Special information was sent as a letter.

The students applied for enrolment to single courses by sending a letter in EKKO to SysOp, stating which courses they wanted to take. SysOp acknowledged receipt of the letter by putting the student into the relevant groups (GDB, SYS and PAS).

To order books, the students sent a letter in EKKO to a student counsellor at the NKI correspondence school. He despatched book parcels and payment slips as the orders were received.

To enter for examinations, the students sent a letter in EKKO to the school's student secretary. She registered the applications and sent out payment slips. It was possible to take the examination at the College of Computer Science or in the student's home town, on condition that they could provide an approved invigilator (supervisor).

Course certificates were issued to all students who completed a course. This work was done by the NKI correspondence school.

Plan of Instruction

Correspondence courses, with official approval, were developed for three courses. Each of the them consisted of six compulsory, individual assignments for submission, each of which had to be approved before the student was issued with a course certificate, or allowed to take the examination. We decided to set deadlines for submission of the assignments. The course started on March 1, and the deadlines for submission were fixed at intervals of 14 days. This was done to ensure that all the students in a class would have approximately the same progression in their studies. In this way the tutor's work would be made easier, and it would stimulate communication between the students.

The students' individual assignments were graded individually by the tutors. This had much in common with traditional correspondence teaching, apart from the fact that we used electronic mail in EKKO instead of the postal service.

After the deadline had expired the tutor was able to give in-depth information, point out common mistakes, and comment generally on the efforts of the class. In addition, suggestions for solutions were given on the class's bulletin board.

During the course, students could ask questions about the subjects in the class's own conference. Fellow students and the tutor could comment on the questions. The teacher could also use this conference to bring up matters with the class.

Completion Rate

Altogether 40 students enrolled on one or more of the 3 courses: *Introduction to Computer Science*, *Structured Programming with Pascal*, and *Systems Analysis*. The majority, 35, completed the assignments, and 12 of the 18 who entered for the voluntary examinations passed.

Use of EKKO

The use of EKKO was logged continuously. It varied greatly from student to student. Among students who completed one or more courses, the amount of usage varied from once a week to several times a day.

Conclusion

I would like to draw attention to the following conclusions, based on questionnaires distributed among the students, written reports from tutors and administrative personnel, as well as other material:

The EKKO project has shown that it is possible to construct a virtual school around a computer conferencing system. We have shown that this is possible with the technology of today, with top professional quality, satisfactory educational organisation and an acceptable administrative work load.

Our distance students have had a relatively good grounding in the use of computers and computer science. Most of them, but not all, have experience of word-processing and/or a PC or microcomputer. However there are remarkably few who had experience of modems and/or conferencing systems before starting the course.

Most of our distance students live in the Oslo area, but many other parts of the country were represented.

Our distance education courses have attracted students with a good educational background and a wide variety of vocations. A great majority of the students are married or cohabit, and have children.

In the tutors' opinion, this has been an interesting but demanding method of instruction. However, the work load should be lighter the next time the courses are run, since many of the texts can be used again.

The text books and assignments for submission were developed for traditional correspondence courses. However, the students, by a large majority, feel that this has not hindered them in their learning. It is therefore possible to offer instruction without materials specially developed for courses of this kind.

The instruction was planned with fixed deadlines for submission of assignments, in order to create a coordinated progression in the courses. This was a positive aspect for both students and teachers. However, we did not succeed in establishing communication between the students as much as we would have wished. It may therefore be necessary to adapt the instruction to meet this need.

The three subjects in which we have offered courses, seem to be well suited for distance education.

In most cases the students give a positive overall assessment of this form of distance education. None of the students who have expressed their views, is dissatisfied with the courses. On a scale from 5 (very good) to 1 (very poor), the students' average estimate of the courses was 3.9, 4.3 and 3.9.

PAPER 8

COMPUTER-MEDIATED WRITING:
THE WRITER IN ELECTRONIC RESIDENCE

Trevor Owen
Riverdale Collegiate Institute, East Toronto, Ontario, Canada

Several years ago, after I purchased my first computer, a student came rushing into my office for details. He was excited and full of questions, but what impressed me most was that he asked for pen and paper to illustrate the concept of telecommunications. First, he drew a small square, and beside it, a large circle.

"This is a modem," he said, pointing to the square.

His pen moved thoughtfully to the circle.

"THIS is the world!"

I hadn't given telecommunications serious consideration before then. To me, the computer was an antidote to my handwriting; a perfect typewriter that produced readable characters on fluidless sheets. Then I began to realise that writers had already embraced the technology, and were very busy using it to produce meaning in our classrooms.

Idea Throwing

Since then, I have been fortunate to participate in several projects which have brought word-processing and telecommunications to the English literature and writing classroom. Some offered students access to contemporary works-in-progress and commentary by Canadian writers, as well as to the writers themselves via electronic mail. Others probed databases and helped students to develop bibliographies. While each of these was worthwhile to some degree, I found that the most exciting projects focused on original student writing and commentary, while offering contact with peers and 'experts'.

The most recent of these, a 'writer-in-electronic-residence' project, was undertaken between February and June, 1988, with poet Lionel Kearns from Vancouver, British Columbia. [1] The project served as a natural extension of the writing program by linking students and writer in a computer-mediated conference. All participants were connected to the host computer system where they could deposit and/or retrieve original writing, commentary and, of course, the writer's responses. The program will continue in 1988-89 with an Ontario-based writer, David McFadden.

It should be stressed here that this program, like the others, is about writing. Our objectives are consistent with those established when we began using word-processing and telecommunications in the English program and advocate the use of technology by students in accordance with Ontario Ministry of Education policy (Program Memorandum 1982, p 47; 1981-82 p 31). This calls for "...creative use of computers by individuals: writing, composing, designing, analysing and other extensions of original thought" while emphasising that computer use is about:

- education and, in particular, curriculum
- equal opportunity of use
- applications in classrooms within an integrative (and *interactive* – emphasis added) context across the curriculum.

as expressed in *Learning With Computers: The Next Few Years* (Toronto Board of Education, 1985).

Based upon the assumption that computer use must be integrated within the context of the existing English program as naturally as possible, the following objectives were emphasised in the report *Computers in Ontario Education*, 1983 pp 26-27:

- to help students learn to use microcomputer technology for enhancing and extending the dynamic processes of learning and self-expression (sensing, creating, synthesising, designing, analysing, and expressing)
- to make the content, process, and pace of learning more adaptable to individual students' needs, and to help students develop the basic knowledge and skills necessary for formulating and expressing ideas through words, numbers, and symbols
- to encourage the development of alternative delivery systems for education
- to help students understand how microcomputer technology is used in everyday life and to foster their ability to use devices based on this technology.

The Writer In Electronic Residence

After a successful pilot project undertaken over the last two years, an English class (Ontario grade ten, 14 to 16 years of age) was timetabled permanently in the school's computer lab.

The students were given several assurances:

- they were free to choose whether to use the computers at all
- those who did were free to decide how they wanted to use them (ie what stages of the writing process would be represented)
- no student would be penalised for choosing to continue with the more traditional instruments of writing.

Some students were more eager to use the machines than others, but most were using the word-processors regularly by the end of the year. Although we had identified composition at the keyboard as a primary element to monitor in this project, students were encouraged to experiment and assess the value of computer use, especially word-processing, at each stage in the writing process. (While most students indicated that they preferred to use the computer for editing and printing, it is interesting to note that those who embraced the idea of composing at the keyboard were more likely to embrace editing and revision.)

Like other, more traditional writer-in-residence programs, the RCI project assumed that the creative writing process could be encouraged in the classroom by the presence of a professional writer working directly with the students. It also assumed that computer-based word processing and on-line communication could be used in this setting by the professional writer to enhance students' creative writing skills, give students added insights into the craft of writing, and increase their writing productivity. Finally, we believed that the computer-mediated conference provided an appropriate forum for a project about writing because

- the nature of on-line interaction is textual and, therefore, appropriate to writing and commentary
- the on-line forum provides a certain equity of use, placing students in control of what to write, when and where to 'send' it, and how to respond.

"What a *wonderful* learning experience it has been," wrote student Yit Yin Tong, who entered grade 11 at Riverdale this year, and was recently recognised by the Board of Education for her creative work on this project. "It has given me a new perspective on learning, and learning how to learn. With other writers of the world, we have all responded and contributed to one another. I see this as something that has changed my life." She adds that "education shouldn't always be within classroom walls."

Taken together, expression and response in the computer-mediated forum provide a meaningful, language-based context for ideas to be offered up in written form. Of course, as worthy a use as this might be for CMC, it is not enough for meaning to occur. The opportunity for equity must also exist.

'Virtual' Equity

The nature of equity in the computer-mediated conference, and the issue of whether computers are, or can be 'neutral' in the virtual world of ASCII lights, is a controversial topic that won't be resolved here. However, I can say that our work with CMC and writing, which was undertaken primarily within the context of the classroom, suggests that technology waits for us to distinguish between participants, and that we can serve equity well by matching meaning and context with safety.

For our project, this meant that there was a clear purpose from the beginning, namely, the ability to correspond with a writer and other students in a creative writing workshop. But it is also true that a software option, which boasts a little controversy of its own, helped to make the process safe. Pseudonymous participation was available as an option to everyone in the conference – including the writer and teacher.

Yit Yin Tong noted this when corresponding with elementary students in the United States in another writing project undertaken on the McGraw-Hill Information Exchange for Education (MIX). "Not only could you send responses and comments more quickly," she wrote, but one could "be 3,000 miles out of reach of somebody who wants to sock your brains out for your 'terrific' remarks..."

Although some did choose nicknames, like 'Whiz Kid', for example, the students tended to see 'initials only' or first name identification as offering a reasonable level of safety in the public arena. Initially, it was clear that the students were as unwilling to assume the sincerity of those not yet known to them as they were hesitant to post their works without the availability of pseudonyms. Over the course of the project, this evolved into a view that the computer-mediated writing conference allowed the work to stand on its own.

I believe that this is a significant shift, and demonstrates the value of CMC as a language adjunct in the classroom environment.

Of course, some people (the student with the pencil) already knew that.

Notes

[1] Documentation of the project, which was edited by two of the students, is available in an eight page newspaper (tabloid format). The complete project, some 150 pages, is available on diskette in MS-DOS or Macintosh format. The project was funded jointly by the Ontario Arts Council (Creative Artists In Schools program), the Toronto Board of Education, and Riverdale Collegiate. Simon Fraser University in Vancouver, British Columbia, donated the host computer and packet-switching services.

PAPER 9

CMC AT ATHABASCA UNIVERSITY

Judith Van Duren
Athabasca University, Alberta, Canada

Athabasca University (AU) is presently in the process of integrating computer-mediated communications into its working environment and delivery system. A number of pilot studies have shown the value and feasibility of CMC and have also indicated some potential problem areas, both educational and institutional.

Background

Athabasca University is an open access, distance learning institution serving approximately 11,000 students who are located primarily in Alberta and across the four western provinces. It employs about sixty faculty, three hundred tutors and over two hundred professional and support staff. The university itself is located in a small town in north central Alberta; most of the tutors are spread across the province and the students are further scattered. The university is highly computerised with a large central capacity and a good networking capability. The present delivery system is based on print-based material with telephone tutor support.

Email is widely and heavily used by the central and regional offices staff. Computer conferencing use is more sporadic but has proven valuable for task-oriented group work. As well, several projects within the university have proven valuable in gaining experience with CMC. The student management system (TRIX), now used institution-wide, incorporates computer conferencing for communication among the tutors, coordinator and secretary of any course. Stand-alone CAL courses incorporate messaging systems for student-tutor communication. The Athabasca CoSy system has been and is being used in several pilot studies by external groups including high school teachers and students, educators from a variety of institutions and a network of business people across the province.

Athabasca University has recently entered into a consortium with AT&T Canada, ACCESS network, Alberta Government Telephones, Alberta Advanced Education and the Ministry of Technology, Research and Telecommunications. This partnership, the Canadian Distance Learning Development Centre, was created with the mandate to develop innovative and improved learning services for educational institutions and industry.

The university is presently in an ideal situation to explore the integration of CMC into its operations: isolated faculty and staff, dispersed tutor and student populations, growing market demands for distance education, well developed existing computer and network infrastructure, a range of experience in the use of CMC and a new source of funds and expertise for project development and evaluation.

Experience Gained

The introduction of the CoSy conferencing system at AU underlines some of the most familiar and obvious problems of computer conferencing adoption and use.
- There was an existing widely used and accepted email system with which it had to compete.
- It represented yet another system to learn with its own conceptual underpinnings, interface and set of commands.
- Its introduction was technology rather than need driven – that is, it was purchased because it existed and might prove valuable, not because a needs assessment had been done and it was the only solution.
- This view of CMC as an additional rather than central system resulted in training which emphasised commands and procedures rather than communication and process.

The present patterns of use of CMC at AU emphasise, yet again, the three basic requirements for successful adoption of this type of system:
- a set of shared goals and objectives (purpose)
- a critical mass of user input (content)
- leadership on the part of the moderator (direction).

From the experience of the various internal and external user groups on the CoSy system it has become apparent that this generic type of conferencing system is unable to meet a full range of needs. However, it is also apparent from experience with a wide range of systems that additional complexity is not the solution to increased use.

Designing for the Future

Computer-mediated communication at Athabasca University is now being viewed as an integral part of a total electronic environment which must be designed to meet the needs of the full range of user groups: students, tutors, academics, staff and external groups with educational and training requirements.

CMC in its broadest sense will include access to email, computer conferencing, file transfer capabilities, national and international networks, CAL courseware and such services as the library and student counselling. A number of the components are presently in place and in use at AU. The task at hand is to design and implement an integrated and consistent operating environment which can be tailored to specific groups and their needs.

Most of the required functionality could be met by the purchase of existing software packages (communications, editors, word and text processors, email and computer conferencing etc) tied together with a single front-end. This approach was considered and rejected for a number of reasons. The major problem resulting from the use of a variety of off-the-shelf utilities is a compounding of the existing email and conferencing situation: different commands, keystrokes, conceptual underpinnings, and screen designs with a confusing and frustrating duplication of functionality. In addition, the existing systems do not meet all of the demands and considerable development and patching would still be required. A third consideration is that of cost where site licensing for a number of systems would have to be arranged.

There are a number of distinct advantages to in-house development.

- With a well-defined goal in mind, all the component parts can be considered from the beginning and consistency at the interface and command level can be maintained.
- Standards can be defined at the outset so that future developments can be more easily slotted in.
- Consistency is also maintained in the underlying system structures such as directory allocation, automated login and student security, usage logging and accounting and data collection for evaluation and institutional research.
- It is important to the usefulness and acceptance of such a system that it can be tailored for specific groups such that a user logging in would have access to a varying subset of available utilities pertinent to their needs – eg. students can access the material only for courses in which they are registered.

These considerations of user needs, functionality, system standards and maintenance helped to clarify the decision to proceed with the in-house development of a powerful and consistent electronic environment for the whole user population.

Problem Areas

It is possible to foresee some of the areas in which problems will arise in the process of design, implementation and adoption of such an electronic environment.

Care must be taken that the open access policy of the university is not endangered by a requirement for expensive and 'high tech' equipment. The possibilities for surmounting this include increased use of regional computer labs, access to local community-based micro-computer equipment, duplications of functions through paper-based versions of on-line material, provision of low cost and/or loaned equipment, computer literacy training for incoming students.

The present tutor model requires telephone access to tutors at a set and limited time each week. The benefit of CMC for the student lies in the immediacy of contact for queries and feedback. The interests of these two groups – tutors and students – are bound to conflict with the changing expectations created by the electronic environment. A new approach to the tutor model will have to emerge such that access can be more immediate for the student without vastly increasing tutor workload.

The role of the course coordinator will also change when students can access their professor electronically. Presently the faculty can select their level of involvement with, or isolation from, individual students in their courses. Policies will have to be established for dealing with 'electronic door knocking'.

In a delivery system based on print-based course materials the revision process is slow and complex. On-line courseware and conferencing create an environment of dynamic content creation and revision based on feedback and evaluation. This change in process has the potential to affect the existing production and distribution systems as well as the individual faculty members in their role of course creators.

Athabasca University has a continuous enrollment policy which results in an absence of student cohort groups and paced student activity. Computer conferencing, although asynchronous within short time periods, is usually used within some kind of temporal framework. It remains to be seen whether this tool can be successfully applied and managed within the AU context where the role of conference moderator will surely take on new dimensions of organisation and creativity.

Conclusion

Athabasca University is embarking on an ambitious and demanding project in the development of its electronic environment. As well as the technical problems to be overcome, the organisational impact will have to be dealt with. It is clear, however, that the educational objectives of the institution, demands of user groups and the existing expertise and experience have combined to indicate the direction in which to move. The success of the project will depend, to a large extent, on institutional vision to carry us forward to create the distance learning system of the future.

PAPER 10

PATTERNS IN COMPUTER-MEDIATED DISCUSSIONS

Richard Riedl
University of Alaska, Fairbanks, Alaska, USA

Patterns in Email Discussions

What kinds of experience do students have when participating in a class discussion via email? It is clearly different from a traditional class setting. On the one hand, we can choose not to worry about whether the experience of an email discussion is as good or better than discussion opportunities in traditional settings. The mere fact that distance education students have an opportunity to interact with peers and instructors, when previously such opportunities were very limited, may be good enough to warrant use of the process. On the other hand, we need to understand how a computer-mediated discussion is different and how to use it to maximum benefit. The following figures represent some descriptive information about one class that used email for discussion. They give us some idea of the nature of computer-mediated discussion, but much needs to be done to further understand the dynamics of the experience.

The class used to develop these figures was a graduate class which was designed to study the use of word-processing and telecommunications in the school classroom, providing some inherent content advantages for it as a computer-mediated class. With only seven students it was relatively easy to keep track of the message flow and discussion topics running throughout the class.

Student Participation

Of the total number of messages,
- the instructor sent 21.9% of them
- Fran 22.9%
- Alice 13.5%
- John 11.5%
- Yi Xin 7.3%
- Andrea, Jian Huai and Gloryann each 6.2%
- Gary 4.2%.

As in most traditional classes, some students participated more than others. The reasons for the variation of participation level can be many, but in a computer-mediated class we must be conscious of particular factors. For instance, Gloryann was a very active participant until her equipment failed, forcing her to complete the class later as an independent study. Gary found it difficult to set aside the time to get to a site that had equipment which allowed him to access the class mailbox and he eventually dropped out. Jian Huai and Yi Xin tended to send joint messages and to utilise the private mailbox of the instructor to a greater extent than the other students, thus taking a relatively inactive part in the overall discussion while remaining active in the class.

This simple statement of percentages also does not take into account the length of each student's messages, the number of topics covered, nor the relevance of the messages to the main topics of discussion. Alice tended to send very long, multi-topic messages, thus having a much higher participation level than is apparent from percentage of messages sent.

It is significant that the instructor, while being very active in the public mailbox, was responsible for only about 22% of the messages. The students were the main participants in the class discussion. The instructor did participate heavily through the private mailboxes of each student, often complimenting student participation or consulting on assignments or student projects, but usually tried to focus the public discussion toward student-to-student interaction.

Another way the simple counting of messages does not present the entire picture of the interactions taking place in the public mailbox, is related to the number of topics covered in each message. Figure 1 shows us that over 36% of the messages carried more than one topic. Because discussions on email systems tend to be multi-dimensional, messages often cover more than one topic with each topic having a separate source. Figure 1 also illustrates that while almost 65% of the messages in the class mailbox were one topic messages, almost 65% of the topics covered were carried in multiple topic messages.

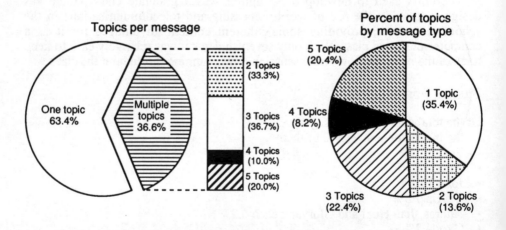

Figure 1 Topics per Message

This multiple topic, multi-level series of interchanges tends to make the discussion much richer than that found in a traditional class setting. It can also be much more difficult to follow unless students take the time to print out messages and read them carefully before reacting to any of the topics. Such multi-level discussion does put significant demands upon students and requires regular participation if the student is going to benefit from the experience.

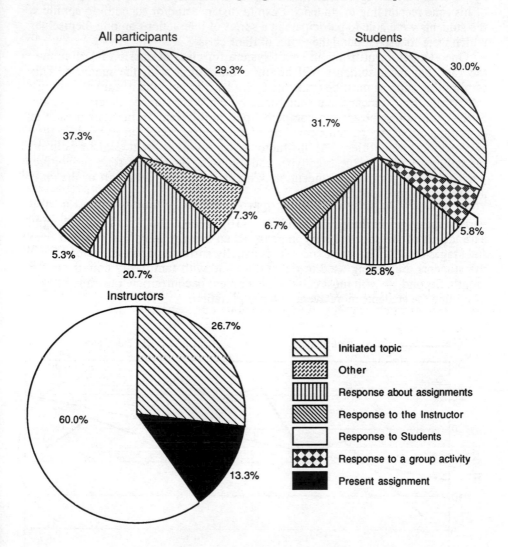

Figure 2 Message Analysis

Figure 2 illustrates the degree to which students were interacting with each other. First of all it shows us that 30% of the topics were initiated by students and almost 32% of the topics discussed were in response to messages of other students. Less than 33% of the topics the students covered in their messages were direct responses to the instructor or class assignments. This would suggest that, once the assignments or the instructor's messages got things started, the students did, indeed, sustain interaction with each other. This can be supported by the final part of Figure 2 in which it is apparent that the instructor spent most of his time responding to students. Despite distance and/or scheduling conflicts, the students were able to participate in a series of interactions among themselves which were focused around the topics of their class.

One element of utilising an email system for class discussion is, of course, the fact that most students will be quite unfamiliar with the medium. This implies that support must be available to students to help them learn how to use the system. It also means that room must be made for student experimentation. Since expressing oneself via computer mail is different from other means of communication, the students must be given guidance and support while they explore the possibilities. The instructor can provide a great deal of help by modelling a variety of message types and by taking the time to send supportive, personal messages to each student, making each student feel a part of the class and encouraging experimentation.

A typical pattern of student participation is illustrated in Figure 3. The earliest messages in the public mailbox (1-10) average about six lines in length. The length of messages rapidly increase to an average length of over 26 lines (messages 60-70). This rapid increase is usually attributable to two factors. First, the students are getting used to the system and with familiarity comes greater length. Second, as with most classes, the content becomes richer as time passes, providing the students more avenues for exploration.

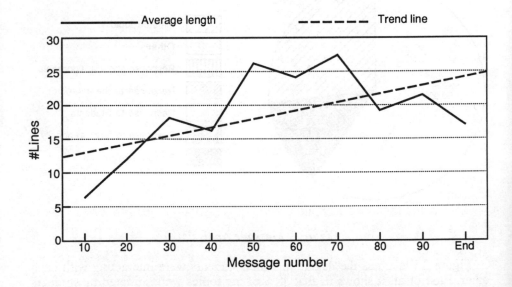

Figure 3 Average Length of Messages

The decrease in the length of messages toward the end of the class is fairly typical. It is explained by the need for the students to turn more of their attention to final class projects and by the many brief, farewell messages the students exchange at the end of a class. The other dips in a generally smooth progression of message length are explained by circumstances particular to this class. The first decrease in message length (messages 30-40) represent a new student just joining the class. She sent several introductory and exploratory messages that very much paralleled messages 1-10 for the students who started earlier. The second dip in message length (messages 50-60) represents a student who began to experiment with using his new computer and word processor to upload messages to the mail system. Because he was experimenting, the messages tended to be much shorter than usual.

Quality of Student Interaction

The fact that distance education students have the opportunity to interact with each other in a class is a positive step, but are these interactions of significant quality to warrant calling them a discussion of class content? This paper will not approach this issue with any direct evidence other than the perceptions of those who have utilised email for class discussion. Scollon and Scollon (1982, September), Quinn et al. (1983), Duranti (1986, April), and Janda (1987, October) have all reported positively on the quality of the interaction available to students through computer conferencing. The class used for this study also demonstrated a quality of interaction that was most satisfactory to the instructor.

Face-to-face discussion and email discussion seem to produce different kinds of student-to-student interaction. The interchanges between students on-line are not as immediate as would be found in discussion in a traditional class setting. However, computer-mediated discussion does provide a degree of depth and diversity that is usually not available in the traditional classroom. Computer-mediated discussions provide the participants with a wide range of topics to pursue at any given time while face-to-face discussions must be limited to one topic at a time. The instructor in the traditional classroom usually controls the student interaction a great deal, whether intentionally or unintentionally, initiating questions and evaluating student responses (Mehan, 1978). The instructor in a computer-mediated discussion certainly can influence the interaction of students, but can also step back and encourage more direct student-to-student interaction.

The instructor using computer-mediated discussion also has the luxury of having the entire discussion recorded. It is easy, therefore, to analyse student contributions for their quality and for any misconceptions a student may have about the course content. It is also easy for the instructor to address students privately to discuss issues of quality or to correct misconceptions. While the instructor's participation may lack the excitement of the give and take of face-to-face interchange, the ability to carefully observe student contributions without the need to control the discussion offers some distinct educational advantages.

The instructor can actually work much more closely with each individual student and provide more guidance and support to the students throughout the class.

Conclusion

There is no doubt that the use of email systems to carry out class discussions holds a number of advantages for the distance education student. The student no longer has to work in virtual isolation, having contact only with the instructor. The opportunity to exchange ideas, questions, interpretations of concepts, etc. with peers is a valuable part of the educational experience and can now be a part of the distance learner's experience. At the same time, the instructor can participate with the students in the interchanges, gaining valuable insight into the students' comprehension of the course content and provide further guidance, stimulation, or correction as needed. The distance education class becomes a much richer environment for the student as a result.The students can actually come to feel a part of a group learning effort. Perhaps that is the highest recommendation that can be made to distance education programs.

PAPER 11

APPLICATIONS OF CMC WITHIN COMMUNITY ORGANISATIONS

Peter Wingfield-Stratford
Wingfield-Polytek, Oxford, UK

No review of education in information technology should omit the huge contribution of the voluntary community organisations. This movement covers interests of a wide range of age-groups, from teenage to the mid-seventy year retired person. The settings for this are:
• the lively computer users' clubs
• the community organisations associated with employment creation and occupying unemployed, volunteers, retired, or handicapped people
• cooperatives.
Throughout this sector, members are constantly getting exposure and training in all aspects of information technology, from computer literacy to word processing, or networked services like email, or computer conferencing.

There are over a score of national clubs, and some hundreds of computer users' clubs in the UK. Most are affiliated to the Association of Computer Clubs. The clubs exist as self-help educational groups working to help members with any problem in use of micros and software, also associated equipment and network and database facilities. Clubs exist as offshoots to all kinds of organisations, from local government, commercial firms, unions, including many private local-interest members' groups. Members' interests may cover a wide range of different makes of machine, or a single brand. Most clubs depend upon members with experience of micros making available their practical rather than theoretical knowledge, by demonstrating actual machines and popular program software they own and use, or that may be available through a club or public-domain software library. Similarly they may show networks and host database systems to which they subscribe. These may be made available on the basis of free trial by other members, having proper respect for copyright and good professional and proprietary requirements.

Amongst other organisations in the voluntary sector that run training courses are the Community Computing Network and the Cooperative Movement.

To those who might decry these organisations as irrelevant to technology or to education, one notes there is already a strong track record. The computer club movement has been responsible for numerous technical innovations in communications and self-help. The Cooperative Movement has long been involved in worker's education. It is possible in self-help groups for the tutoring to be flexible in how things are done according to individuals needs, both by using live demonstrations and by the members with experience answering telephone enquiries. The larger clubs and voluntary groups publish journals full of useful instructional material contributed by members; also they run seminars of an evening, or several days at a residential venue. Members get access to a large software library and pooled support for older operating systems and software packages that have wide circulation, but that are now discontinued commercial products. Some clubs or their members operate databases and bulletin-board systems for members and are now accustomed to use these on-line services for publicising and resolving a wide variety of problems with information technology.

The voluntary movement has proven ability to find members of a calibre and responsibility to teach and manage. Voluntary workers train managers for Prestel and volunteers help manage the National Viewdata Host, one of the largest host database network systems in the world. Their efforts and innovations have raised community usership of Prestel to levels of readership in the top ten information providers nationwide while maintaining around 10,000 pages of information. Members also manage several hundred independent host information systems, including operation of FIDO, a global amateur automatic-forwarding low-cost electronic mail system.

Vocational Training through the Club Movement

The Association of Computer Clubs has discussed making a more formal commitment among clubs so that selected clubs might be recognised as a place of vocational training, even leading to some grade or credit to a formal qualification in some aspect of information technology. One idea was to establish a project under the programs of the European Communities, whereby clubs and voluntary groups might participate in vocational training in return for facilities needed to do this. This idea could make available some of the most experienced amateurs, having skills in applied information technology, for training work throughout the country. It also offers a way to bring experience of the latest technology and its use into formal education, where many people have little contact with such facilities or skills. This could be used to broaden education curricula, train or up-grade teachers and link out into adult education in a community setting.

Among the facilities the clubs and voluntary groups need is access to modern kinds of micros and to a library of software of the type widely used in commerce. Another vital facility would be access to venues for meeting which were convenient and equipped for information technology work. These are problems that are currently a major constraint to the education work of clubs in community locations.

It was suggested that participant clubs could be identified and a committee set up to work with a sponsor such as a distance-learning educational institution. They would define and obtain a curriculum for an informal course for vocational training and a structure of support for members. There is a precedent for this. The Radio Society of Great Britain is now in the midst of an anniversary year project, aimed to encourage young people of school-age in electronics hobbies and use of amateur radio. This project allows a wide variety of experiments, and direct education using both amateur and digital packet radio. Course materials are published through club journals and youth operators can run a bulletin board like a conference system, which becomes accessible to other users both amateur radio enthusiasts, school radio clubs and even outsiders. In practice computer clubs and other voluntary groups might use prepared tutor materials and face-to-face meetings to distribute the vocational course materials. The project could be administered via community networks using host information systems linked with the association. This could involve an existing structure serving clubs needs for a headquarter base and supporting software library and administration. Such voluntary structures have many precedents in Britain.

As the clubs have small money resources, they would expect special consideration of the value of their role putting in resources in kind, not cash. Sponsorship would need to cover the equipment and network facilities, and provide means for headquarter services and access to suitable venues for the clubs to use. At present suitable sponsors have not been identified, but individuals in the main clubs have expressed interest in participating.

Uses of Amateur Digital Packet Radio and Satellite Links

The technology linking amateur radio with computers is called digital packet radio. Text transfer is possible which transforms the medium and makes it feasible for direct support of school to school information exchanges. The Amateur Radio movement has mounted seminars at which packet radio has been mooted to help in distance learning. The use of the digital radio network for exchange in education is virtually nil-cost. For the developing countries, this medium may be the only economic way to improve distance learning, given the numbers of schools, teachers and potential pupils to be served. It may be most valuable in the role of teacher support in the developing countries.

Schools have used amateur radio for some years. A new development is the linking of countries by this means, with the collaboration of schools in the developing countries for their benefit. This is a form of technical aid, which has become very much a topic of concern for children and youth in general worldwide. Frensham Heights, a private sector school, has an enthusiastic amateur radio station, with several experienced radio amateurs helping the teacher/operator. They have made links with amateurs in many countries worldwide, using voice and morse-code. Several other schools have set up links with partner schools in developing countries. It is hoped that these links might be made more effective by better communications, such as packet radio, or even use of amateur bulletin boards connected to the telephone.

It is hoped to find local contacts in the countries that will lend or donate facilities, like computers, telephone costs, modems, radio sets etc. There are many problems to overcome, such as the restrictions of the countries to use of data communications, but it is known that the technology of the link itself can be made very effective with quite low-cost equipment at each end, even when power is uncertain. The technical equipment can be donated, or built from kits, or use made available from friendly residents who have it for some other reason.

Telehouses in Scandinavia – Voluntary Education at Village Level

In Scandinavia a novel concept has been created called the 'Telehouse'. This is a network of community-based facilities, each like an electronic village hall. There are Telehouses in Denmark, Sweden and Norway. They each have equipment like micros, printers and communications, and a person is delegated to be responsible called the 'telehouse-keeper'. The costs are disbursed by the community, with a bursary for part-time work by the telehouse-keeper. The keeper can add to his income by training and other small jobs; otherwise people use the facilities directly and pay for materials.

This telehouse concept has been very successful in rural areas, cut off by geographic factors, or the weather or season. Groups participating have co-operated across frontiers and many hundreds of kilometres. The network enables people to help others anywhere, so developing self-help in many professional capacities and in managing the community and its small business.

Telehouses could easily be included in programs of formal education, such as correspondence courses, or distance teaching. This would be useful with conferencing and could also extend scarce teaching resources and teacher-support. The concept could also be integrated with the vocational training program envisaged by the Computer Users' Clubs. This way many highly motivated teachers could be found and enabled to help train in the remotest country or island, irrespective of base.

Conclusions

Educators should listen to such experience, and work with the people in clubs and other community organisations. They offer very interesting ideas that can help formal education reach out into the community. The voluntary and informal sector has a resource of know-how with enormous flexibility and technical skill available to help education expand. It may be the best means to take information technology into the older groups of the population, ie those past school and university age. Secondly, the staff from formal education benefit from informal training through working with voluntary groups. Such contacts with skilled amateurs tap a scarce resource of teachers of information technologies. They raise the educators understanding, and up-date their own knowledge in tune with applications of computing and computing equipment with communications, now coming into wide use in the business, commercial and voluntary arena. This way formal education can better serve the holistic needs of the community in the information age.

REFLECTIONS ON CMC AS A MEDIUM FOR EDUCATION

PAPER 12

THE LIFE-WORLDS OF COMPUTER-MEDIATED DISTANCE EDUCATION

Gary Boyd
Concordia University, Montreal, Quebec, Canada

This brief paper on CMC in distance education attempts to incorporate perspectives from the works of Jurgen Habermas and Mary Douglas. Educational activity can and does occur on a number of levels at once; while one is learning to do sums one may be learning neatness, one may be learning how to learn, and one may even be learning who one is part of.

The relevance of Jurgen Habermas and Mary Douglas to computer mediated distance education (CMDE) lies at the higher levels of learning, or what could be called the 'hidden curriculum' aspects of distance education. 'Communicative discourse' as Habermas (1987) uses the term has to do with constituting the human 'Life-world', or to put it more simply: with defining the game and inventing the rules. However, the 'Life-world' games are the games which establish who we are, which establish both our individual and collective identities so that they function coherently.

Habermas emphasises undominative discourse designed to promote understanding, as the quintessential human characteristic. It enables us to understand who we have been, who we are becoming. It enables us to set up mutually agreed norms and rules, and it enables us to adjudicate their use fairly. This is true, but not for everybody.

Mary Douglas (1973) the anthropologist, following Basil Bernstein's lead, shows that many people in many cultures live largely in worlds of 'restricted code' speech. In other words they live in worlds which have not been created, and are not reproduced through 'rational discourse promoting understanding'. Habermas' construction is an ideal one which can appeal most strongly to academic and professional intellectuals; it is not a universal human property.

The importance of Habermas' ideal type of discourse is that it may be the only way to deal with the two main problems of our age, problems which are reflected in each everyday learning or teaching activity.

First Problem
The first problem and the one which most concerns Habermas, (also Adorno, Benjamin and Marcuse) is what he calls the colonisation of the Life-world by the steering media technical systems. More simply put, this is the intrusion of the bureaucratic requirements of the global money-power commercial-industrial system into the way we define and regulate our interpersonal performances and games. When the big system's laws say it can't be done, there is nobody to argue with.

Our Life-world making is what is most important to us – doing science, doing theatre, playing nourishing games. In order to support these activities we have created the global industrial-commercial-legal-bureaucratic complex. And now it is spoiling our games (eg literally, by paying ten million dollars to the winner of a footrace, making it a superhuman requirement to avoid the steroids temptation).

Discourse designed and protected so that its main thrust is the promotion of understanding of all our technical-commercial systems and of our personal plays and games, seems to be the only avenue available to recover from what I call 'lexitechonomic' systems hegemony.

Second Problem
The second central problem which strongly implicates education (especially here in Quebec) is the imperative for heretical modifications of our traditional cultures so that they can in future thrive symbiotically, rather than by attempting to proselytise or exterminate each other.

Mary Douglas's work is particularly relevant to this problem because her studies (of for example the 'bog Irish' in London) elucidate the precise nature of the failures of imagination and communication. These have to be overcome before we can re-create our traditional Life-worlds and live symbiotically, while retaining most of our traditional ethno-religious variety.

Practical Implications for CMC in Distance Education

Computer-mediated communications are unique in their options for flexible intimidation-free norm-respecting participation. This is because of their editability, censorability, vote collecting capabilities, and also because they can support pseudonymity and or anonymity (eg Stodolsky, 1988).

Consequently it should be possible to set up conferences with the functions of:
• defining the nature of curriculum and instructional plays and games
• specifying acceptable norms and rules
• adjudicating acts of illegitimate communication, and acts of illegitimate censorship.

As it were: a constitutional convention conference, a legislature conference, and a court conference.

Such institutions should enable our educational activities to be really democratic and really variety conserving.

Open to Whom?

The British Open University was set up by Labour to provide open access to post-secondary education for adults from all sectors of society, particularly those who had missed the opportunity of pursuing full-time higher education on leaving school. The main beneficiaries in the first decade, however, were teachers and other middle class people who were kept out of regular university by job commitments. This is quite understandable from the Mary Douglas/Basil Bernstein perspective. Marginal people tend to communicate spontaneously and in ways with the minimum of structure (eg the glossolalia of some of the charismatic or evangelistic churches). They also tend to use a lot of body language – kinesthetic communication. The media of the Open University are print, radio, and television (and now CMC). All are highly structured. The TV is one-way, so the acted out understandings of learners who depend on body language have no place. Such media do not readily accommodate the Life-worlds of a large proportion of the population. Moreover if such people do work through the Open University they are likely to become estranged from their native culture rather than being enabled to help its evolution.

The provision of 'cafe' spaces of the sort Levinson provides for his Connected Education courses is a step toward the accommodation of the dramatic and informal Life worlds of learners. When we are able to include up-loaded MIDI music, and digitised videoclips perhaps we will use this capability to really open out distance education to most people, not just the literate, and rhetorically skillful.

PAPER 13

COMPUTER-SUPPORTED COOPERATIVE LEARNING: INTERACTIVE GROUP TECHNOLOGIES AND DISTANCE LEARNING SYSTEMS

Dick Davies
CECOMM, Southampton Institute of Higher Education, UK

Cooperative Learning

There is now increasing evidence and argument for the view that effective learning should be both active and cooperative. The active component is developed both by workers in mainstream education (Beckwith, 1983) and by those in the commercial training field (Carroll, 1985) and the cooperative element by Bruner (1986) amongst others (see Davies, 1988 for details of proponents of the above).

Initially, this view of active, cooperative learning seems to pose problems for distance learning systems. The mediating technologies traditionally used to deliver open learning – text, broadcast linear video and audio – seem to offer only passive learning experiences.

Whilst it seems very probable that instructional designers could handle the active component of learning through innovative design methodologies with existing media, the cooperative component, which implies interaction, is a little more difficult to fix. One route is expensive and time sensitive. This is real-time interactive small-group technologies such as audio and video conferencing. In addition to being expensive and so unavailable to mainstream education at this time, their synchronicity is inappropriate to the needs of many distance learners. The alternatives are computer-based interactive group technologies. These technologies are the subject of this paper.

Communication and Coordination.

Computer-Supported Cooperative Work (CSCW) is a set of emerging concepts, practices and technologies that have been categorised by Wilson (1988) as containing two common strands: cooperative activity and computer-based support. Examples are message systems, Office Automation systems, Speech Act Theory-based products and Collaboration Research. Some of these CSCW technologies will have an impact on computer-supported group learning.

This section focuses on the current most widely used cooperative technology – computer-based message systems, in particular, computer conferencing. From our own experience at CECOMM [1] and from the reports of numerous workers (see Chang, 1987), it would seem that computer conferencing, where used for structured communication tasks such as problem solving is not wholly effective.

Chang argues that 'time coherence' is a critical factor in task focused conferences. He quotes Fisher (1974) in arguing that a minimum amount of social cohesiveness is necessary for the effective performance of a task. This cohesiveness is usually obtained through the regulation and coordination that occurs in the effective performance of a task. The unpredictable time occurring between message sending and response makes this cohesiveness difficult to achieve. This absence of time coherence among its users is a major flaw of the computer conferencing environment (p 317). He goes on to paraphrase Johansen and Vallee (1979) saying that "people take their old, unconscious rules for a meeting from their familiar cultural surroundings into a new medium." Therefore "electronic meetings such as computer conferences do not deal well with other aspects of group interaction such as the use of physical space, a shared understanding of time, social structures that can integrate divergent views and initiatives, nonverbal messages and the control of group interaction." The result, as pointed out in the introduction, is that the communication medium directly affects the coordination rules of the group. The inability of the medium to offer (or provide tools for offering) a key coordination element – time coherence – undermines cohesiveness and affects the group's ability to perform structured tasks. It is exactly these kinds of tasks that we are addressing in this paper.

Structuring Coordination and Communication In Group Learning

Communication in formal learning is mainly task-oriented and so is structured according to particular sets of coordination rules. CSCW would, *de facto*, seem to have at least some application here. However, it is the nature of the group communication structures in formal learning environments that need to be investigated before these technologies, mostly developed for the office environments, can be seen to be directly applicable.

It is worth standing back at this point to try to understand the nature of communication in groups. Communication is *a priori* social and is the basis of social interaction. It can be verbal, paraverbal and non-verbal. It always occurs in a context and of course can be mediated by a range of technologies. In the context of groups the term 'communication' itself can be unpacked to reveal two further main elements (Decker,1987): communication and coordination.

Communication refers here to the semantic content of information, the medium in which communication takes place and how information is distributed. Coordination refers to the degree of cooperation, how the group organises itself and how the dynamics of coherent cooperation are achieved. In real life interaction these two elements usually intertwine seamlessly.

We can now return to our original problem, that is the nature of group communication structures in formal learning environments, and add the concept of active, cooperative learning. The question now is: what computer support is needed to assist collaborative problem solving?

Computer-Supported Cooperative Learning

Earlier some of the inadequacies of CMCS were highlighted. However, the problem is more serious than simple technical limitation. Message systems are simply that – message passing technologies – whether configured for person-to-person or group communication. As a paradigm for group communication in all its richness it is inadequate. The functionality of current messaging systems does not mesh with the wide range of needs of communicating groups. "Humans do not work together via one system but use a variety of tools and media – letter, phone, face-to-face meetings, conferences, facsimile. So, too, will it be in the CSCW world." (Wilson, 1988).

In the last part of this paper, I feel it is worth exploring what kinds of functionality a computer-supported group communication technology should have. I have termed this area of exploration 'Computer-Supported Cooperative Learning' (CSCL) partly to acknowledge its genesis in CSCW, but also to establish its claim to distinct needs.

CSCL systems must aim to offer a degree of functionality that will support the components of communication and coordination outlined above in the context of the needs of learners in groups.This whole area of the learning needs of groups has been extensively researched (see Johnson and Johnson, 1985). This research however has not focussed on computer support.

Ford and Morriscoe (1987), in the context of the DELTA Project, argue that "learning is not confined to a single philosophy" and that each learning philosophy (discovery learning, simulation, gaming, drill and practice, tutoring) will require its own form of learner support. CSCL systems could be designed with a single approach in mind, but as good tutors use a variety of teaching strategies which may well be philosophically eclectic, it seems wise not to close design possibilities at this stage. A brief outline of the functional requirements of a general purpose CSCL system follows:

CSCL Communication:
- Semantic content: the content and context of information should be made available. This includes contextual information such as time, spatial position, relevance, completeness, etc.
- Medium: the medium should be able to integrate the communication needs of the group. This may mean that text, image and voice should be available.
- Distribution: information should be able to be broadcast, personalised, targeted. It can be directed to individuals, lists of individuals or groups. It can be private or public.

CSCL Coordination:
- Degree of cooperation: from close knit project group or team game to irregular semi-formal discussions.
- Organisation: if cooperation is assumed how is it organised – through groups, all of whose members have the same role and work on the same material, or through teams in which the participants' roles differ?

- Dynamics of coherence: cooperating groups are dynamic and can reorganise themselves into a number of forms. Any system must be capable of either adapting or being reconfigured to these new forms.

Whilst the above speculative specification may appear to point to a constraining technology this is not intended; rather I would agree with Wilson (1988). The question is: what minimum degree of organisation can you get away with to achieve results? To underline this in terms of the construction of any CSCL system I would in general agree with the approaches to the use of interactive technologies advocated by Flores and Winograd (1986) and Suchman (1987). In both cases and from different perspectives they argue that "actions are always situated in context" and that "plans are resources for action." From this it follows that the role of interactive technologies is to support action – in this case, action from learners rather than the prepackaged pedagogies of CAL.

Conclusion

This paper is an attempt to set down markers towards the development of a framework for interactive group technologies. If education is to be in a position to handle the emergent interactive group technologies in any coherent way, then it needs to be able to analyse the communication structures of existing distance learning systems and so be in a position to proactively assess these technologies. The alternative, as in the past, is to allow education to be driven by the technology and imported applications.

Notes

[1] See for example Paper 2 by Gray. (ed)

PAPER 14

THE INSTITUTIONAL CONTEXT
FOR COMPUTER CONFERENCING

Barbara Florini and Daniel Vertrees
Syracuse University, New York, USA

Computer conferencing is one of the more promising communications technologies available for use in higher education. Unfortunately, the promise of computer conferencing may not be realised in many institutions that might benefit from its use. As both Bates (1985) and Bacsich (1985) have indicated, organisational or institutional problems can hinder the introduction of new technologies. The introduction of computer conferencing is no different; it too requires attention to the institutional context.

Too often when attempts are made to introduce and maintain a new technology in an institution, insufficient attention is paid to critical contextual variables like institutional politics, comprehensive costs, and the need for new alliances. These variables are often inextricably mixed in various combinations, but are highlighted separately in this paper for purposes of discussion. The paper concludes by suggesting that a visionary project manager can facilitate the introduction of computer conferencing into an institution and help ensure its adoption by people there. The particular context addressed in this paper is that of a post-secondary institution offering a mix of on-campus, extended campus, and distance learning opportunities, but much of the discussion is relevant for other types of institutions.

Institutional Politics

Institutions and their respective sub-units have missions to accomplish. To gain their support, the key decision makers at various institutional levels need to see proposed new programs or media as supporting their individual missions. In the case of media especially, difficulties can arise because decision-makers frequently lack understanding of the newer technologies. This is neither surprising nor insurmountable. With technology evolving so rapidly that people in related fields have trouble keeping up, administrators cannot be expected to have any special awareness of the field. But they can be educated, particularly when the potential of a technology like computer conferencing is presented in relation to the overall institutional mission and that of selected sub-units. A demonstrated relationship between mission and use of the proposed medium is more likely to win support for the necessary budgetary and other requirements of the technology.

A second potential political problem can arise in those instances where the activities or responsibilities of different sub-units of the university overlap. One unit can easily construe the introduction of new media as an attempt by another component to invade its domain. Maybe in some cases that is exactly true. More likely, the people introducing the new technology are so caught up in their enthusiasm for it and in learning to work with it that they have given no thought to how others might perceive the situation. Because of its potential for use in distance education, the introduction of computer conferencing is especially likely to draw the attention of any unit involved in that practice. Attending to such intra-institutional concerns by keeping appropriate units abreast of plans, providing them with demonstrations, and assisting them in becoming familiar with conferencing can reduce enmity and win additional supporters for the technology.

Faculty form a third group who need attention when new media are introduced, whether intended for use by the academic community at large or by a segment of it. For one thing, faculty in higher education are notoriously hostile to media, especially that proposed for instructional use. Disappointed over many decades by failed promises of media that would revolutionise education, faculty have developed a sturdy skepticism toward all such promises. Some faculty also feel threatened by the advent of some of the newer communications technologies: "Can they replace me? What will happen to *my* course? Must I substantially alter my teaching style?" Failure to address faculty concerns immediately places a powerful group in opposition to the new medium. Involving representatives of the faculty most likely to be affected by the new technology in the decision-making process can minimise opposition.

Student rumour mills generate information, and too often misinformation, faster than the speed of light. When word begins circulating that a new technology will be used for instructional purposes, both unrealistic expectations and anxieties are often fueled by mere unfounded rumour. Like faculty, students have legitimate concerns as to possible alterations in the way academic programs are offered. Students also reasonably might wonder about what new skills they may have to learn due to the introduction of the technology. Certainly, many students will wonder about access to the technology itself. In the case of computer conferencing, for instance, will only students having personal computers and modems be able to participate in some course offerings?

Costs

Technology costs money, time, and resources. Beyond the initial purchase price, technology has installation, maintenance, and support costs. Highly skilled computer staff are needed to install software on the institution's computer. Their skills are also required to maintain the software and to upgrade it as the vendor issues updates. Whose budget should be tapped for these services – the computing unit's, the department needing the services, or some other? The answers will undoubtedly vary from one institution to another, but the question needs to be raised in discussions about buying the software. Installation and maintenance costs are just some of those associated with computer conferencing. Training is another.

Even with fairly easy-to-use software, people need various kinds of training in order to use it efficiently and effectively. In the case of computer conferencing, both faculty and students usually require assistance in learning certain features of the operating system of the computer housing the conferencing software so they can sign on and off, change passwords, and upload and download files. Faculty and students will also need an introduction to the conferencing program. Materials will probably have to be developed, produced, and made available on an on-going basis in order to facilitate the training. Against whose budget should all these training-related costs be charged? A well-conceived policy can help ensure that this and other cost questions are addressed rationally and fairly.

New Alliances: Support

Vital as the matter of cost is, it is not the only important variable to consider when introducing a new technology. Use of most of today's communication technology requires new alliances that go beyond cost-sharing. In the case of computer conferencing, one requisite alliance is with the institutional unit responsible for the campus computing services. The interest and willing cooperation of the computing services administration and staff is crucial in facilitating the smooth introduction and initial use of the conferencing software as well as in using it over a period of time. People in that agency are the ones who will install and maintain the original program as well as any software upgrades. They or people in affiliated offices also have the responsibility for assigning computer accounts and passwords to users and to allocating storage space on the computer. A good working relationship between representatives of the computing centre and those managing the conferencing program can ensure that mutually satisfactory decisions are implemented and reasonable priorities given to requests for service. Computing personnel also stand to benefit from such an alliance. The new approaches and demands made by users of their services will provide the computing staff with opportunities to explore their technology in new ways and to find practical and useful answers to significant questions.

A good working relationship with the vendor of the technology is a second important alliance. Vendors are coming to realise that reputations are built by supporting those who buy their sophisticated products. Because computer conferencing programs are complex pieces of software, each new installation may well raise different problems or questions. Good will on both sides keeps communication channels open and provides quick access to people having answers to critical questions. Vendors also benefit by gathering useful information that can lead directly to product improvement.

New Alliances: Interdisciplinary

One way to help institutionalise the adoption of a new technology is to broaden the base of its users, a far from insurmountable task. A time of change provides an opportunity to forge alliances with different academic disciplines as well as with the world outside. Education, business, and the professions can be working side by side to develop programs to be offered through the conferencing system. Increased understanding and shared expertise among disciplines will be fostered through such close proximity. Issues important to all with similar interests in the education of students and in the continuing education of members of their respective communities will be evident. Common efforts to address these issues should be mutually beneficial.

For example, the social and psychological concerns surrounding the introduction and utilisation of a recent technology like computer conferencing can shed new insights into human behaviour, social interaction, and the impact of technological change on individuals, groups, and institutions. Social scientists allied with conferencing efforts can both benefit from and contribute to the generation of new knowledge resulting from use of the technology. Similarly, hardware and software engineers can help meet needs by new designs that are responsive to users' concerns. New technology also raises new legal questions. Law school professors and students can collaborate on the legal ramifications that surround the new access and new freedoms that manifest themselves with computer communications.

Other previously unexplored relations may also prove fruitful. For those accustomed to preparing their own courses, one attractive alliance worth forming is with instructional developers or designers. Like all media, conferencing functions best as a means of delivering instruction when lessons are designed in keeping with the particular characteristics of the medium. Instructional developers are accustomed to identifying media characteristics and designing efficient and effective instruction that makes best use of the characteristics. Some of the lessons they have learned in working with other media can be applied to help avoid common mistakes in the use of a new technology.

The permutations are endless for the involvement of different disciplines in the use of computer conferencing. As each group joins the conferencing activity, each brings its own agenda and point of view. Those varied points of view can help all of us develop new visions and forge productive, collaborative efforts.

The Role of a Project Manager

The introduction of a major technology like computer conferencing has many institutional ramifications. In the short space of this paper, it was only possible to highlight several important variables and to suggest how they might be addressed. Clearly, if the implementation is to be successful, the adoption of the technology assured, and the promise of computer conferencing realised to the greatest extent, myriad factors call for attention. We strongly believe that a project manager has to oversee the process. Who should this person be? What attributes are important? Because of the tasks involved, good management skills are preferable to technical expertise. Well-developed interpersonal skills are important, too, especially due to the need to cross disciplinary boundaries. The person chosen as project manager should also be placed high enough in the institutional hierarchy to ensure ready access to key decision makers. Finally, the manager should be a person of vision, imagination, and industry – one who can see the possibilities inherent in computer conferencing and help realise them.

PAPER 15

SOME CMC DISCOURSE PROPERTIES AND THEIR EDUCATIONAL SIGNIFICANCE

David Graddol
Open University, Milton Keynes, UK

Users of computer conferencing systems often claim that although the medium involves written language it possesses a number of features which are more like speech. Many computer conferences are much like conversations; that is, they are informal turn taking activities. The cause of such informality, which seems to be a tendency on all CoSy conferences, is not clear. Does it relate, for instance, to properties of the software (which encourages certain behaviours and inhibits others) or to the psychology of interpersonal communication? It is also unclear whether the tendency is to be regarded as a weakness of computer-mediated communication or a strength. Usually, it is regarded as a problem, and the informal discourse which results is dismissively referred to as 'chat', 'unstructured', or 'off-topic'. Such conferences are imagined to provide a poor context for students' learning; contributions are said to lack substance, to provide an obstacle to students through their bulk and lack of relevance, and so on. This paper presents an opposing view: that informal talk is highly structured and represents a valuable context for learning, and that a close examination of the discourse structure on some conferences on the Open University's CoSy conferencing system reveals certain properties which are not found in either written or spoken language, but which have special implications for the participation of students who may be marginalised in conventional educational settings.

The Structure of Teacher-Mediated Discourse

Traditional classroom discourse is controlled by a teacher with whom the students are in an unequal power relation. This relationship is often supported by the physical arrangement of the class; by various nonverbal asymmetries (the teacher may be standing and free to move whereas the class may be seated and confined); by the teacher's role in evaluating and grading students' written work; in the teacher's ability to resort to institutional sanctions and penalties in order to control behaviour. One gross effect of this power asymmetry is that a teacher in class usually talks far more than all the students put together. Flanders, in a well known study of USA schools, proposed the 'two thirds rule' which suggests that two thirds of classroom talk is by the teacher, and only one third pupil talk. This figure has proved a conservative estimate, but such inequality in talk is found in educational settings in all age groups, including adult classes. This inequality in talk derives from specific features of discourse structure. The teacher, for example, has privileged speaking rights and controls the turns of other speakers. That is, rather like a chair in a formal meeting, the teacher has responsibility for selecting the next person who will speak and this ensures that the teacher will take a turn after each other speaker – twice as many turns as all other participants together. The teacher's role in evaluating or giving feedback on each student turn gives rise to a turn structure peculiar to classrooms, sometimes called 'initiation, response, follow-up (Sinclair and Coulthard, 1975). The IRF pattern allows the teacher to control the flow of the topic by rejecting turns until a suitable one is found.

Such institutionalised power relations are not just reflected in talk, they are also in part established through talk. The IRF pattern, for example, is a powerful way in which a teacher can establish a claim to rights over controlling the discourse and determining what is to be regarded as legitimate knowledge. However, we can note that the mechanism depends on every other turn being taken by the teacher who must be able to respond to a student contribution before any further contribution is made. Such teacher-mediated discourse is often an inefficient environment for learning: students have very little opportunity to talk themselves; most questions are asked by the teacher, rather than the learner; learners are given no opportunity to define and articulate their own needs and problems; and so on. The learner has little control over either the curriculum or the mode and pace of learning.

Characteristics of Informal Talk

Since the early 1960s a great emphasis has been placed by educators in Britain and many other countries on the role of informal talk between pupils. Pupils could only learn, it was argued, if they were able to talk freely. The rationale was twofold: first, the act of planning and uttering was regarded as psychologically beneficial to thinking and problem solving. Second, it allowed the joint negotiation of knowledge, and co-operative learning. Even talk which appears to be off the topic may provide a vital forum for adventitious learning (see Phillips, 1987). "It is as talkers, questioners, arguers, gossips, chatterboxes, that our pupils do much of their important learning" claimed one of the leading exponents of this approach (Harold Rosen in Barnes *et al.*, 1971).

The primary curriculum has long been structured according to this student centred view of learning-through-language, with extensive use of small group work, especially in the science curriculum (see Barnes and Todd, 1977) and it is fast becoming an orthodoxy amongst teachers of older pupils and adults. It forms, for example, a principle method of face-to-face teaching at Open University Summer Schools, at both foundation and post-graduate level.

Although conversation and chat is often regarded as unstructured and chaotic, conversation analysts have documented the orderliness that informal multi-party discourse displays, and how such order is maintained by the participants. Participants do have to work to maintain such order. For example, in order to ensure a smooth change of speaker, the person finishing a turn gives out signals which allow the new speaker to synchronise their entry. Each new turn must be topically tied, usually to the immediately forgoing turn, so that the conversation maintains a coherent thread. There are many examples of the way in which the meaning or function of a statement depends crucially on how it is placed in relation to other turns. As a simple example, 'Hello' means something different if said at the beginning of a telephone conversation rather than in the middle. Informal talk can, in this way, be shown to be a highly structured activity, in which the format and ordering of turns is conventional and understood by all participants. The coherence of a conversation relies on the way each turn is closely bound to the foregoing turn in various ways (see Graddol *et al.*, 1987, for a fuller discussion of turn exchange mechanisms and discourse structure).

The dynamics of face-to-face talk allow for many inequalities, however. The turn-taking mechanism is such that successful participation in conversation is often a competitive business requiring speed and confidence: a maxim of 'first in gets the floor' seems to operate; one person can interrupt another and prevent them from taking or completing a turn. The need for contributions to be topically tied to the current topic means that those who cannot or do not wish to participate in that topic have limited powers to change the topic to another. There is, instead, a continuous thread in which current participants have more control than those listening and a current speaker has first rights to select the next speaker.

In summary, research shows that both talk mediated by a teacher and informal peer group talk is highly structured, but that both suffer from inequalities which may have educational significance. For example, boys and men routinely get to say much more than girls or women; within each gender group there will also be great differences in the participation rates of individual learners (see, for example, Swann and Graddol, 1988).

CoSy Discourse

Such research raises several interesting questions with regard to how computer-mediated communication can best be used to provide a context for student learning. What kind of 'work' has to be done by participants in a CoSy discourse and how is this different from face-to-face? CMC still requires a certain burden of social maintenance, both in terms of metalinguistic comments that organise the flow of the discourse and in terms of maintaining a sense of community and belonging amongst participants. Much of this is done through nonverbal communication (NVC) in ordinary talk and the lack of NVC on computer conferencing has both advantages and disadvantages. Some of the 'idle gossip' which characterised the conferences analysed for this paper probably serves purposes which would otherwise be handled by NVC. For example, the gender of a speaker is normally apparent in face to face interaction, and participants' gender identities may be continuously apparent through the different styles of speech used by women and men (see Graddol and Swann, forthcoming, for a review of such differences); in CoSy discourse participants' gender is not immediately apparent from their usernames. Nevertheless, some women have complained that men often indicate their gender through what they say, with phrases such as 'now, lads' and so on. However, the lack of NVC may make it difficult to maintain and negotiate power differentials, since the usual technology of accent, dress, location of speaker and so on, is missing.

However, it is in terms of the discourse structure and the dynamics of turn-taking and topic development that interaction on CoSy differs most from other media. Below are listed a number of such observed differences.

Turn-Taking
Turn taking on CoSy does not require skills or special management in the same way as in face to face interaction. There is no such thing as an interruption and there is no way in which one participant can prevent another from taking a turn (other than by a moderator 'withdrawing' a contribution after it has been made).

The maxim of 'first in gets the floor' which operates in both teacher-mediated discourse and informal conversation does not apply on CoSy. In an ordinary conversation, the first person to respond also determines the topic flow of the discourse, and the requirement for coherence between adjacent contributions means that it soon becomes too late to say something different. Not so on CoSy, where the complaint 'someone beat me to it' means someone else said what I wanted to say and deprived me of the credit.

On CoSy, unlike conversation, the current speaker has no special rights to select the next speaker. A clique of participants cannot bounce the conversation between themselves and, in principle, any person can always contribute next. One person may take several turns in sequence, taking up points made by a variety of earlier contributors or dealing with both the assertions and the assumptions made by an earlier contributor. In face-to-face discourse, such multiple turns are usually a feature only of very formal situations, where a contributor has been called upon to speak and given special local speaking rights.

Topic Development
In ordinary discourse if a question is not answered or a topic not taken up in the very next turn, then it is unlikely ever to be so. The close bound nature of 'chat' means that a convention of 'relevance' must be satisfied in the very next turn. Not so in CoSy where a contribution can be commented upon days later.

Cohesion between adjacent contributions is broken down in favour of a more complex cohesion pattern that extends over a longer discourse domain. This cohesion is supported by the 'comment' function within CoSy which marks a contribution as tied to a particular earlier one, but many of the shorter, apparently vacuous messages may also serve to maintain this pattern of cohesion.

Because of the irregular pattern of logging on, later arrivals will scan all subsequent contributions in one go and will take up for further comment those that seem of interest and substance rather than whichever happened to be last. Where mean time between log-ons is small, one can expect that adjacent entries will be more closely tied, topic development will be less dispersed, entries will begin to feel out of date faster (the discourse has 'moved on') and fewer topics will be handled simultaneously. Hence the stochastic behaviour of students logging on to the system is likely to have far reaching effects on the discourse structure.

The lack of the requirement for close tying with the forgoing turn means that CoSy is able to handle simultaneous topic flows. The ability to take multiple turns means that each participant can engage with as many of these topics as desired. Participants cannot be disenfranchised by a particular topic dominating.

Some Educational Implications

Formulating contributions in text, off line, may be a better aid to learning even than talk. The conversational nature of CoSy also discourages too great a polish from contributors which would lead to more of a set piece debate and thereby lose the interactional and 'joint negotiation' of learning that CoSy engenders.

Such learning is often adventitious and divergent, so many apparent digressions from a set topic can be expected. However, such digressions are not nearly so injurious to a CoSy conference as they would be in a formal classroom. The loose bound cohesion of CMC not only encourages divergent talk but also supports it. Hence one can argue that CoSy is uniquely equipped to provide a context for adventitious learning.

Support of Minority Topics
The ability of CoSy discourse to maintain several topics simultaneously means that minority interests can be represented within the mainstream community. For example, women and disabled students have been able to draw out specific implications of contributions without appearing to divert the flow of the discourse. Women have also been able to make metalinguistic comments, pointing out for example, the sexist assumptions or language used by a contributor. Such comment would appear hostile and damaging in a discourse where strong ties existed between adjacent contributions and where a contributor could only take one turn before yielding the floor to another speaker.

Support of Late Arrivals and Lurkers
All discourse, to be successful, requires certain assumptions to be made about shared knowledge. The start of many conferences shows participants negotiating a shared or usable social reality. The flow of discourse also needs participants to be able to build on and tie to earlier contributions. A late-comer to a face to face interaction, whether a classroom or a chat, is in an unprivileged position compared with existing members and this may create a power inequality which can take a long time to repair. This inequality manifests itself in the restricted ability of the newcomer to contribute, or in the ability of existing members to give put downs such as "yeah, we've been through all that weeks ago."

Most conferences contain a very large number of lurkers. A lurker may only log on occasionally to a particular conference, nevertheless such a person is able to scan through the history of the discourse and contribute as a fully experienced participant who knows all the protagonists and their histories, and is a full party to shared knowledge.

Discourse Genres on CoSy
I have assumed that there exists a single style of computer discourse but this, not surprisingly, is a simplification. Already we can see several 'genres' developing within CoSy. Users are typically not familiar with the subtleties of such genres; CMC represents a new cultural context for which they need to develop a new communicative competence. In this respect the architectural metaphors used to describe the areas on CoSy may not help. Traditional registers of talk do not always map on to those found in CoSy, and the metaphors of 'common room' or 'tutorial' suggest too much of a continuity between familiar discourse styles and CMC. An ordinary speaker who knows how and when to be 'formal' or 'informal', encouraging or hostile, and so on, in speech does not necessarily know how and when to do these things appropriately in CoSy. Both the dynamics and structure of CoSy discourse differ from those found in more familiar kinds of written or oral interaction.

PAPER 16

THE HUMAN INTERFACE:
HIDDEN ISSUES IN CMC AFFECTING USE IN SCHOOLS

Bridget Somekh
University of East Anglia, UK

The experience so far gained of CMC, at least in Britain, suggests that one of the main problems lies in getting people to use it. This paper is about that part of CMC which constitutes the relationship of people to the machine. The term 'human interface' is used as a metaphor for that relationship, a metaphor which suggests a techno-human hybrid, because that is how many people *feel* about CMC. The paper reflects on this human interface as I have observed it, drawing on my research with the UK/USA Communications Project during 1986-87 and my continuing experience of using CMC in the course of my work (for a full account of the former see Somekh and Groundwater-Smith, 1988, and National Union of Teachers, 1988). The purpose of the paper is to open up discussion about how people approach CMC in order to capitalise more fully on the opportunities it provides for human communication.

The key factor in establishing an individual as a user of CMC seems to be the social context which surrounds its use. The social context is considered here under two headings: (i) the individual and (ii) the institutional, with particular emphasis in the case of the latter, on British schools.

CMC and the Individual

CMC is a tool for people to use. Just like the telephone, CMC can bring people closer together. Yet, the majority don't see it like that before they use it. For many, using a computer itself does not fit their self-image; for others who are computer users the notion of communicating via a computer seems to be perverse, since communication is about human relationships in which they can see no place for a machine.

Much of human behaviour is ritualistic. We sleep on the same side of the bed, dry our bodies bit by bit in the same order after taking a bath or shower... Rituals simplify life so that departing from them takes thought and reduces time for other things. More fundamentally, though, these rituals are closely bound to our personal self-image; they symbolise the way we present ourselves to ourselves and the world. It is not just convenient to have our desk arranged in a particular way, it also indicates our acceptance or rejection of order, and some under-currents of attitude to our work. Those few people who refuse to own cars or television sets are making proud statements about themselves and their attitude to life. So too are those who reject the very notion of using CMC. It would cut across the familiar rituals of their daily life on two counts: first it would be more time consuming (yes, it would at first) and less familiar than the telephone or letters; secondly it would cut across their self-image as non-technology people – they would not feel good about using it. What becomes crucial is that their concept of themselves as non-technology people prevents them trying out CMC; whereas only through use can they establish new rituals which make CMC integral to the social context (as has happened with radio and television).

For some whose self-image is strongly non-technological the barrier can be broken down. If the terminal literally becomes 'part of the furniture' on someone's desk it loses its cold technological aura. Then, going on-line is endowed with feelings much like those we experience when lifting mail from door mat or pigeon hole. Once over the initial barrier, with the system beginning to feel familiar, it is possible for individuals to reach a decision about the usefulness or otherwise of CMC. Until that time any rational decision may be impossible.

There is some confirmation of the importance of this human interface in acting as a barrier to use of CMC in the difference between the ways in which email and fax have been adopted. It seems that, almost accidentally, different patterns of use make fax fit more easily than email into existing behaviour rituals. A fax machine is often dealt with by a specialist operator, and becomes a magic device for transporting pieces of paper produced in the normal way. Email and computer conferencing by contrast are not normally filtered through operators – they demand an intimate 'hands on' relationship with the machine so that side-stepping the human interface is not possible.

In order to establish the use of CMC we need, therefore, to provide access to on-line facilities on every desk to create an environment in which individuals can adapt the machine easily to their own self-image and personal rituals. This goes further than the usual notion of 'user friendliness' and involves looking at the machine in the context of the whole personal work space. Far from reaching this ideal, CMC as it now operates in Britain, almost perversely caters to the prejudices of the non-technology self-image. We still have to key in a twenty digit series of code in order to use JANET internationally; and we generally use systems which are command rather than menu driven, in small print, without colour, and without the support of a good on-line HELP service.

CMC in the Context of British Schools

When introducing CMC to a school, there is a further series of institutional assumptions and expectations which strongly affect its use.

The Siting of CMC Equipment
Apart from the obvious and important consideration of ease of access, there seem to be two main factors about CMC which strongly affect the siting of equipment: the link with the telephone and the high prestige value of computer hardware.

Telephones are strongly linked to emotions in British schools. They tend to be in short supply, and access to a telephone is a status symbol for teachers, as well as considerably easing their administrative tasks. Telephone bills are relatively high and difficult to justify as value for money: so, telephones represent one of the items of expenditure which it is felt can and must be controlled. Siting a telephone line in a classroom, and/or giving students access to it, is, therefore, contrary to accepted institutional norms. Computer hardware is expensive and has high prestige value in terms of the school's public relations with parents, local industry and the community. In this context, security considerations and the perceived opportunities to enhance prestige can play a large part in deciding where to site CMC equipment.

Issues of Autonomy and Control
The need for teachers to establish control over their students is embedded in the culture of British schools, particularly in the secondary age range. This, together with attitudes to the use of telephones, may account for the assumption made by many teachers that they should retain responsibility for the use of CMC – by spooling their students' word-processed files, transmitting them to other schools and downloading in-coming files. This results in a considerable extra work load for teachers which can only be handled out of school hours. In consequence, it results in major blocks in the chain of communications and loss of the vital spontaneity offered by CMC. It seems that initially teachers want to use CMC in privacy after school, so that they do not risk loss of authority and control by exposing their lack of expertise in front of students. However, a significant factor may be the ritualistic quality of their pattern of control. Once having done the 'work' by writing the word processed files, the students 'give it in' and the teachers have the responsibility of sending it off as part of the usual 'marking' procedures. Thus new technology is simply being fitted into existing rituals of behaviour in which the teachers habitually assume a controlling role through the setting and marking of work.

Assumptions about the Nature of Email Communications
Email can be used in two different ways:
• for short on-line messages
• for the exchange of lengthier word processed pieces.
These two types of use have considerable bearing on the nature of the communications and, although there are variations of the first pattern with software capable of downloading mail and transmitting mail in batches, these two types of communication remain quite distinct from each other. Short on-line messages tend to be written without formal patterns of addressing or signing off, without careful attention to spelling or punctuation and with an immediacy and informality half way between a memo and a phone conversation. Whereas, word-processed pieces are no different from any other form of writing and adopt style and form appropriate to their purpose and audience in the normal way.

Within schools the assumption tends to be made that communications will always be of word processed files. Partly, this is because of the nexus of control and cost implications outlined above, but another significant factor may be institutional attitudes to students' work.

Writing is the main constituent of a student's classroom activity in Britain. Despite the importance of reading, listening and talking there is overwhelming evidence (see for example Bullock, 1975) that students spend an inordinate proportion of their time on writing. There is an assumption that a carefully constructed piece of prose is of more 'worth' for assessment purposes than a memo, a jotting, or a short message. Consequently, teachers can see a piece of word processed writing sent electronically as purposeful and therefore part of the curriculum. They may feel much more uncomfortable about letting a student loose to write brief notes and 'chat' on-line.

Communicating within the Curriculum – Issues of Classroom Interaction
In using email to communicate between classrooms a strong influence seems to be the nature of internal classroom interactions. Despite many ideas for joint projects, the most successful communications are often pen pal letters, 'relay stories' (in which one group begins a story, the next continues it and so on), and communications with an 'outside adult', perhaps taking a mystery role of some kind. In each of these examples there is little in-built conflict of purpose. Writing pen pal letters leaves students at both ends entirely free to write as they wish. The task becomes one of interesting the unknown partner (which is not an easy one, but the parameters of pen pal letters are familiar and students know exactly what is expected). Similarly, continuing the writing of a story begun by someone else is relatively straight forward – there may be problems of unmatched interest, but with sufficient ingenuity even an entirely unpalatable plot and characters can be subverted to a new purpose. Similarly, too, one outside adult is likely to be very responsive to students' interests.

Other tasks prove much more problematic. The stated curricula of different schools do not match, making it hard to carry out joint work on the same curriculum content. Even at the simplest level a recurring problem is delay or straight failure to reply. I have written elsewhere (*op cit*) of my realisation that classrooms are not structured around the notion of communicating interactively with others. They are closed boxes from which information can be published or into which information can be drawn, but they are not able to interact spontaneously with other closed boxes. CMC between two classrooms is a complex business – in effect team teaching at a distance – and requires extensive and detailed planning between the teachers concerned.

I should like here to elaborate on this a little. Within a typical classroom the teacher will nominally control the curriculum and activities by selecting the topics for study, planning the activities, giving out the books and resources, setting the tasks and assessing the work done. However, in reality a great deal of negotiation goes on between the teacher and students as to the level of noise, the time spent on task, and even the nature of classroom tasks and activities. The work of Doyle (1979) and others has shown that students engage in an 'exchange of grades for compliance' in which they negotiate the level of difficulty of each task. Within this context, only the most careful planning of collaborative CMC can involve the students in both classes so that there is a real commonality of priorities for the teachers concerned. Even quite careful planning is likely to fall by the wayside if an uninvolved class doesn't like the look of the communications when they arrive. No teacher can put a responsibility to other students and another teacher in a remote classroom before the interests of those for whom s/he has a specific responsibility. It will never be worth risking violation to the fragile balance of the negotiated curriculum.

Collaborating at a Distance – the Human End of the Human Interface
In the end, even when individuals and schools come to terms with CMC and use it successfully, there remains a remoteness which makes collaboration difficult. If there is a shared purpose, as with colleagues working for the same company or on the same research project, or between a student working at a distance and his/her tutor, CMC will be an excellent addition to other available means of communication. Conversely, when there is no shared purpose at all there may be a sense of adventure in ranging across the mailboxes and making unexpected friends – lets see who's out there to 'chat' to (a kind of 'ham radio' phenomenon). For those like teachers and their students whose purposes are neither urgent nor serendipitous there is the very human problem of depending heavily on other people. On reflecting why it is that I have sometimes been so badly let down by others over CMC links between schools, I realise that it is not an uncommon experience except in that the consequences have been more serious because my reliance has been greater than normal! It is human to promise, with good intentions, to do something and sometimes to fail. With the colleagues we work with from day to day we know them well enough to gauge their dependability and will pick up the job for ourselves when we judge it will not be done after all in any other way. At a distance we do not have the same personal knowledge of colleagues and cannot gauge when our priority is slipping beneath the weight of another's work load. It has nothing to do with technology, only a human failing masquerading as part of the human interface.

Conclusion

Establishing the use of CMC is a complex process involving changes to the personal and social context of daily life. For many there is a barrier to the use of CMC in their self-image as non-technology people. Within schools, there are further institutional assumptions and rituals of behaviour which create an extra layer of complexity. Following the government initiatives which have introduced CMC equipment into British schools there are considerable opportunities to enhance learning, and it is hoped that this paper may give some insights which will enable teachers to overcome problems and capitalise on these opportunities.

PAPER 17

COMPUTER CONFERENCING AND ELECTRONIC PUBLISHING: COOPERATION OR COMPETITION

Paul Bacsich
Open University, Milton Keynes, UK

Some people use the term 'electronic publishing' to mean any method of using digital computing technology to disseminate information, and in that wide sense, computer conferencing becomes a mere part of electronic publishing. I shall use the term in the narrower sense of using digital computing technology to assist the creation of paper documents. Desk Top Publishing (often called DTP) is one type of electronic publishing; there are others.

An immediate contrast between electronic publishing and computer conferencing can be made by plotting their applications areas on a quality/timeliness diagram. See Figure 1.

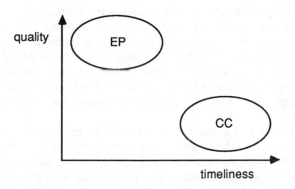

Figure 1 Electronic Publishing and Computer Conferencing

These juxtapositions are based on the current levels of the technologies. But both are changing. A major trend in electronic publishing is the move to the production of shorter and shorter print runs, as the large mechanical printing presses of the past are replaced by high-speed xerographic copiers and laser printers. Indeed, this is leading to the end-goal of the 'on-demand' book, each copy different from the next (like a Readers Digest letter). Another trend, though only just starting, is the replacement of the book by some other form of package, such as a CD-ROM optical disc.

Of course, there are other axes of classification, in particular that of interactivity. Electronic publishing, like all conventional publishing is essentially one-way, whereas computer conferencing is naturally two-way. Some of the other differences are shown below in Table 1. You can add others.

Table 1   Major Differences between EP and CMC

	Electronic Publishing	Computer Conferencing
Document quality	Can be high	Low
Timeliness	Weeks or days	Minutes
Interactivity	None	High
Specificity	Audience can be large groups	Usually small
Authority	Expertise at centre distributed	Expertise may be
Purchase method	Buy a product	Rent a service

Computer conferencing is also changing. The average speed of data communication is rising each year, as faster and cheaper modems come on to the market. Already, 9600 bits per second modems are available for under $1500. In the next few years, the Integrated Service Digital Network will bring the reality of 64000 bits per second communication to home-based users in much of the developed world (at least, the wealthier ones). But what to do with these higher speeds? It's easy to buy *quantity*, ie send larger and larger text files through the system. It's slightly less easy to buy *quality*, ie send better-looking documents through the system. (But look how fax has developed into a major force over the last few years.)

So far we have looked at the two media from the point of the *consumer*, ie the student (more exactly, the system manager reflecting on the needs of the student). From the point of view of the *producer*, ie the author, the systems are closely related. In particular, when an organisation like the Open University invests in electronic publishing, it spreads a network of microcomputers among authors and typists in order to capture information at source. This creates a vast electronic bank of material which can be distributed in various ways: much of it can be organised into published paper documents; some of it, especially the material which is either more time-critical or has a higher 'information density', can be pumped out through the computer conferencing system. More radically (for many organisations) the computer conferencing system permits an inflow of material from students, tutors, experts, etc. which can be used as input to new editions of paper documents, to the planning function, to the updating by the authors, and so on.

Thus electronic publishing and computer conferencing are to some extent mutually beneficial to the authors. To the students, they are still too far apart in media terms to compete; but they are beginning to converge. Nevertheless, there is this large middle ground which is waiting to be occupied by a medium with some of the characteristics of both – probably the CD-ROM optical disc.

Evolution of Computer Conferencing

I would now like to come back in more detail to the likely evolution of computer conferencing systems. Currently their output looks very different from that of an electronic publishing (or conventional publishing) system: typically monospaced text on screen or on a dot-matrix printer, versus laser-printed (or typeset) high-quality text and diagrams. (I accept that the difference in educational effectiveness is less than the difference in appearance, but the difference is still there.) Current computer conferencing systems mostly suffer from the following limitations:

- a limited range of characters (not all European roman letters, no Greek, etc)
- no text attributes (**bold**, *italic*, <u>underline</u>, etc)
- no choice of fonts (Times, Helvetica, script, etc)
- no real mathematics capability
- no diagrams.

Figure 2 shows some of what is missing.

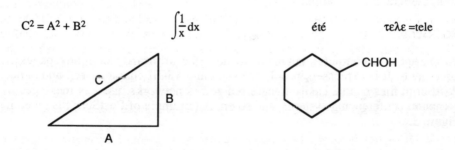

$$C^2 = A^2 + B^2 \qquad \int \frac{1}{x}\,dx \qquad\qquad \text{été} \qquad \tau\epsilon\lambda\epsilon = \text{tele}$$

Figure 2 Missing Features in Computer Conferencing Systems

Again I accept my implicit bias in favour of authors. Maybe a student could not or would not want to cope with a system which let him create such a wide variety of messages. (Indeed, one of the difficulties with telewriting systems seems to be the unwillingness of students, and tutors, to write and draw to each other, especially when they feel they must reach some 'professional standard'.) But surely students can cope with some of these? After all, they do so on the Macintosh in many universities across the world.

There are two ways of 'improving' computer conferencing systems in such a direction. The revolutionary way proposes a total scrapping of existing systems and their rewrite according to international standards, of which the most relevant are X25, OSI, X400, ODA, SGML and GKS. This is unlikely to yield results within the next couple of years. The evolutionary way is based on two premises:

1   Higher-speed modems (plus data compression) allow more complex
    documents to be transmitted.
2   Users are moving to micros, which can act as intelligent terminals. These can
    not only allow a transformation of traditional systems into a more friendly
    form (the classic use, as in the OU on DT200); they can also allow the
    translation of complex documents between a *transmission format* which
    appears to the system to be a normal message (even if unintelligible to the
    human reader), and a *representation format* which may be a complex
    document with fonts, attributes, diagrams, etc.

Before proposing a specific technical solution one must take a view on a very
important issue:

In the design of a computer conferencing system, is the screen more
important than the paper?

I take the view that, at least in distance education circles, paper is the dominant
medium. (Even on computer conferencing systems, many people print their
messages out in order to 'read them carefully'.) This view implies that a paper-
oriented technical approach should be preferred to a screen-oriented approach.
And this implies that the low-level document description language used should
be PostScript (by far the most important Page Description Language for laser
printers) rather than the GKS graphics standard beloved by the (screen-oriented)
computer graphics community.

PostScript

PostScript is a computer language to describe arbitrarily complex pages in
documents. It is expressed in only the standard ASCII character set, and hence
PostScript files can be easily transferred across networks, used as messages in
computer conferencing systems, and so on. An example of PostScript is given in
Figure 3.

```
newpath
270 360 moveto
0 72 rlineto
72 0 rlineto
0 -72 rlineto
closepath
.5 setgray
fill
```

Figure 3 A Simple Diagram and its PostScript Form

The main problem with PostScript is its verbosity, as the above example
shows. However, most modern word processing packages write a reasonably
economical form of PostScript, and with the development of higher-speed
modems, modest verbosity ceases to be a great problem. (And even simple data

compression schemes can considerably compress the kind of PostScript files found in practice.)

It will be relatively straightforward to graft a 'PostScript' message type on to existing computer conferencing systems so that arbitrarily complex documents, short or long, can be transferred from author to student, or student to student, or student to author. I predict that in many circumstances, this will be a useful feature.

However, it has not captured one essential aspect of a computer conferencing system: the fact that I can edit a message received from somebody before sending it on its way to a third party. In other words, PostScript is not a *revisable* format: it replicates the *layout* of the document, not its *structure* (not even the words).

Revisable Document Formats

There has been a great deal of interest in the last few years in revisable document formats, much of it in connection with standards work for Office Document Architecture. The standard proposed by ISO is the Standard Generalised Mark-up Language, or SGML for short. Like many standards, SGML is far from fully worked out, and so far tends to be found only on very expensive systems. Thus there is an interim requirement for more down-to-earth revisable text formats.

In the scientific academic community, a de facto standard can be found in the TeX language, developed originally by Professor Knuth of Stanford. However, this has not found favour in the general market place. As an alternative, there is the standard *Rich Text Format* (RTF) proposed by Microsoft. Since Microsoft dominate the IBM PC operating system market (MS DOS, Windows, OS/2, Presentation Manager), and also are one of the foremost developers of applications software for both PC and Macintosh (Word, Excel, MS Works), RTF has to be an industry standard of some significance. Certainly we have focussed on it to good effect in our own electronic publishing system.

Formats like RTF are reasonably economical. For example, each phrase in boldface (or italic, or underline, etc) incurs an overhead of only 5 or 6 characters, likewise for each font change. Figure 4 gives some examples of RTF coding.

This is a **bold** word	This is a {\b bold} word\par
This is an <u>underlined</u> word	This is an {\ul underlined} word\par
Italic phrases are useful	{\i Italic phrases} are useful\par
A change of `font` is nice.	A change of {\f22 font} is nice.\par

Figure 4 Examples of Attributes and their Coding in RTF

Unfortunately, the various revisable text formats do not adopt a standardised approach for graphics. It is true that simple vector graphics formats are all more or less interconvertible, but as one climbs up the scale of rounded rectangles, Bezier curves, fill patterns, and so on, this interconvertibility breaks down. However, if one is prepared to focus on a particular class of microcomputers (such as the ubiquitous IBM PC and clones), then a standard format is usually available.

Despite the worries about graphics, it will be straightforward to add one or more of the revisable formats to a conferencing system so as to provide a high-quality document plus the ability to revise documents.

Conclusion

- There is a large degree of synergy, and complementarity rather than competitiveness, between computer conferencing and electronic publishing.
- It will be relatively straightforward over the next couple of years to enhance existing computer conferencing systems to the level of document quality expected from a electronic publishing system, whether the documents are 5 lines long or 50 pages long.

PAPER 18

PRINT vs CRT:
A COMPARISON OF READING MODALITIES

Jim Dunn
Guttenberg, New Jersey, USA

The history of the alphabet details its movement from less to more flexible and transportable media, maximising dissemination at every turn. For the last five hundred years, or so, our words in letters have resided primarily on the printed page. The synergy of paper and moveable type generated a powerful explosion of ideas... the shock waves still reverberate today.

In its most recent adventure, the alphabet has escaped the technology of Gutenberg for the medium of Franklin – *electricity* (hence the Franklin Home Library). If the printing press owes its success to flexibility and economical dissemination, then, from this contemporary saltation, [1] we may reasonably anticipate comparable cognitive and socio-political impacts. For the first time, this new mode of textual discourse renders the alphabet as a 'light through' medium (as opposed to 'light on'). For the first time in the epoch of literacy, people are 'dimming' the lights to read more clearly. And for the first time in the age of television, children can watch the tube and read their homework at the same time.

This subtle, yet profound, shift in the physical nature of the code may just be significant enough to justify the replication, in electronic text, of the research conducted on reading and literacy in traditional print environments. The results of this preliminary study suggest that distinctions between the two environments are worth looking into. The objective here was to isolate and define the relative efficiency of CRT (Cathode Ray Tube) and print environments as display media in tests of pre-reading skills and early reading comprehension.

The two text environments were juxtaposed in a within-subjects experimental design: single variable with two levels.

All participants were tested in both print and CRT environments. The two pre-reading tests and the two reading comprehension tests were presented an equal number of times, in both modes, to minimise the effect of any discrepancy in the difficulty level between them. The order of presentation of the media was also counterbalanced to minimise any task learning or first order interferences.

Both the pre-reading and reading groups followed the same procedure. The testing took place in a period lasting two days.

The teachers ranked the children in three tiers, according to their academic performance. The three tiers were arbitrarily separated into two groups to counterbalance presentation order while distributing the level of performance evenly. Half of the children took a CRT test first, and the other half took a print test first.

The CRT tests were administered by a teacher as follows. The participant was seated in front of a computer and CRT. They were told only that they were taking a test and no other context was given. The teacher then explained the test instructions.

In the case of the pre-reading test, the children were asked to count how many of each shape, letter or number they saw on the screen. The shapes, letters and numerals were represented on the answer sheet, followed by the numbers 1 through 5. The answer sheet represented the test objects in a different form (in lower case and in script) than on screen to minimise matching by shape alone. They were told to circle the correct number next to each object. A total of five screens comprised this test, each screen had an associated answer sheet with ten questions. When the participant finished one screen, the teacher accessed the next one. The children were timed for each screen.

The instructions for the CRT versions of the reading comprehension test involved a demonstration of text scrolling and manipulation of the up and down arrow keys. After the participant felt comfortable with the task, the teacher provided the answer sheet and explained that the questions were on the screen, but the answers are recorded on the paper by filling in the circle in front of the right choice. Then she loaded the test onto the screen. The children were timed for the total duration of the test.

After half of each group, pre-reading and reading, had taken a CRT test, print versions were administered to all the participants in both groups. This was done to emulate the typical environment of standardised competence tests. Again, the teacher told the children only that they were about to take a test, and she gave no other context.

The instructions for the pre-reading print version were, for the most part, the same as the CRT test. There was no need to explain the relationship of the answer sheet to the test material. The five screens were printed out into five sheets with ten questions at the bottom of each page. The sheets were distributed in sequence and times were recorded for each child on each sheet.

The instructions for the print mode of the reading comprehension test were similarly more self evident. The questions followed the test passages immediately, and they comprised a single booklet. Again, the children were timed for the total duration of the test.

After the print versions were administered to all participants, the second half of each group took the CRT tests.

Combined Results

At the end of the testing phase, each child was asked which medium they preferred. The children overwhelmingly preferred the CRT environment.

The CRT environment was also the more efficient display medium for reading and pre-reading comprehension material. The children scored significantly higher when they were tested on CRTs.

An analysis of variation of the combined scores of both the pre-reading and the early reading groups indicates that the results are significant at the 0.01 level.

The reasons for this are not easily identified, but four possibilities immediately suggest themselves:
- It may be the different testing environments: the group atmosphere of standardised tests as practiced today, versus the relatively private CRT environment.
- Simple excitement about the medium.
- Luminosity.
- McLuhan's 'participatory factors'.

In this study these elements could not be independently evaluated. From this very preliminary work, the only conclusions one may reasonably draw are: something's afoot, and it's worth a look.

Notes

[1] 'Saltation' means a sudden, unexpected leap – a discontinuous jump as distinct from a gradual move forward. The term is frequently used in evolution theory; for example, Stephen Jay Gould's theory of 'punctuated equilibria' is a theory of saltations. (Paul Levinson)

PAPER 19

IMPROVING A DISTRIBUTED LEARNING ENVIRONMENT WITH COMPUTERS AND TELECOMMUNICATIONS

Stephen Ehrmann
The Annenberg / CPB Project, Washington DC, USA

The Challenge: Simultaneous Improvement of Access and Quality

Critics of distance learning often begin their challenge with the unspoken assumption that quality and accessibility are antithetical values. Learning resources are inherently scarce, they assume, and therefore any attempt to bring more people into the fold will dilute quality, while any attempt to improve some of the resources is an inherently exclusionary act.

Fortunately, however, technological advances have often made possible the development of learning resources that are both better and more accessible than their predecessors. The printed book, mass produced calculators, lecture halls, telephones, cars, paperback books, photocopiers, and interlibrary loan systems are among the innovations that have enlarged access for the many and enriched quality for even the best learners simultaneously.

Each of these innovations has made possible the creation of a superior learning resource that is also more readily distributed across a wider network of learners and teachers. In cases like the printed book, the technology makes possible a superior resource that can also be more readily distributed to learners. Other innovations help learners travel to a site and share a resource (eg roads and libraries), so that its benefits can be distributed. Still other innovations, such as telecommunications, allow learners to use and share resources without physical movement by any of the parties in the transaction. In this paper, all the resources within the learner's reach, and all the means of reaching them, will be termed the learner's *distributed learning environment*.

Interacting with One's Distributed Learning Environment

Technologies seem to be used to enhance four distinctive, complementary types of interaction by the learner with the distributed learning environment:

*   Learners study *instructive messages* about the field under study, messages that are embodied in and transmitted through media. Technological advances have enhanced the diversity and portability of such messages. Traditional technologies for this task include the lecture hall and the textbook. New technologies include videotape, audio tape, desktop publishing, and faculty-crafted computer-aided instruction. Each of these technological advances can

support both improved access (inexpensive media or transmission) and quality (eg improved images, dynamic displays, branching instruction).

• Technology can enhance the portability and power of the *tools and resources* with which students can work on the open-ended problems of the field. Traditional tools and resources for analysis and composition/design include paper, typewriters, calculators, libraries of primary source materials, telephones for administering social science surveys, and science laboratories. Accessible new technologies include personal computer software such as word processing, computer-aided design, statistical packages, and tools for musical composition, as well as video cameras and tape editing facilities. The technology again both enhances access (in that the new tools can often be more readily financed and amortised than their precursors) and quality. (Balestri and Ehrmann, 1987, describe how computers enable undergraduates to design and compose across a wider range of problems and disciplines.)

• Technology enhances the student's ability to conduct *conversations* with others in *real time*. Formal recognition of the crucial role of real-time conversation goes back at least to Socrates: it can help untie knots of ambiguity, provide the stimulus of brainstorming, and surface and challenge assumptions of both learner and teacher. Traditional technologies for supporting real-time conversations include the seminar room with its blackboard, the architecture studio with its sketch pads and tracing papers (Schön, 1987), the faculty office, and the dormitory corridor. New technologies include audio conferencing, text-based conferencing (Batson, 1988), and audiographic conferencing (Gilcher and Johnstone, 1988). Each technology that supports real-time conversation changes its character as well as its accessibility (Baron, 1984; Peyton and Batson, 1986).

• Technology can also enhance *time-delayed conversation*. Homework assignments and other time-delayed conversations usually require the parties to think at length and move around during the hours, days or weeks of the exchange. Traditional technologies for supporting time-delayed conversation include not only the paper on which assignments are written but also the residential campus (technologies which help ensure that students are close enough to the faculty to exchange work frequently) and the mails (for distant learners). New technologies include the more malleable documents created by computer, electronic transfer of those files, asynchronous computer conferencing, and fax. Once again the technology has the potential to improve both access (more students can exchange work) and quality, since the exchange can occur more frequently, giving both students and their coach-critics the potential for a wider range of expression and exploration [FIPSE Technology Study Group (1988, p 16-18); Kaplan (1987)].

So certain advances in technology have supported improvements in both access and quality by enhancing one or more of four complementary types of interaction between the learner and the distributed learning environment. A single technological innovation can sometimes support more than one type of interaction. For example, the residential campus made real-time and time-delayed conversations more feasible, clustered tools and resources for greater availability, and enabled good faculty to serve more students.

Lacking the equivalent of a campus in their distributed learning environments, distant learners have historically been offered a reasonable supply of instructive messages (print; broadcast audio or video) but relatively little in the way of tools and resources (print sources; typewriter); time-delayed conversation (mail); and real-time conversation (optional telephone and several face-to-face meetings a semester). Because their environment is usually deficient in three of the four forms of interaction, distant learners probably suffer barriers to learning, especially in the area of higher order reasoning and open-ended problem-solving, that might be alleviated with more coordinated support. Which new technologies might be most cost-effective in achieving improved quality and access?

Extending the Environment with the Telecommunicating Computer

Like the residential campus, the computer linked to a telecommunications network can support improvements in all four types of interaction. Significantly, this enhanced environment can then be used by a variety of academic programs pursuing quite different goals:

- When students are equipped with computers and modems, institutions should be able to provide *access* to more diverse populations, especially students who have trouble matching their schedules to institutional norms. Houston Community College reports that their modem-based program, which supports all four forms of interaction, is bringing in computer-owning students who would not have been able to participate before, while simultaneously improving the level of achievement. (*Distant Learning...*, 1988) The new technology should help redefine the boundaries of the campus, including distant students, distant experts, distant resources.

- Some academic programs must keep pace with rapid shifts in technology if they wish to attract students. Computers can support or simulate a wide variety of tools, resources, and instructional packages, so one needn't buy new hardware with every change in methods. Also, telecommunications can support improved faculty and student contact with experts in the work world and at other universities.

- Some academic programs emphasise skills and values that can only be acquired through experiential learning. By using computer-based tools and resources, students can work on more complex and interesting problems (eg Balestri and Ehrmann, 1987). Also, the telecommunicating computer has already begun to help students out in the field on an internship, cooperative assignment, or research project to maintain contact with the campus; in the future they could even continue to take campus-based courses.

- Networked computers can also be helpful to those academic programs that employ seminars, problem solving groups, and other teaching-learning strategies that emphasise the social construction of knowledge. Students using computers to work on open-ended problems particularly need to compare notes with faculty and peers. Time-delayed communication allows the involvement of faculty and students who have difficulty coordinating their schedules with one another. Advances in time-delayed communication also allow a new rhythm for learning. A seminar can take forward steps several times a day over a period of weeks (Hiltz, 1988). Students can submit drafts on diskettes for critique as often as two or three times a week.

• In order to maximise coverage of content, computers and networks enlarge each individual's access to data and stored instruction. Optical discs and new methods of information manipulation such as hypermedia make it more possible for individual students to obtain the information and instruction that they need (Crane, 1988; Mylonas *et al.*, 1988). Desktop publication and presentation make it easier for faculty to create their own instructional resources for individual student use, as well as for enhancing classroom presentation. By allowing students to ask questions and faculty to modify materials, telecommunications can reduce the investment needed in pre-designed instructive messages about each element of content, thereby expanding the content that can be covered with a given budget.

Challenges to Come

Attempts to add computers and networks to the distributed learning environment will encounter at least three types of challenge: problems of invention, problems of definition, and problems of sharing.

Problems of Invention
Students need all four types of interaction but most academics seem to focus their technological investments on just one or another of the four. There are technical difficulties in integrating technologies, and it is easier to train staff and students for one new application than for several. Even more challenging is inventing what to do with the *tabula rasa* offered by the telecommunicating computer; the shapes of success will become obvious only in retrospect.

Problems of Definition
One implication of enlarging the distributed learning environment with telecommunicating computers is that it will matter less where the learner is, and when the learner chooses to study. As that becomes true, should we continue to define and budget 'distance learning' in the same way? In the US, distance learning programs receive only a tiny share of total academic spending, yet the majority of learners face barriers of space and time, despite living within a few miles of a campus. They have jobs or other impediments to reaching class meetings and study facilities, and their campuses may not offer the course or study approach that they really need. 'Majority' problems such as these may not be amenable to solution so long as our budgets and staffing categories make traditional distinctions between the mythical majority of 'haves' on campus and the minority 'have nots' at a distance.

Problems of Sharing

Who pays for improvements in a distributed learning environment? And who gets the returns when the new environment can be used to advantage? Libraries are struggling with this issue: when should information be expensive, and when free? Networked campuses are struggling: who pays for the network, and how much? The wider the web is spread across people with unequal ability to pay, the more troublesome this question becomes. The wider the network is spread across some programs that take rewarding advantage of it, and some that do not, the more troublesome this question becomes.

Final Thought

Distributed learning environments are not new. However, the networked computer offers a rather spectacular enlargement of the learner's reach. It can support real tools to work real problems, the means for quick chat and considered exchange, and more cost-effective instructive messages as well.

Improving something as transparent and 'taken for granted' as the basic learning environment will not happen overnight. The challenges are enormous, the bills steep, and who is to pay them a question yet unresolved. But the rewards for enhanced teaching are so significant that the web of learning is already growing.

PAPER 20

CMC IN DISTANCE EDUCATION AND TRAINING: THE BROADER CONTEXT

Peter Zorkoczy
Open University, Milton Keynes, UK

What is meant by the term 'broader context'? Broader than what? Well, broader than the topic of computer-mediated communication (CMC), which has been the focus of interest of the preceding contributions. The intention here is to regard CMC as just one of several methods of communication available to distance learners and course providers, and to try to point to some of the achievements, problems and future directions in integrating CMC into the multi-media environment of distance learning.

To help with this task I should like to introduce a framework which, for simplicity, is confined to only three aspects:
- the features and characteristics of the technology itself
- the applications

• the characteristics of the users and their environment.

If we combine these dimensions with views of the past achievements, present problems and future directions, we end up with an imaginary 3 by 3 grid to guide our thinking throughout this discussion. (This framework can also be used with media other than CMC for comparison.)

But before we start, just a few words on what it is we are really talking about: 'computer-mediated communication in distance learning'. We must be careful not to use the term in either too narrow or too broad a sense. CMC is clearly more than electronic mail, but it is also less than all computer applications in distance education and training. I think perhaps what the term 'CMC' is lacking, is some precision in the use of the word 'communication'.

Historically, in the context of CMC 'communication' often meant 'the use of a telecommunications network'. As we shall see, the notion has been extended recently to cooperative working, decision-making, etc, where the distance element is missing, and the emphasis is on direct human communication augmented by computer. So, here is an area where some thinking is needed: just what is CMC – and what isn't.

Past Achievements

While on a historical note, let us follow up the first column of our 3-by-3 grid: the achievements in the technology, applications and user population of CMC.

The technology of CMC goes back to the late 1960s when the Office of Emergency Preparedness in the USA introduced the 'Party-Line' and 'Discussion' systems, leading to the EMISARI system. Together with PLANET and EIES (1975) these formed the first generation of CMC software – very much in the computer conferencing mould, using a free-form discussion structure. By contrast, there were also some first generation systems like FORUM, which introduced highly structured communication processes – Delphi structures, voting, etc. (For a more complete historical view refer, for example, to Johansen *et al.*, 1979 which itself contains a useful bibliography.)

The second generation, represented by products like Participate, CoSy, and COM extended the range of features of the earlier systems, introduced electronic mail facilities, and catered for larger user populations – but at the expense of requiring significant computer power for reasonable response time. The third generation, currently with us, retains these features, but relegates many of the functions to 'intelligent' workstations so that powerful central engines are no longer necessary. Examples here are the WBSI version of VaxNotes, CAUCUS, TEIES, etc. There is definitely progress here, but no quantum leap, over a period of some 20 years. Effectively, the technical development of CMC has reflected developments in computer and telecommunication technologies.

More noticeable has been·the progress in the applications of the concept. It has moved from being a decision-support tool for a select few (eg EMISARI), to a learning-support component in a multi media system for thousands (eg the Open University implementation of CoSy, see for example, Kaye, 1987b).

In the context of open and distance education we see CMC today in three main application areas: academic, management and research. In the academic area, other papers in this book describe CMC in roles like information giving, active group interaction support, etc. In the management area we have examples like community formation, message handling, etc. In research it serves as the prime vehicle for a range of exciting projects in the technology of educational communication, and in social and cognitive aspects of human communication.

The most important contribution of CMC to distance education is seen by many as providing attractive means for 'closing the loop' between the tutor and the learner, that frees them both from the constraints of time and place. Good examples here are the use of PortaCOM by EuroPACE (a European programme for advanced and continuing education, see eg Zorkoczy, 1988), and of CoSy by the Open University.

The user population for CMC has grown significantly in range and number over the last 20 years: from computer scientists and other computer specialists to managers to educational technologists, teachers, trainers and, at last, learners.

Present Problems

With the increase of experience coming from the various application and user areas, there has been a corresponding accumulation of experience with the problems of CMC. So let us turn now to the second column of the grid, and look first at some of the problematic areas of current CMC systems. Since so much progress had been made with the hardware, the outdated characteristics of much of today's computer conferencing software and of the human interface become strikingly evident.

A metaphor which was used to good effect by Andrew Feenberg (see Chapter 2) is the 'crowded hall' into which the would-be users of a conferencing system arrive. The system provides only minimal guidance to effective navigation for novice users. They are often overwhelmed by the vast amount of relatively unstructured information at their disposal. They find the conventions of the communication process rather complex and cumbersome.

Early conferencing software had the imprint of computer science specialists, wanting a relatively unpolished but workable tool for person-to-person or person-to-group messaging. As producing a suite of conferencing software is still not a routine task for non-computer specialists, much of the early problems remain: the messages are text-only, the layout is compact but difficult to read, and the command syntax is unnatural.

In the area of applications, perhaps the biggest problem is that CMC has not yet found a clear role with a clearly demonstrable advantage for itself. Some say that systems are often 'cluttered up with junk' – irrelevant, light-weight stuff. For others, that is the *raison d'etre* of the concept – the social glue which holds groups and communities together. [1]

Many non-specialist users find that conferencing systems do not provide value in terms of time or money invested – at least until they are thoroughly conversant with the system, and until it is tailored to their needs. The need for access to a terminal or PC with modem, plus telecommunication costs must be counterbalanced by personally relevant information and convenience of use before conferencing systems can become a routine component of multi-media distance learning systems.

Future Directions

Several contributions in this volume raise these and other problems in far more detail and with more supporting evidence than I am able to fit into this brief overview. However, their appreciation leads us to the consideration of possible directions for development and future work – the last column of our grid.

In the technical arena, it is clear that there is parallel work going on in the field of hypertext and hypermedia, as well as in electronic publishing. [2] A convergence of CMC work with these developments would be a useful direction to pursue.

Other desirable short-term developments, in my view, include:
- modularisation of CMC software so that systems can be configured (tailored) to specific requirements, and also that improvements can be made to, say, the database handler or the user interface without necessarily having to modify the rest of the system in a major way
- efficient downloading and local structuring of the database, or parts of it, to allow individual users to establish their own views and cross- reference in the material, and to display its contents in a way that suits the user
- improved interfaces, with greater use of icons, navigation aids, search facilities, dynamic menus, and overcoming the small-window effect of current displays. [3]

In the application field, the main requirement is for more experience with the use of CMC in the distance learning environment, so as to uncover its strengths and weaknesses. We need also to discover the joint characteristics of CMC, when used in combination with other components of a multi-media learning environment. We must further develop the uses of CMC in the management of distance learning and in joint authoring, cooperative working, and decision-making. [4] In this way, we shall extend the range of applications of CMC and its attractiveness to a larger user community. That, in turn, will attract the necessary commercial interest and marketing activity needed to exploit the research and development effort in CMC.

Finally, in the user arena, we need to continue to do, and to make use of, fundamental work on the characteristics and processes of human communication, at the individual (cognitive and psycho-affective) level as well as on the social (group interaction and cooperative working) level.

Notes

[1] See for example Paper 15 by Graddol. (ed)
[2] See Paper 17 by Bacsich. (ed)
[3] See Chapter 7 by Alexander and Lincoln. (ed)
[4] See Paper 13 by Davies. (ed)

REFERENCES

Ambron, S. and K. Hooper (1988). *Interactive Multimedia*. Microsoft Press, Redmond, Washington.

Austin, J.L. (1961). Performative Utterances. In: *Philosophical Papers*. Oxford University Press, Oxford.

Austin, J.L. (1971). *How to do things with words*. Oxford University Press.

Bacsich, P. D. (1985). *Teleconferencing for distance education and training: Is the Open University experience typical?* (Optel Report No. 16). The Open University, Milton Keynes (ERIC Document Reproduction Service No. ED 273 258).

Bales, R. F. and P. E. Slater (1955). *Role Differentiation in Small Decision-Making Groups*. In: (T. Parsons, R. F.Bales *et al.*, eds.), pp. 259-306. Free Press, New York.

Balestri, D. and S. Ehrmann, (eds) (1987). *Machine Mediated Learning*, **II:1**, January.

Baltz, C. (1984). Gretel: Un Nouveau Média de Communication. In: *Télématique: Promenades dans les Usages* (M. Marchand and C. Ançelin, eds). La Documentation Française, Paris.

Barnes, D. and F. Todd (1977). *Communication and Learning in Small Groups*. Routledge and Kegan Paul, London.

Barnes, D., J. Britton and H. Rosen (1971). *Language, the Learner and the School*. Penguin, Harmondsworth.

Baron, N. (1984). Computer-mediated communication as a force in language change. *Visible Language*, **XVIII:2** (Spring), 118-141.

Bates, A.W. (1985). *New media in higher education*. (Papers on Information Technology No. 241) The Open University, Milton Keynes (ERIC Document Reproduction Service No. ED274 322).

Batson, T. (1988). The ENFI Project: A Networked Classroom Approach to Writing Instruction. *Academic Computing*, **II:5** (February), 55-56.

Beckwith, D. (1983). The nature of learners as total systems with implications for research and instructional development: A theoretical/conceptual paradigm. *Journal of Visual Verbal Languaging*, Fall, 9-28.

Benne, K D. and P. Sheats (1978). Functional Roles of Group Members. In: *Group Development* (L P. Bradford, ed.), 2nd ed,.pp.52-61. University Associates Inc., San Diego.

Bernstein, B. (1975). *Class, Codes and Control*. Routledge and Kegan Paul, London.

Bertho, C. (1981). *Télégraphes et Téléphones: de Valmy au Microprocesseur*. Livre de Poche, Paris.

Bouton, C. and R. Garth, (eds) (1983). *Learning in Groups. New Directions in Teaching and Learning*. Jossey-Bass, San Francisco.

Boyd, G.M. (1987). Emancipative Educational Technology. *Canadian Journal of Educational Communications*, **16**(2), 167-172.

Brown, J.S. (1985). Process versus product: A perspective on tools for communal and informal electronic learning. *Journal of Educational Computing Research*, **1**(2), 179-201.

Bruhat, T. (1984). Messageries Electroniques: Gretel à Strasbourg et Télétel à Velizy. In: *Télématique: Promenades dans les Usages* (M. Marchand and C. Ançelin, eds). La Documentation Française, Paris.

Bruner, J. (1986). *Actual Minds, Possible Worlds*. Harvard University, Cambridge, Mass.

Bullock Report (1975). *A Language for Life*. HMSO, London.

Carroll, J. M. (1985). Minimalist Design for Active Users. In: *Human Computer Interaction* (B. Shackel, ed). INTERACT '84. Elsevier, North-Holland.

Chang (1987). Participant Systems for Cooperative Work. In: *Distributed Artificial Intelligence* (M. N. Huhns, ed). Pitman, London.

Coombs, N. (1988). History by Teleconference. *History Microcomputer Review*, Spring, pp. 37-39.

Coombs, N., and A. Friedman (1987). Computer Conferencing and Electronic Mail as 'Classroom Communication'. *Proceedings of the Third Annual Conference "Computer Technology/Special Education/Rehabilitation"*. California State University, Northridge.

Coopers and Lybrand Associates Ltd. (1987). Further Education Costing: Final Report. A report produced for the Department of Education and Science and the Manpower Services Commission, Manpower Services Commission, Further Education Unit. [2 volumes: *Final Report and the Final Report Manual of Guidance*.].

Crane, G. (1988). Redefining the book: Some preliminary problems. *Academic Computing*, **II:5** (February).

Crittenden, W.J. (1988). Political Participation: Self-Development and Self-Interest. University of Oxford. Mimeo.

Davie, L. E. (1987). Learning Through Networks: A Graduate Course Using Computer Conferencing. *Canadian Journal of University Continuing Education*, **XIII**(2), pp. 11-26.

Davie, L. E. (1988). The Facilitation of Adult Learning Through Computer-Mediated Distance Education. *Journal of Distance Education*, Fall.

Davie, L. E. and P. Palmer (1985). Computer-Teleconferencing for Advanced Distance Education. *Canadian Journal of University Continuing Education*, **XI**(2), pp. 56-66.

Davies, D. (1988). Computer-Supported Cooperative Learning Systems. *PLET*, **25**(3).

De Certeau, M. and L. Giard (1983). L'Ordinaire de la Communication. *Réseaux*, **3**.

DeCincio, F., G. DeMichelis and C. Simone (1987). The Communication Disciplines of CHAOS. In: *Concurrency and Nets* (K. Voss, H.J. Genrich and G. Rosenberg, eds). Springer-Verlag, Berlin.

Decker, K.S. (1987). Distributed Problem-Solving Techniques: a Survey. *IEEE Trans. on Systems, Man and Cybernetics*, **17**(5).

Dell Hymes, H. (1972). On communicative competence. In: *Sociolinguistics* (J. Pride and J. Holmes, eds). Penguin, Harmondsworth.

Derrida, J. (1972a). La Pharmacie de Platon. In: *La Dissemination*. Seuil, Paris.

Derrida, J. (1972b). Signature Evènement Contexte. In: *Marges de la Philosophie*. Editions de Minuit, Paris.

Diebold Group (1983). *From Pilots to Contagion in Telecommunications*. Diebold Group, New York and London.

Dietrich, I. (1979). *Kommunikation and Mitestimmung im Fremdsprachenunterricht*. Scriptor.

Dieuzeide, H. (1985). Les enjeux politiques. In: *Le Savoir à Domicile: pédagogie et problématique de la formation à distance* (F. Henri and A. Kaye, eds). Presses de l'Université du Québec, Québec.

Distance Learning: Courses by Computer Modem (1988). *The Academic Administrator*, **VII:**14, July 25.

Douglas, M. (1973). *Natural Symbols*. Penguin Books, Harmondsworth.

Doyle, W. (1979). The Tasks of Teaching and Learning in Classrooms. R & D Report, no 4103. North Texas State University.

Dunkin, M. and B. Biddle (1974). *The Study of Teaching*. Holt Reinhart and Winston, New York.

Duranti, A. (1986, April). Framing discourse in a new medium: Openings in electronic mail. *The Quarterly Newsletter of the Laboratory of Comparative Human Cognition*, 8(2), 64-71.

Ehrmann, S. (1988). Specifications and Strategies: A Sustainable Investment in Technology. In: *Telelearning*. New Jersey Institute of Technology. Eastern Educational Consortium, Newark, NJ.

Eicher, J.C. *et al.* (1982). The economics of new educational media, Vol. 3: *Cost and Effectiveness Overview and Synthesis*. The Unesco Press, Paris.

Electronic University Network (1987). *Catalog*. TeleLearning Inc., San Francisco.

Emms, J. and D. McConnell (1988). An evaluation of tutorial support provided by electronic mail and computer conferencing. In: *Aspects of Educational Technology XXI: Designing New Systems and Technologies for Learning*. Kogan Page, London.

Feenberg, A. (1986). Network Design: An Operating Manual for Computer Conferencing. *IEEE Transactions on Professional Communications*, 29(1).

Feenberg, A. (1987). Computer Conferencing and the Humanities. *Instructional Science*, 16(2), 169-186.

Feenberg, A. (1989). The Planetary Classroom. *Proceedings of the IFIP Conference on Message Handling*, 6.5. North Holland Publishing Co, Amsterdam.

Fielden, J. and P.K. Pearson (1978). *Costing Educational Practice*. Council for Educational Technology, London.

FIPSE Technology Study Group (1988). Ivory Towers, Silicon Basements: Learner-Centered Computing in Postsecondary Education. McKinney, TX: Academic Computing.

Fisher, B.A. (1974). *Small Group Decision Making*. McGraw-Hill, New York.

Flanders, N. (1970). *Analyzing Teaching Behavior*. Addison-Wesley, Reading, Ma.

Ford, L. and F. Morriscoe (1987). Support for the User in Open and Distance Learning. In: *Tutoring and Monitoring Facilities for European Open Learning* (J. Whiting and D.A. Bell, eds). Elsevier, Amsterdam.

Gilcher, K. and S. Johnstone (1988). A Critical Review of the Use of Audiographic Conferencing Systems by Educational Institutions for Instructional Delivery. College Park, MD, University of Maryland University College.

Goffman, E. (1961). Fun in Games. In: *Encounters*. Bobbs-Merrill, New York.

Goffman, E. (1982). *Interaction Ritual*. Pantheon, New York.

Goodwin, N.C. (1987). Functionality and Usability. *Communications of the ACM*, 30(3).

Goody, J. and I. Watt (1986). The consequences of Literacy. In: *Literacy in Traditional Societies* (J. Goody, ed.). Cambridge University Press, Cambridge.

Graddol, D., C. Cheshire and J. Swann (1987). *Describing Language*. Open University Press, Milton Keynes.

Graddol,D. and J. Swann (forthcoming). *Gender Voices*. Blackwell, Oxford.

Guillaume, M. (1982). Téléspectres. *Traverse*, 26.

Habermas, J. (1971). *Knowledge and Human Interests*. Heinemann, London.

Habermas, J. (1981). *Theorien des kimmunikativen Handelns*. Bände 1-2. Suhrkamp, Frankfurt am Main.

Habermas, J. (1987). *The Theory of Communicative Action*. trans, T. McCarthy (2 vols.). Beacon Press, Boston.

Haile, P.J. (1986, April). An analysis of computer conferences supporting the distance learner. Paper presented at the annual conference of the American Educational Research Association. San Francisco.

Harasim, L. (1987a). Teaching and Learning Online: Issues in computer-mediated graduate courses. *Canadian Journal for Educational Communication*, 16(2).

Harasim, L. (1987b). Computer-mediated cooperation in education: Group learning networks. *Proceedings of the Second Guelph Symposium on Computer Conferencing*. University of Guelph, Ontario.

Harasim, L. (1988). Designing the online educational environment: Group teaching methods. Paper presented to the Electronic Networking Association Conference. Philadelphia.

Harasim, L. (1989). Online Education: A new domain for collaborative learning and knowledge networking. In: *Online Education: Perspectives on a New Medium* (L. Harasim, ed.) in press.

Harasim, L. and R. Wolfe (1988). Research analysis and evaluation of computer conferencing and networking in education. Final Report. OISE/Ontario Ministry of Education.

Harasim, L. and T. Winkelmans (1988). Computer-mediated scholarly collaboration: A case study of the 'International Online Educational Research Workshop'. Technical Paper #9. Ontario Institute for Studies in Education. Spring, 1988.

Harris, D. (1987). *Openness and Closure in Distance Education*. The Falmer Press, Lewes.

Harry, K. and G. Rumble (1982). *The Distance Teaching Universities*. Croom Helm, London.

Held, D. (1987). *Models of Democracy*. Polity Press, Cambridge.

Henry, J. (1986). D309 Electronic Mail Evaluation. Open University Institute of Educational Technology, Milton Keynes. mimeo.

Hiltz, S R. and M. Turoff (1986). Remote learning: technologies and opportunities. Paper given at the World conference on Continuing Engineering Education. Lake Buena Vista, Florida.

Hiltz, S.R (1986). The 'virtual classroom': Using computer-mediated communication for university teaching. *Journal of Communication*, 36(2).

Hiltz, S.R. (1984). *Online Communities: A Case Study of the Office of the Future*. Ablex Publishing Corp, New Jersey.

Hiltz, S.R. (1987). Learning in a Virtual Classroom. Vol 1 of A Virtual Classroom on EIES: Final Evaluation Report. *Research Report 25 and 26*. Computerized Conferencing and Communication Centre. New Jersey Institute of Technology, New Jersey.

Hiltz, S.R. and M. Turoff (1978). *The Network Nation*. Addison-Wesley, Reading, Ma.

Hiltz, S.R., K. Johnson and M. Turoff (1982). The effects of formal human leadership and computer generated decision aids on problem solving via a computer: a controlled experiment. New Jersey Institute of Technology Computerized Conferencing and Communications Centre. New Jersey Institute of Technology, New Jersey.

Inglis, P. (1987). Distance Teaching is Dead! Long Live Distance Learning!. 56th ANZAAS Conference, New Zealand.

Jamison, D.T., S.J. Klees and S.J. Wells (1978). *The Costs of Educational Media. Guidelines for planning and evaluation*. Sage Publications, Beverly Hills.

Janda, K. (1987, October). Computer augmented teaching in large lecture courses: The case of the American government. *Academic Computing*, 2(2), 34-35, 42-43.

Johansen, R. (1988). *Groupware: Computer Support for Business Teams*. The Free Press, New York.

Johansen, R., J. Vallee and K. Spangler (1979). *Electronic Meetings: Technical Alternatives and Social Choices*. Addison-Wesley, Reading, Ma.

Johnson, D. and R. Johnson (1975). *Learning Together and Alone: Cooperation, Competition, and Individualization*. Prentice-Hall, Englewood Cliffs, NJ.

Johnson, D.W. and R.T. Johnson (1985). The Internal Dynamics of Cooperative Learning Groups. In: *Learning to Cooperate, Cooperating to Learn* (R. Slavin, ed). Plenum, New York.

Johnson-Lenz, P. and T. Johnson-Lenz (1982). Consider the Groupware; Design and Group Process Impacts on Communication in the Electronic Medium. In: *Computer-Mediated Communication Systems: Status and Evaluation* (S.R. Hiltz and E. Kerr, eds). Academic Press, New York.

Kaplan, N. (1987). Writing Courses in the Electronic Age. *EDUCOM Bulletin*. Fall, 10-12.

Katz, E. (1980). Media Events: The Sense of Occasion. *Studies in Visual Communication*, **6**.

Kaye, A. R. (1985). Computer-mediated communication systems for distance education: report of a study visit to North America. Institute of Educational Technology, Milton Keynes. mimeo.

Kaye, A. R. (1986). La Télématique comme outil de communication en formation à distance. *Le Bulletin de L'IDATE*, **23**. Montpellier.

Kaye, A R. (1987a). Introducing Computer-Mediated Communication into Distance Education. *Canadian Journal of Educational Communication*, **16**(2), pp. 153-166.

Kaye, A. R. (1987b). Integrating Computer Conferencing into Distance Education Courses: A Discussion Paper. *The Second Guelph Symposium on Computer Conferencing*. University of Guelph, Ontario.

Kaye, A. R. (1988). Distance Education: the State of the Art. *Prospects*, **xviii**,1, pp.43-54. Unesco, Paris.

Kerr, E. (1986). Electronic Leadership: A Guide to Moderating On-Line Conferences. *IEEE Transactions on Professional Communications*, **29**(1).

Kerr, E. and S.R. Hiltz (1982). *Computer-Mediated Communication Systems: Status and Evaluation*. Academic Press, New York.

Kiesler, S., J. Siegel and W. McGuire (1984). Social psychological aspects of computer-mediated communication. *American Psychologist, 39.*(10).

Levin, H.M. (1983). *Cost-effectiveness: a primer*. Sage Publications, Beverly Hills.

Levin, J., K. Haesun, and M. Riel (1989). Analysing Instructional Interactions on Electronic Message Networks. In: *Online Education: Perspectives on a New Medium* (L. Harasim, ed). in press.

Levinson P. (1988). *Mind at Large: Knowing in the Technological Age*. JAI Press, Greenwich, CT.

Levinson, P. (1979). Human replay: a theory of the evolution of media. PhD Dissertation, New York University.

Levinson, P. (1988). CMC in the Context of the Evolution of Media. In: Proceedings of the Research Workshop on Educational Applications and Implications of CMC (L. Harasim and C. Montgomerie, eds). OISE, Toronto. in press.

Lorentsen, A., L. Dirckinck-Holmfeld and K. Andersen (1988). Picnic – Project in Computer Networks in Distance Education Curricula. University of Aalborg.

Lyotard, J-F. (1979). *La Condition Postmoderne*. Editions de Minuit, Paris.

Mansbridge, J.J. (1983). *Beyond Adversary Democracy*. Chicago University Press, Chicago.

Marchand, M. (1987). *La Grande Aventure du Minitel*. Larousse, Paris.

Marchand, M. (1988). *A French Success Story: The Minitel Saga*. translated by M. Murphy. Larousse, Paris.

Marcuse, J. (1964). *One Dimensional Man*. Beacon Press, Boston.

Mason, R. (1988). Computer conferencing: a Contribution to Self-directed Learning. *British Journal of Educational Technology*, **19**(1).

Mason, R. and A. Kaye (1989). New Paradigms for Distance Education. In: *Online Education: Perspectives on a New Medium* (L. Harasim, ed). in press.

Masuda, Y. (1980). *The Information Society As Post-Industrial Society*. Institute for Information Society, Tokyo.

McCreary, E.K. and J. Van Duren (1987). Educational Applications of Computer Conferencing. *Canadian Journal of Educational Communication*, **16**(2), pp. 107-115.

McDonald, F. and P. Elias (1976). Beginning teacher evaluation study: Phase II *Final Report*, Vol 1, Chapter 10. Educational Testing Service, Princeton, NJ.

McLuhan, M. (1962). *The Gutenberg Galaxy*. Mentor, New York.

Meeks, B. (1987). The Quiet Revolution – On-line education becomes a real alternative. *BYTE*, February.

Mehan, H. (1978). Structuring school structure. *Harvard Educational Review*, **48**, 32-64.

Mills, C. (1963). *Kritik der soziologischen Denkweise*. Neuweid.

Mintzberg, H. (1979). *The Structuring of Organizations: a Synthesis of the Research*. Prentice-Hall, Englewood Cliffs, N.J.

Mylonas, Elli, (ed) (1988). Assignments in Hypertext. The Annenberg/CPB Project, Washington, DC.

National Union of Teachers (1988). *We Did It Our Way*. Tape no 2. Video available from Focus in Education Ltd., 65 High Street, Hampton Hill, Middlesex TW12 1NH.

Negt, D. (1971). *Soziologische Phantasie and Exemplarisches Lernen*. Frankfurt am Main-Köln.

Ong, W. (1971). The Literate Orality of Popular Culture Today. In: *Rhetoric, Romance, and Technology*. Cornell University Press, Ithaca and London.

Ong, W. (1977). From Mimesis to Irony. In: *Interfaces of the Word*. Cornell University Press, Ithaca and London.

Open University (1987). Comparative costs of the OU. Internal Planning Office paper.

Orivel, F. (1987). Analysing costs in distance education systems: a methodological approach. Dijon, IREDU, Université de Bourgogne. mimeo.

Paulsen, M. (1987/88). In Search of a Virtual School. *T.H.E. Journal*, Dec/Jan.

Peyton, J. and T. Batson (1986). Computer Networking: Making Connections Between Speech and Writing. *ERIC/CLL Bulletin*. **X:1**(September), 1-7.

Phillips, T. (1987). On a related matter: why successful small group talk depends on NOT keeping to the point. Paper presented at the International Oracy Convention, University of East Anglia.

Piepho, H-E. (1974). *Kommunikative Kompetenz als Übergeordnetes Lernziel im Englischunterricht*. Dornburg-Frickhofen.

Postman, N. (1979). *Teaching as a Conserving Activity*. Delacorte, New York.

Prinz, W. and R. Speth (1988). Group Communication and Related Aspects in Office Automation. In: *Proceedings of the IFIP 6.5 International Conference on Message Handling Systems* (R. Speth, ed). Elsevier, North-Holland.

Quinn, C.N., H. Mehan, J.A. Levin and S.D. Black (1983). Real education in non-real time: The use of electronic message systems for instruction. *Instructional Science*, **11**(4), 313-327.

Rowan, R. (1986). The Intuitive Manager. Little, New York.

Rumble, G. (1986). *The Planning and Management of Distance Education*. Croom Helm, London.

Rumble, G. (1988a). The economics of mass distance education. *Prospects*. **18**(1), 91-102.

Rumble, G. (1988b). The costs and costing of distance education. In: *Commonwealth Co-operation in Open Learning: Background Papers* (J. Jenkins, ed.). Commonwealth Secretariat, London.

Schön, D. (1987). *Educating the Reflective Practitioner*. Jossey-Bass, San Francisco.

Scollon, S. and R. Scollon (1982, Sept). Computer conferencing in instruction. Unpublished manuscript. Center for Cross Cultural Studies, University of Alaska Fairbanks, (9pp).

Searle, J. (1969). *Speech Acts*. Cambridge.

Shimanoff (1984). Coordinating Group Interaction via Communication Rules. In: *Small Group Communication* (4th Edition) (R.S. Cathcart and L.A. Samovar, eds). Wm. C. Brown, Dubuque, Iowa.

Simondon, G. (1958). *La Mode d'Existence des Objets Techniques*. Aubier, Paris.

Sinclair, J McH. and R.M. Coulthard (1975). *Towards an Analysis of Discourse*. Oxford University Press, London.

Slavin, R. (1986, April). Cooperative Learning: Where behavioural and humanistic approaches to classroom motivation meet. Paper presented to the AERA, San Francisco.

Smith, P. and M. Kelly (1987). *Distance Education and the Mainstream*. Croom Helm, London.

Sniderman, P. (1974). *Personality and Democratic Politics*. University of California Press.

Somekh, B. and S. Groundwater-Smith (1988). Take a Balloon and a Piece of String. In: *New Technologies and Professional Communications in Education* (D. Smith, ed). Occasional paper 13, National Council for Educational Technology.

Stefik, M. *et al.* (1988). Beyond the chalkboard: Computer support for collaboration and problem solving in meeting. In: *Computer-Supported Cooperative Work: A Book of Readings* (I. Grief, ed). Morgan Kaufmann Publishers, San Mateo.

Stodolsky, D.S. (1988). Protecting expression in teleconferencing; pseudonym-based peer review journals. *Proceedings of the 14th World Conference on Distance Education.* I.C.D.E., Oslo.

Suchman, L.A. (1987). Plans and Situated Actions: the Problem of Human-Computer Communication. *CUP.* Cambridge.

Swann, J. and D. Graddol (1988). Gender inequalities in classroom discourse. *English in Education,* 22, pp 48-65.

Turkle, S. (1984). *The Second Self.* Simon and Schuster, New York.

Turner, R. (1970). Words, Utterances and Activities. In: *Understanding Everyday Life* (J. Douglas ed.). Aldine, New York.

Turoff, M. (1982). On the Design of an Electronic University. In: Telecommunications and Higher Education: Conference Briefs. New Jersey Institute of Technology, Department of Higher Education, New Jersey.

Turoff, M. (1987). TEIES: Tailorable Electronic Information Exchange System. *CCCC.* New Jersey Institute of Technology, New Jersey.

Umpleby, S. (1986). Online Education Techniques. *ENA Netweaver,* 2(1).

Vallee, J. (1984). *Computer Message Systems.* McGraw Hill, New York.

Wagenschein, M. (1956). Zum Begriff des exemplarischen Lehrens. 1: Zeitschrift für Pädagognik. 2. Jahrgang.

Wagner, L. (1982). *The Economics of Educational Media.* Macmillan, London.

Whetmore, E.J. (1988). *Mediamerica.* Wadsworth Publishing Co., Belmont, CA.

Wilson, P. (1988). Key Research in Computer-Supported Cooperative Work (CSCW). *European Teleinformatics Conference.* EUTECO '88. Vienna.

Winkelmans, T. (1988). Educational Computer Conferencing: An application of analysis methodologies to a structured small group activity. Unpublished Master's Thesis, University of Toronto.

Winograd, T. and F. Flores (1986). *Understanding Computers and Cognition: A New Foundation for Design.* Albex, New Jersey.

Wolfe, R. (1989). Hypertext perspectives on educational computer conferences. In: *Online Education: Perspectives on a New Medium* (L. Harasim, ed). in press.

Woodley, A. *et al.* (1987). *Choosing to Learn: Adults in Education.* Milton Keynes: SRHE and Open University Press, p. 160.

Wunderlich, D. (ed) (1972). *Linguistische Pragmatik.* Athenaeum.

Yates, F. (1966). *The Art of Memory.* University of Chicago, Chicago.

Zorkoczy, P. (1988). PACE – A satellite- and terrestrial network-based international educational service. 2nd Eurotelecom 88, Madrid.

Zuboff, S. (1988). *In the Age of the Smart Machine.* Basic Books, New York.

INDEX